前　　言

天壇，建於1421年(明永樂十八年)。是世界上最大的祭天建築群。它占地273萬平方米，由兩座祭壇構成——南爲圜(yuan)丘，北有祈谷壇。

郊祀祭天是我國古代最盛大的典禮，它反映了古代人們的理想和觀念，這種儀禮在中國延綿了大約五千年。明淸兩代曾有22位皇帝親自在這裏舉行過654次祭天儀式。1918年天壇被辟爲公園，它以恢宏的規制，獨特的建築和深厚的祭天歷史文化內涵，吸引着中外廣大遊人。

天壇壇域廣濶，古柏森森，芳草茸茸，在碧樹藍天的掩映下，潔白無暇的圜丘、輝煌壯麗的祈年殿，“崇基石欄紫翠重，不是天宮似天宮”。進入天壇，一種庄嚴、肅穆、神聖、幽幻的意境會油然而生，當你望見那美麗的祭壇時，彷彿你的靈魂立刻得到了凈化，思想得到升華。

天壇有五組建築，各有特色，而宏偉壯麗的祈年殿是天壇的主要標志，它璀巍嵯峨是泱泱大國的氣度，燦爛輝煌是古都北京的形象。它記述着民族五千年的文明，也寄託中華騰飛的希望。在圜丘建築群中有三組奇特的傳聲現象：回音壁、三音石、億兆景從石，是世上絕無僅有的，若大的圜丘台，所有石質構件都由九和九的倍數組成，精妙絕倫，也是舉世無雙的。

天壇是一座祭天文化的博物館。它集建築學、美學、聲學、天文、歷法、音樂、舞蹈等爲一體。它展現給人們的祭天禮儀、祭天樂舞、祭天供奉、祭天祭品、祭天齋戒等是我們認識中國歷史的一個重要窗口。

一聲音回友誼傳遍四海，億頃松濤芳菲飄過五洋。天壇正以嶄新的面貌迎接着廣大中外遊客的到來。

天壇公園園長：景長順

Foreword

Built 1421 (the 18th year of the reign of Eperor Yongle, Ming Dynasty), is the largest architectural group where sacrifices were offered to Heaven. Covering an area of 2.73 million m^2, it includes 2 sacrificial altars: The Circular Mound Altar in the south and Altar for the God of Grains in the north.

The ceremony offering sacrifices to Heaven is the most magnificent celebration in ancient China. Such a ceremony reflecting the ideal and conception of ancient people had lasted for about 5000 years. In Ming and Qing Dynasties, 22 emperors held 654 ceremonies offering sacrifices to Heaven. In 1918, Temple of Heaven was turn into a park. It attracted masses of visitors from home and abroad by the grand scales, unique buildings and profound connotation of historic culture of offering sacrifices to Heaven.

The spacious Temple of Heaven is well-afforested. Set of by verdant trees and blue sky, the snow-white Circular Mound Altar and magnificent Hall of Prayer for Bumper Harvests look like a palace in the Heaven. When going into the Temple, a feeling of solemnity, respectfulness, holiness and quietness will well up in the mind. When looking at the beautiful sacrificial altars, one will feel the his soul is purified and his thoughts sublimed.

The 5 architecture groups in the Temple are given respective features, while the magnificent Hall of Prayers for Bumper Harvests is the major symbol. The resplendence and magnificence show the bearing of a great and proud country, and the splendour and brilliance present the image of Beijing, the ancient capital. It records the 5000-year civilization of the Chinese nation, and is the object on which the soaring of China find sustenence. In Yuanqiu architecture group, there are 3 wonderful phenomenons of sound transmission; The Echo Wall, the Triple Sound Stone and Yizhao Jingcong tone, all unique even in the world. Large as the Circular Mound Altar is, all the stone components are in the number of 9 or the multiples of nine. The exquisite compositions are also unique through the world.

The Temple is a cultural museum of offering sacrifices to Heaven, which merges architecture, aethetics, acoustics, astronomy, calendar, music and dancing into an integral whole. What it show (such as the sacrificial ceremony, sacrificial music and dance, sacrificial offerings and fastings) comprise an important window through which we can learn the history of China.

Beautiful scenes help in establishing friendships among peoples all through the world. The Temple of Heaven is greeting masses of visitors from home and abroad.

Jing Changshun
Director, Tiantan Park

まえがき

天壇は、紀元1421年(明代永楽18年)にたてら北、面積は273万平方メートルで、世界にある祭壇の中でも一番大きいものである。天壇は、二つの祭壇からなっている——南にある圜丘と北の祈穀壇である。

天を祭るは、中国古代の一番盛大な儀式で、古代の人人の理想と観念を反映した。このようの儀式が、中国にだいたい五千年も続いて絶えなかった。明と清の両代のあいだに、双皇帝がみずからここて654度天を祭る儀式をおこなわった。1918年、天壇は公園にかわった。その偉大な制度と独特な建築とふかい天を祭る歴史文化の内包をもって、おうぜいな旅行者をひきつけていた。

天壇の領域は広広として、古い柏と草があおあおし、あおい木とあおそらに映えて、真白い圜丘と雄大で美しい祈年殿は、天堂のようとみる気持をでてくる。天壇へはいると、荘厳、粛穆、神聖、奥深い感情が油然として起る。あの美しい祭壇をみたら、霊魂が清浄になれる、思想も昇華にできた。

天壇は五組の建物を包含して、それぞれ特色をもっている。雄人で美しい祈年殿は天壇の主要な標識で、その高くそびえるさまは大国の気概で、その光り輝くさまは古い都北京の形姿である。中華民族五千年文明が記載されて、中華活躍する希望も預けていた。圜丘の建築群において、三組の特別な声音をパスする現象がある——回音壁、三音石と億兆景叢石は皆極めて少ないものだ。そんな大きい圜丘台の上に、すべての石の部材は皆九と九の倍数でできて精巧で比較を絶する。または、世にならぶものがないのだ。

天壇は祭天文化の博物館で、建築学、美学、声学、天文、暦法、音楽とダンスを一体としている、かれによって人口展示した祭天儀礼、楽舞、供奉、祭品、斎戒なとは、中国歴史を認識するまどである。

旅行は、友誼のたてることをたすけている。天壇は、新しい姿でおうぜいな中国と外国の客さまをむかっている。

天壇公園園長　景長順

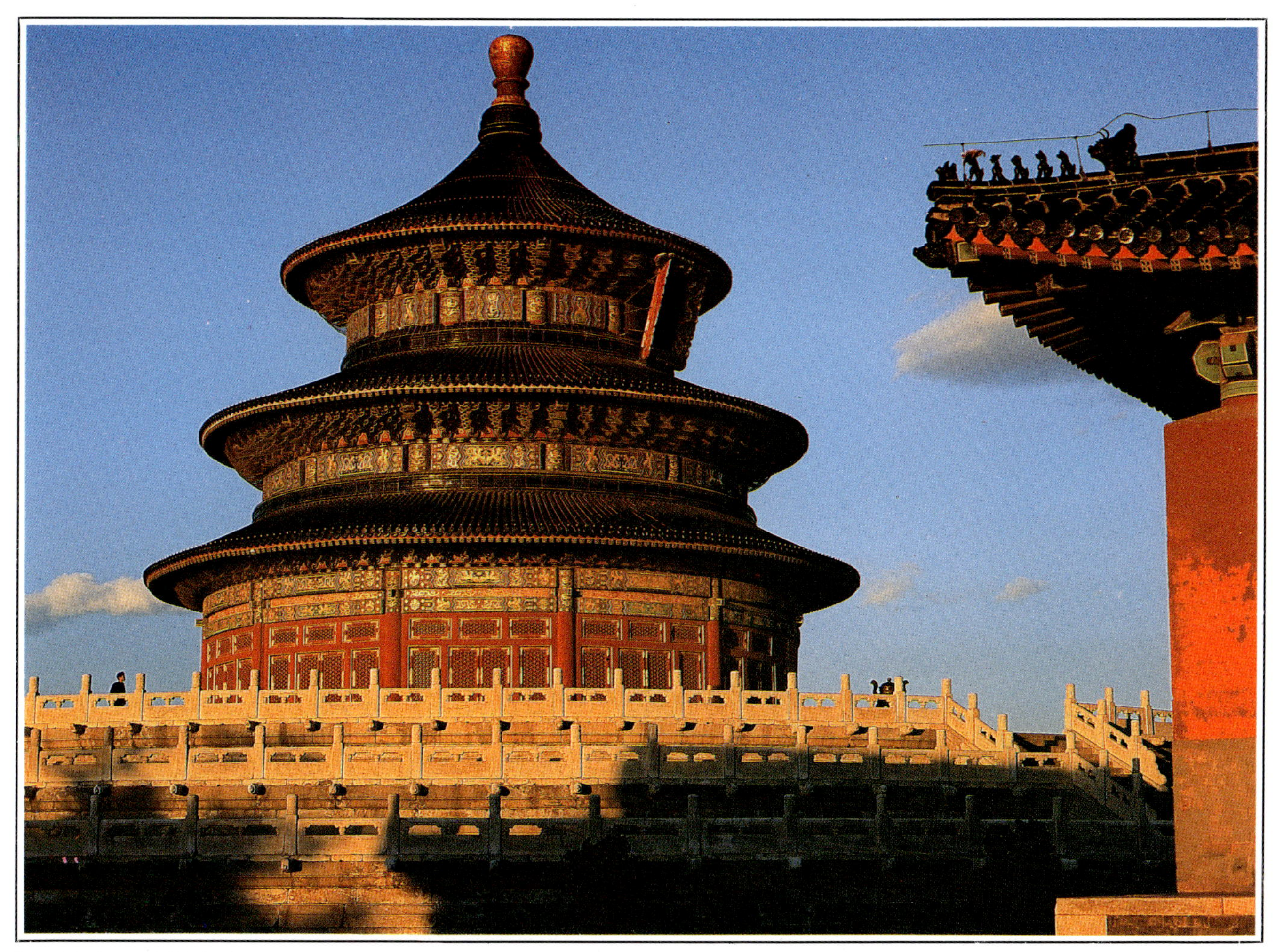

祈年殿　坐落在三層白石壇基上，圓形三層檐，攢尖頂建築。壇基上共出八道台階，南、北各三道，東、西各一道，每道九級。每層壇基均由帶浮雕漢白玉欄板及望柱圍護。所刻飾紋由下至上爲雲紋、鳳紋及龍紋。大殿內外滿飾中國古建彩畫中等級最高的龍鳳和璽彩畫。大殿覆三層靑琉璃瓦，上安金頂。整座建築充分寓示了中國古代天地人共爲一體，陰陽兩極自然和諧的觀念。

Hall of Prayers for Bumper Harvests　Situated on a 3-tiered white marble base, the Hall is a circular building with triple eaves and an obliquely pointed top. On the base are 8 flights of stairs (3 each in the south and north, and one each in the east and west), and there are 9 steps on each flight. Each tier of the base is surrounded by white marble boards and balustrades with reliefs. The reliefs, arranging from lower parts up, are patterns of clouds, of phoenix and of dragon. Inside and outside of the Hall, the walls and the columns are all decorated with coloured paintings of dragons, phoenixes and seals, which are the highest grade decorations in coloured paintings on Chinese ancient buildings. The 3 tiers of roofs are covered with glazed tiles, and a golden top is on the pointed end. The building fully presents the conceptions of the integration of Heaven, earth and human being, which prevails in ancient China, and that of the natural harmony of the positive and negative.

祈年殿　祈年殿は三階建白石壇基の上におけた、まるい三重檐、とかった頂ある建物である。壇基に八つの階段がでて（南と北のほうが三つつず、東と西にはひとつつず）、毎階段に九段ある。壇基は皆浮きぼりあゐ漢白玉でできた欄板と柱にかこんでいる。その飾り模様が、一階から三階まで順順に雲、鳳と竜である。殿の内外が中国古い建築に写いたもっとも高級な竜、鳳と璽の彩画がいっぱい。殿の屋根に三重の青い琉璃瓦が敷き、うえに金色の頂がある。この建築は，充分に，中国古代の“天地人は一体にする”と“陰極と陽極が自然に調和する”の観念を示させている。

祈年殿　始建成於明朝永樂十八年(1421年)。明、清兩朝均作較大更改。現存建築爲1890年遭雷火後依原樣重建。祈年殿基座直徑90米、大殿直徑32米，基座高6米，大殿高38米。白壇，紅殿、藍檐、金頂，是中國古建築中的代表作。

Hall of Prayers for Bumper Harvests First completed in 1421 (the 18th year of the reign of Emperor Yongle, Ming Dynasty), the Hall went though larger changes in Ming and Qing dynasties respectively. The present building was one rebuilt in 1890 after it was struck and destroyed by a thunder fire. The base of the Hall is 90m in diameter, and that of the Hall is 32m. The height of the base is 6m, and that of the Hall 38m. Composed by a white base, a red hall, blue eaves and a golden top, it is the representative work of ancient Chinese buildings.

祈年殿は、1421年(明代永楽18年)に建て始まり、明代と清代はともに大きい改建の工程をおこなわれた。いまの建物は、1890年に、もとの殿は雷火に毀れてから再建したものである。祈年殿の基座の直径は90メートル、殿の直径は32メートル，基座の高さは6メートル、殿の高さは38メートルである。白い壇、紅い殿、あおい檐と金色の項を持っている祈年殿は、中国古い建築の代表作品である。

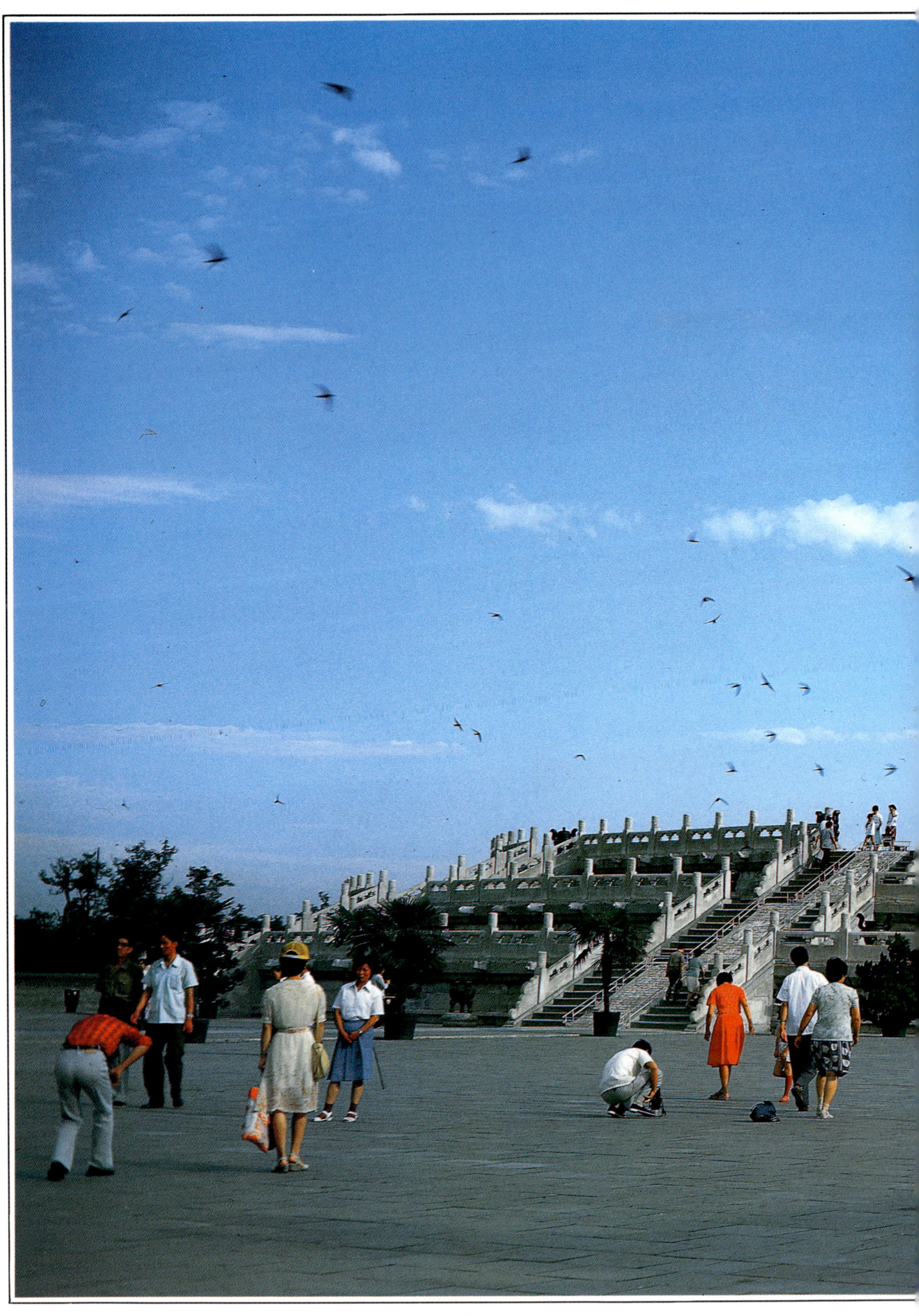

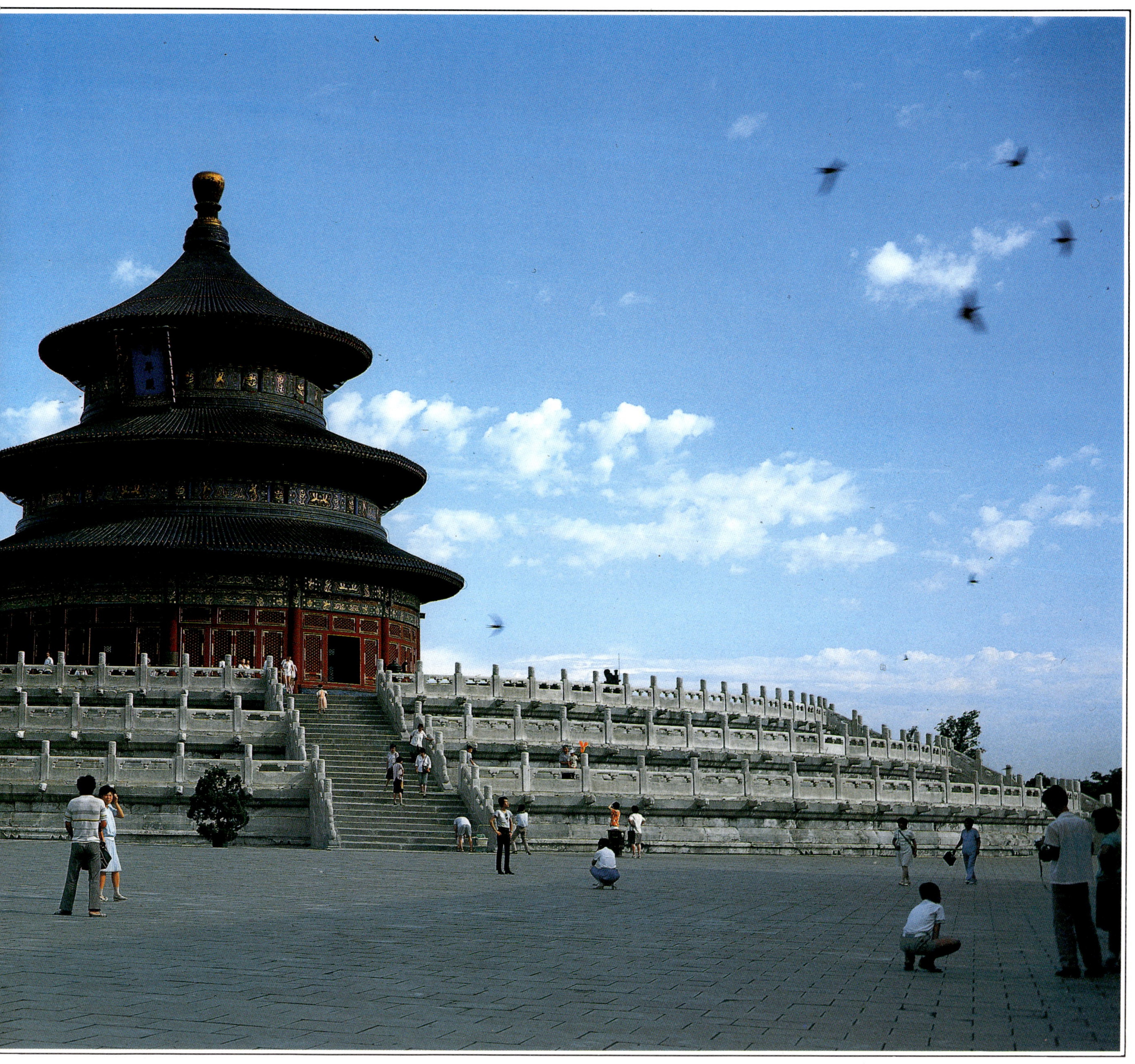

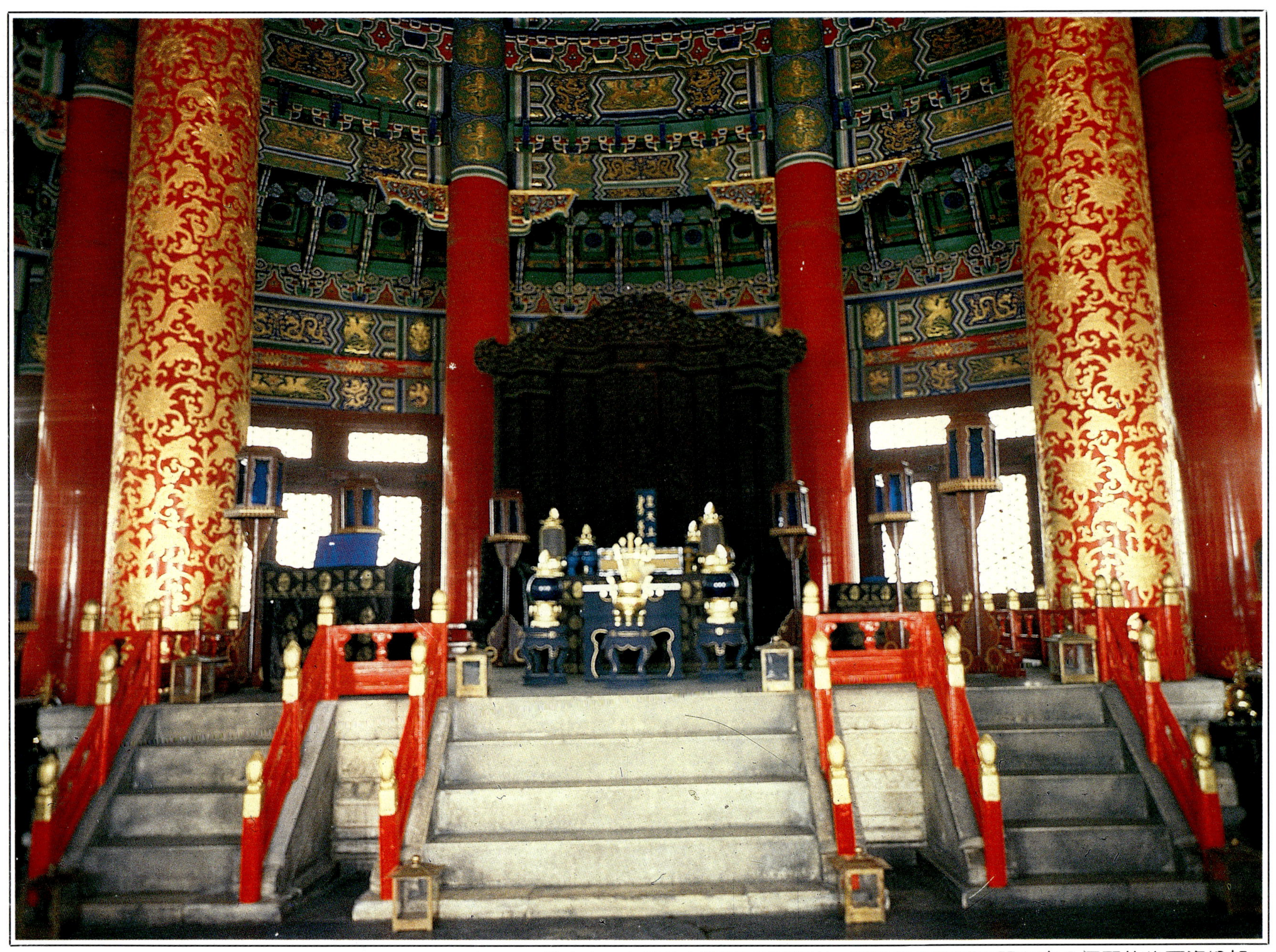

祈年殿是清朝舉行孟春祈谷大典的祭祀場所。祭祀時，殿內供奉皇天上帝及清代列祖列宗神位。至道光帝達到三祖五宗八個配位後再沒增加。圖爲大殿正中皇天上帝正位供奉陳設情況。

The Hall of Prayers for Bumper Harvests was the place where ceremonies praying for bumper grain harvests were held in the first month of spring. When ceremonies were held, tablet of Heaven and God and those of ancestors of the Qing imperial household were set. By the reign of Emperor Daoguang, the tablets involved 3“zu”, 5 “zong” and 8 matching ones, and nothing had been added ever since. Picture shows the proper setting of the tablets of Heaven and God in the middle of the Hall.

祈年殿は、清代に、春の最初の月に祈穀の儀式をおこなわれるところである。祭りをするときに、殿内に皇天上帝ならび清皇室の祖宗の神位を供える。道光皇帝の時，それ神位は三祖五宗と八つの配位に限りとして，あとには，いつでも増加しなかった。写真は、殿のまんなかに皇天上帝の正位を供えている状況。

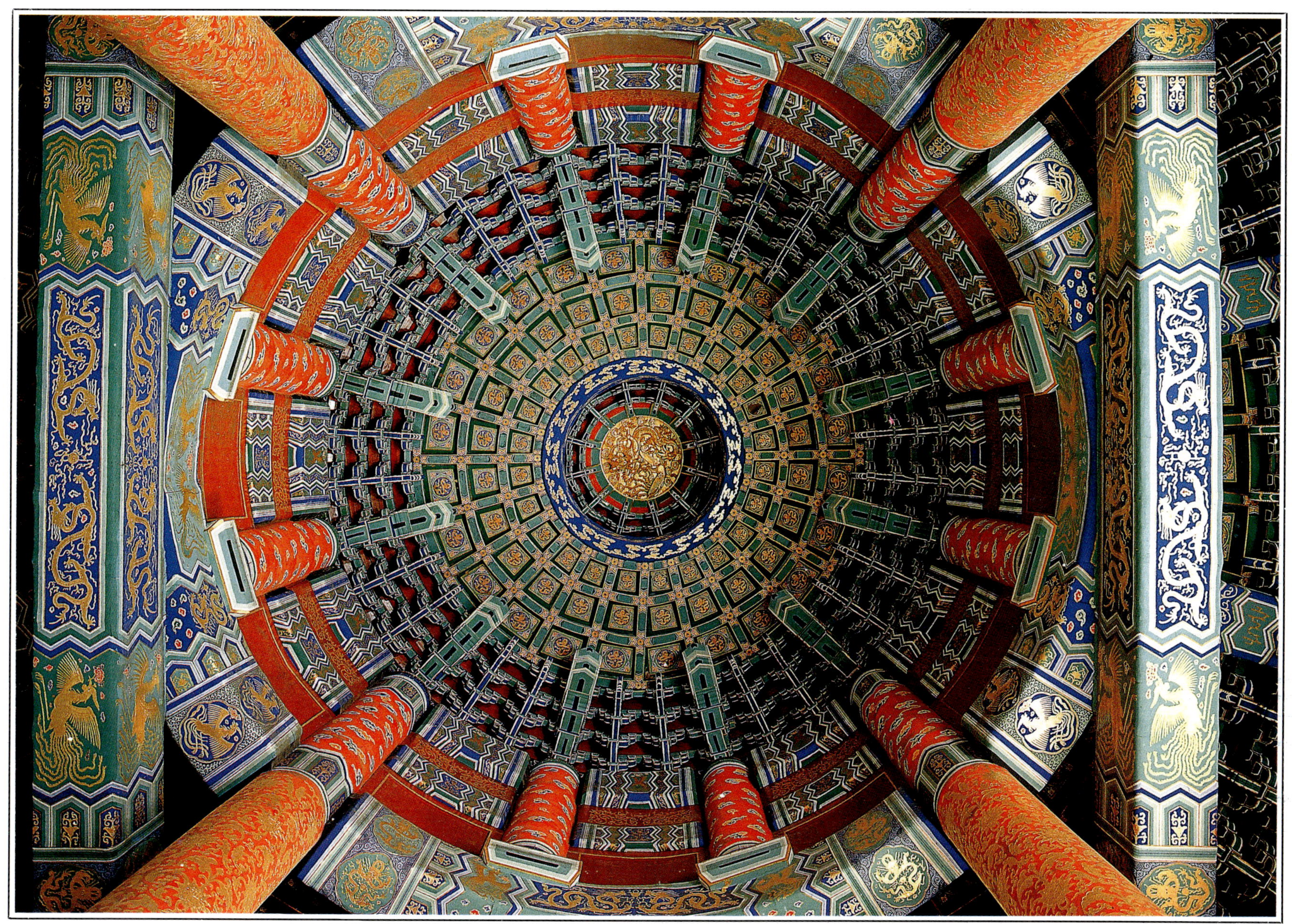

祈年殿是中國木結構建築中的精品。中間藻井由四根龍井柱支撐。柱子上接方形的地樑和圓形的天梁，天梁上另增八根雷公柱，加龍井柱共十二柱一起承受藻井。藻井由兩層斗拱及一層天花組成，中間爲金色龍鳳浮雕，結構精巧，富麗華貴。

The hall of Prayers for Bumper Harvests is the excellent work among cinese wooken constructions. The caisson ceiling in the centre is supported by 4 Longjing columns which contact the square lower beam and round upper beam. On the upper beam are 8 Leigong pillar which, together with the Longjing columns, support the ceiling which is composed by 2 layers of brackets and 1 layer of caisson, and goledn reliefs of dragons and phoenixes decorate the middle. The construction is meticulous and looks splendid and luxurious.

祈年殿は、中国の木結構建物の中の優良品である。まんなかの天井が四つの竜井柱で支えて、柱の上は四角形の地樑とまるい天樑があり、天樑の上に八つの雷公柱が加えされている。雷公柱と竜井柱とともに天井を受ける。天井は、二層のとがたと一層の天井板で作くられ、まんなかには金色の竜と鳳の浮彫で、結構は精巧で、立派である。

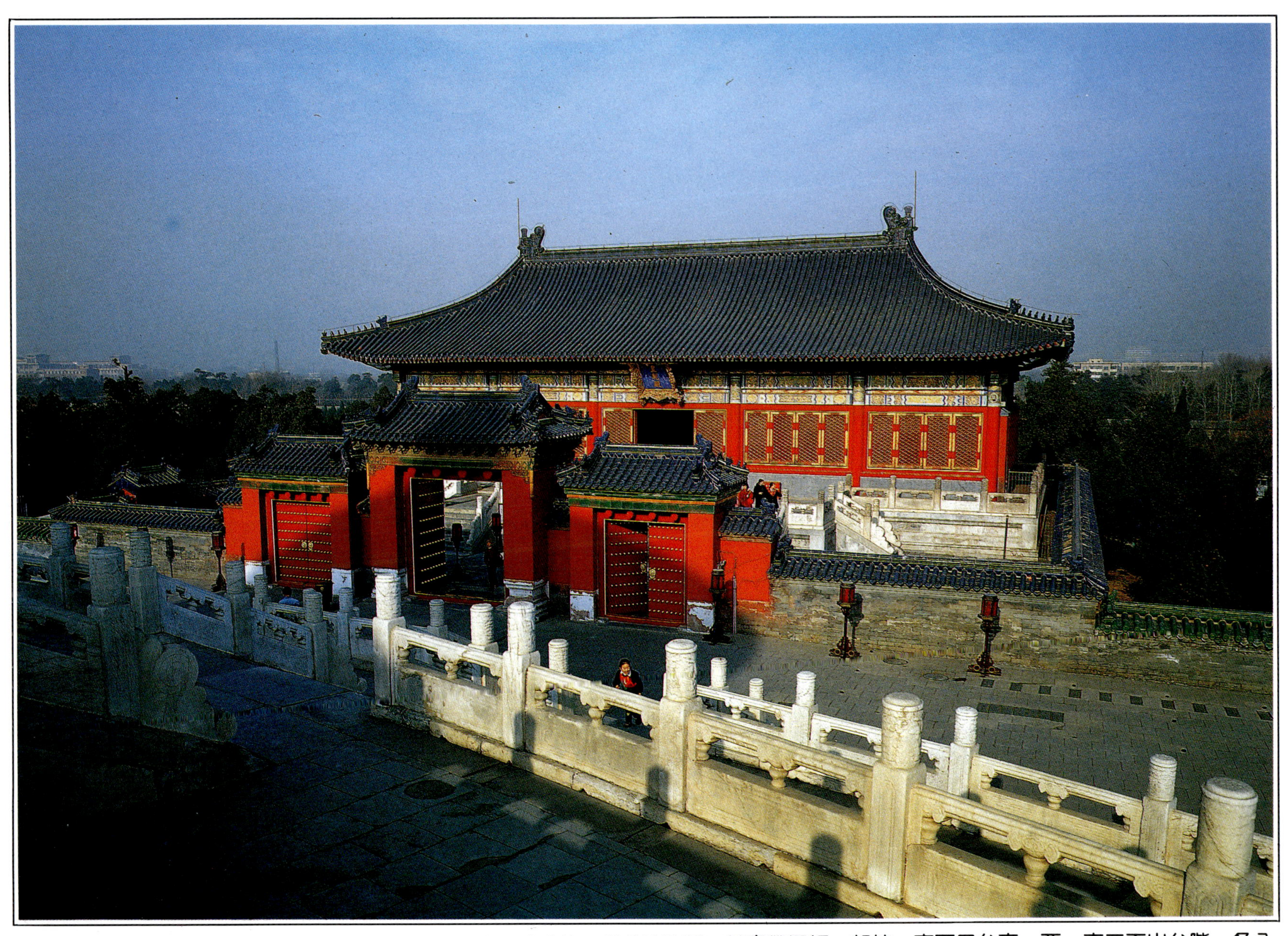

皇乾殿建成於明朝永樂十八年(1421年)、五開間，廡殿式建築，藍色琉璃頂，基座帶欄板、望柱，南面月台東、西、南三面出台階，各八級，望柱浮雕龍、鳳紋相間，大殿內外飾龍鳳和諧彩畫。殿前琉璃三座門是中國古建中的珍品。

Buill in 1421 (the 18th year of the reign of Yongle, Ming Dynasty), the Hall of Imperial Heaven is a construction 5-bay across, with blue glazed-tiled roof. The base is surrounded by blocking boards and balustrades. The terrace in the south is equipped by stairs in the east, west and south, 8 steps each. The balustrades are carved with alternating reliefs of patterns of dragon and phoenix. The outer and inner sides of wall of the Hall are decorated with harmonious coloured paintings of dragon and phoenix. The 3-bayed glazed gate is the masterpiece among ancient Chinese buildings.

皇乾殿は、1421年(明代永楽18年)に建てられ、五軒幅の廡殿式の建物で、屋根に藍色の琉璃瓦が敷きられ、基台の項部は板と望柱がある。南の月台の東、西、南の三つのほうに階段がでて、毎階段に八段ある。望柱の上は、竜、鳳模様の浮彫がかわるがわるにあり、殿の内外の塀などには竜鳳和諧の彩色絵画がかざれている。殿の前にある琉璃三軒幅鳥居は、中国古代建築中の珍しい品である。

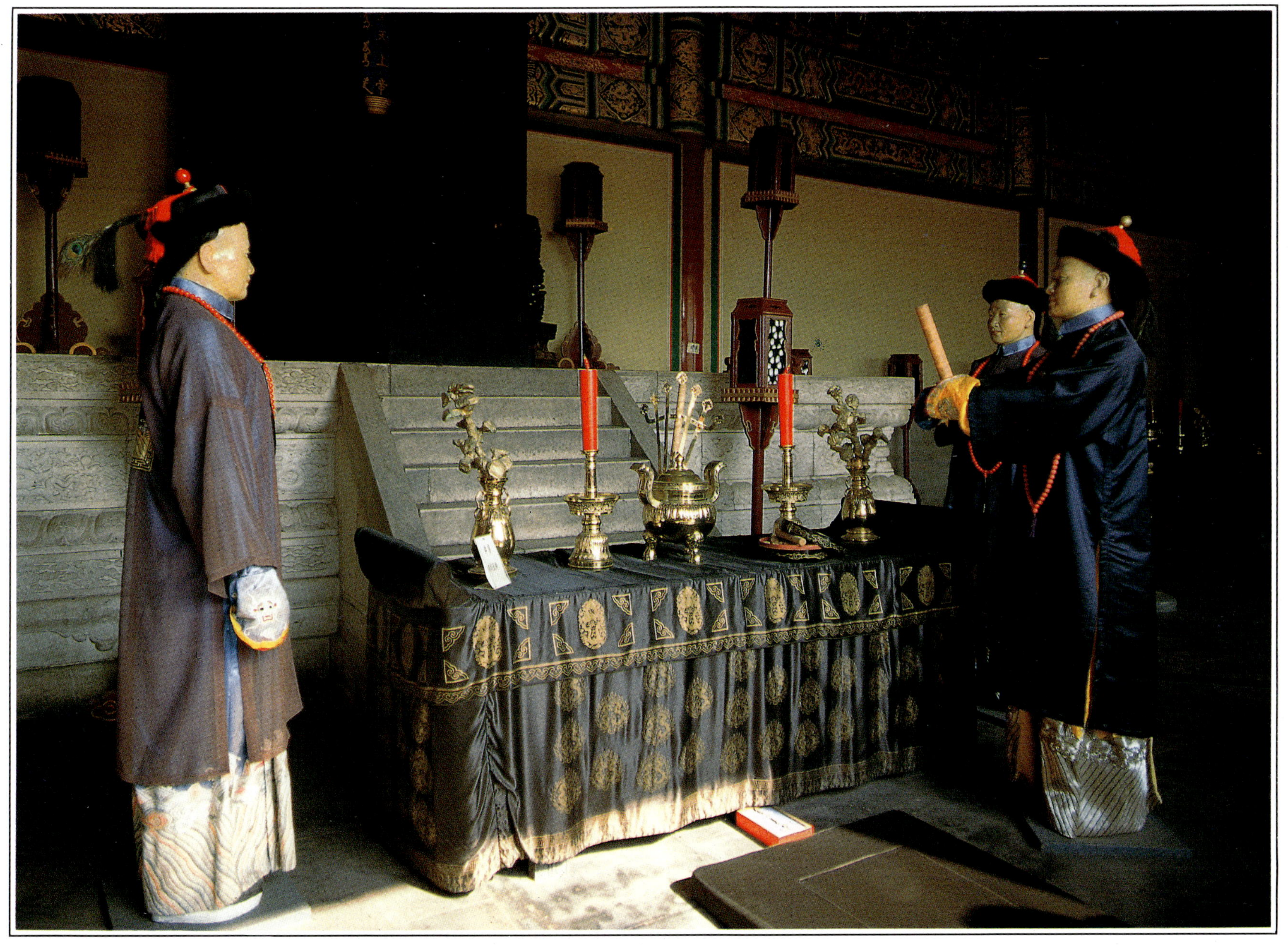

皇乾殿是平時供奉正位及配位神版的地方。祭祀時皇帝先赴這裏上香，再赴齋宮齋戒。圖中所示爲清朝咸豐皇帝至此上香之情景。

The Hall of Imperial Heaven was the place where tablets of proper and matching ancestors were kept. When a ceremony was held, the emperor burnt incense here first, and then went fasting in the Fasting Palace. Picture shows the scene when Emperor Xianfeng came burning incense here.

皇乾殿は、平素正位ならび配位神の神位を供えるところである。祭りをするとき、皇帝はまづここで線香をあげてから、斎宮へ斎戒するにゆく。写真は、清代咸豊皇帝が皇乾殿に線香をあげている状況。

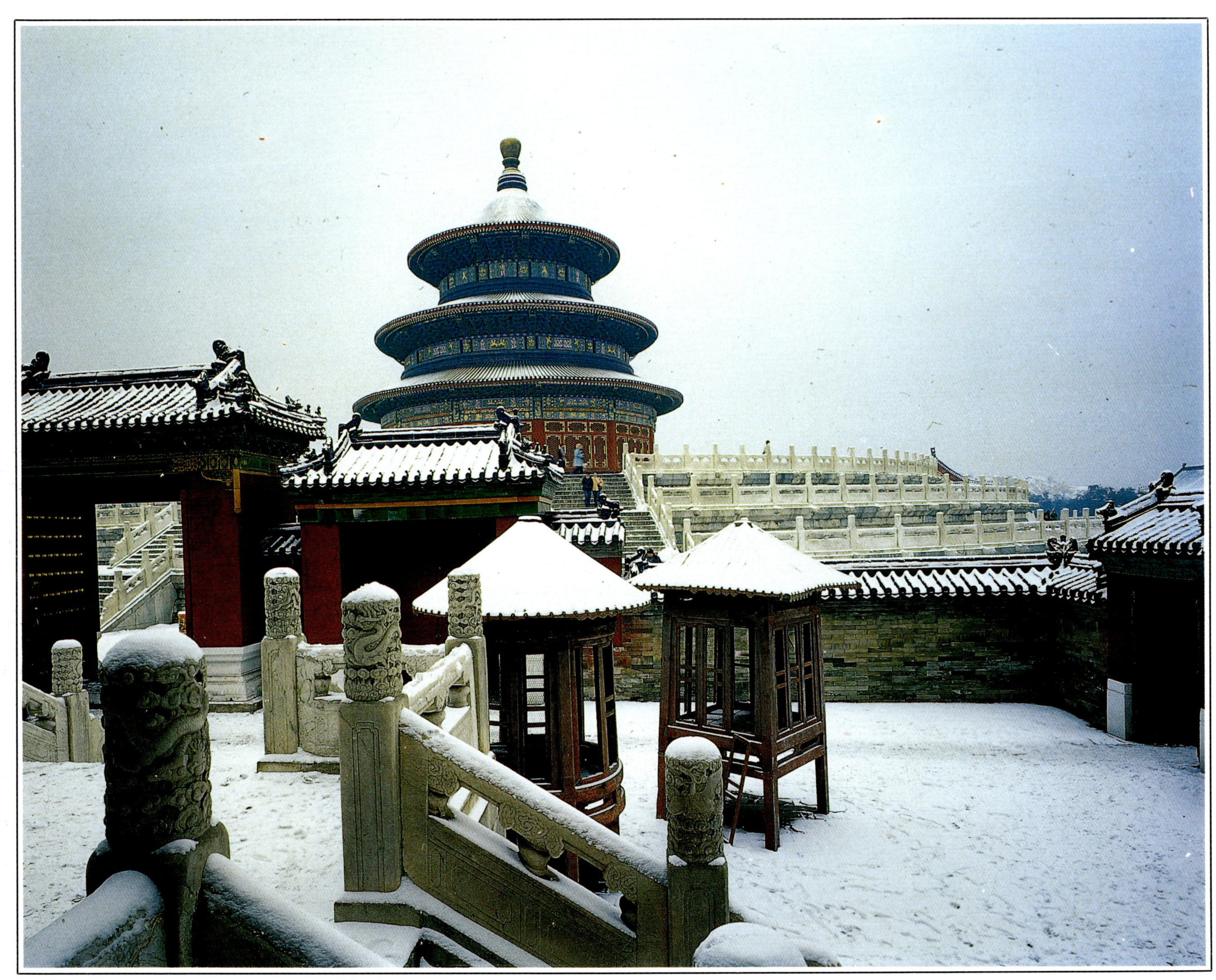

祈年殿
Hall of Prayers for Bumper Harvests
祈年殿

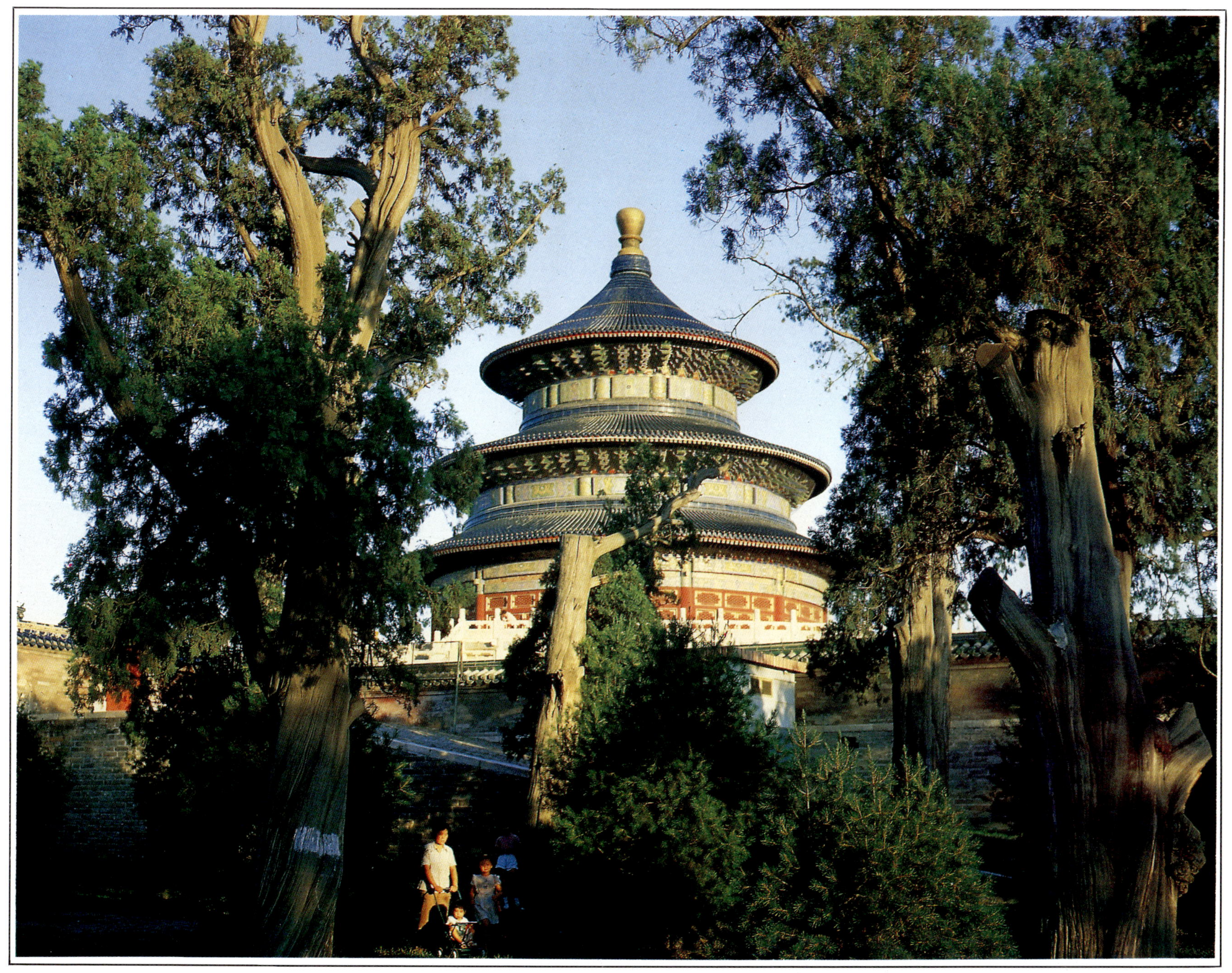

祈年殿周圍，明清兩代遍植松柏，現已歷數百年，蔚然成林，置身其間，氣氛自然，祥和，清幽，寧靜。眞正“松柏閱世風霜古，老壇沐春歲月新”。

In Ming and Qing Dynasties, pines and cypresses were planted around the Hall of Prayers for Bumper Harvests. Through several hundred years, those trees have formed forests. Standing among them, one can feel the atmosphere natural, harmonious, quiet and peaceful. The ancient forests is providing a really new environment for people to wander in.

明代と清代の時、祈年殿の周辺に松と柏の木を植元た。数百年のあいだに，あおあお森になってきた。そのところにたって、あの氛囲は自然、祥和、清幽、寧静で、古い森が、新時代の春風を受けているとおもい。

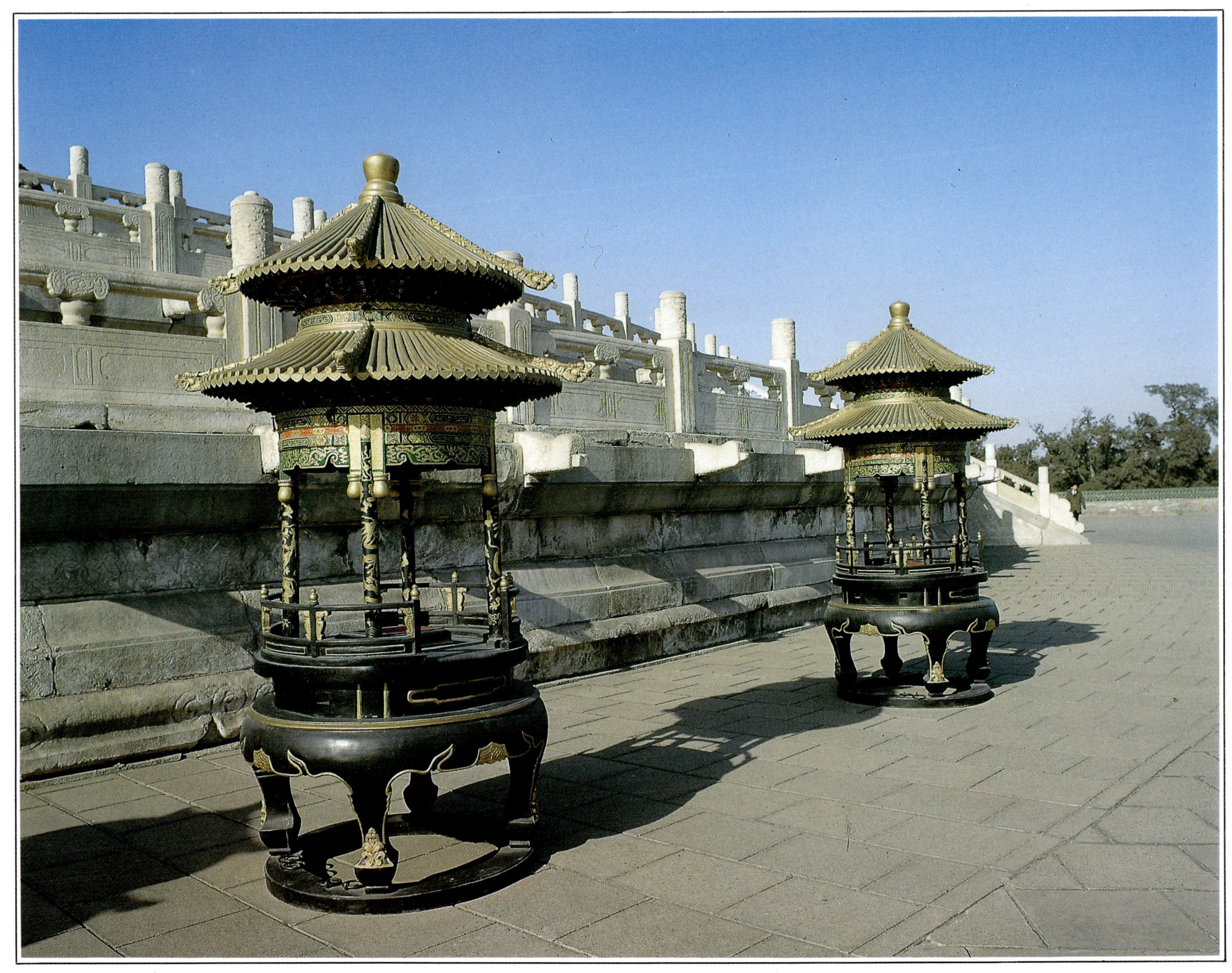

當年舉行祭祀禮時，由校尉把供奉在皇乾殿的正位，配位神版，抬至祈年殿內供奉。這是升抬神版時用的龍亭。亭內有安放神版的木坑，正位爲圓形，配位爲方形。

When sacrificial ceremonies were held, The proper and matching tablets kept in the Hall of Imperial Heaven were carried into the Hall of Prayers for Bumper Harvests by some officers, where they were worshipped. Picture shows the Dragon Pavilion in which are wooden troughs for placing the tablets——Round troughs for proper ones, and square for the matching.

昔、祭りをするときに、校尉によって、皇乾殿に供えている正位と配位神位を祈年殿へ運搬して供える。写真は、神位をはこぶときにつかっていた竜亭である。亭の中には、神位をおく木槽があり，正位は丸い槽におく、配位は方形槽をつかう。

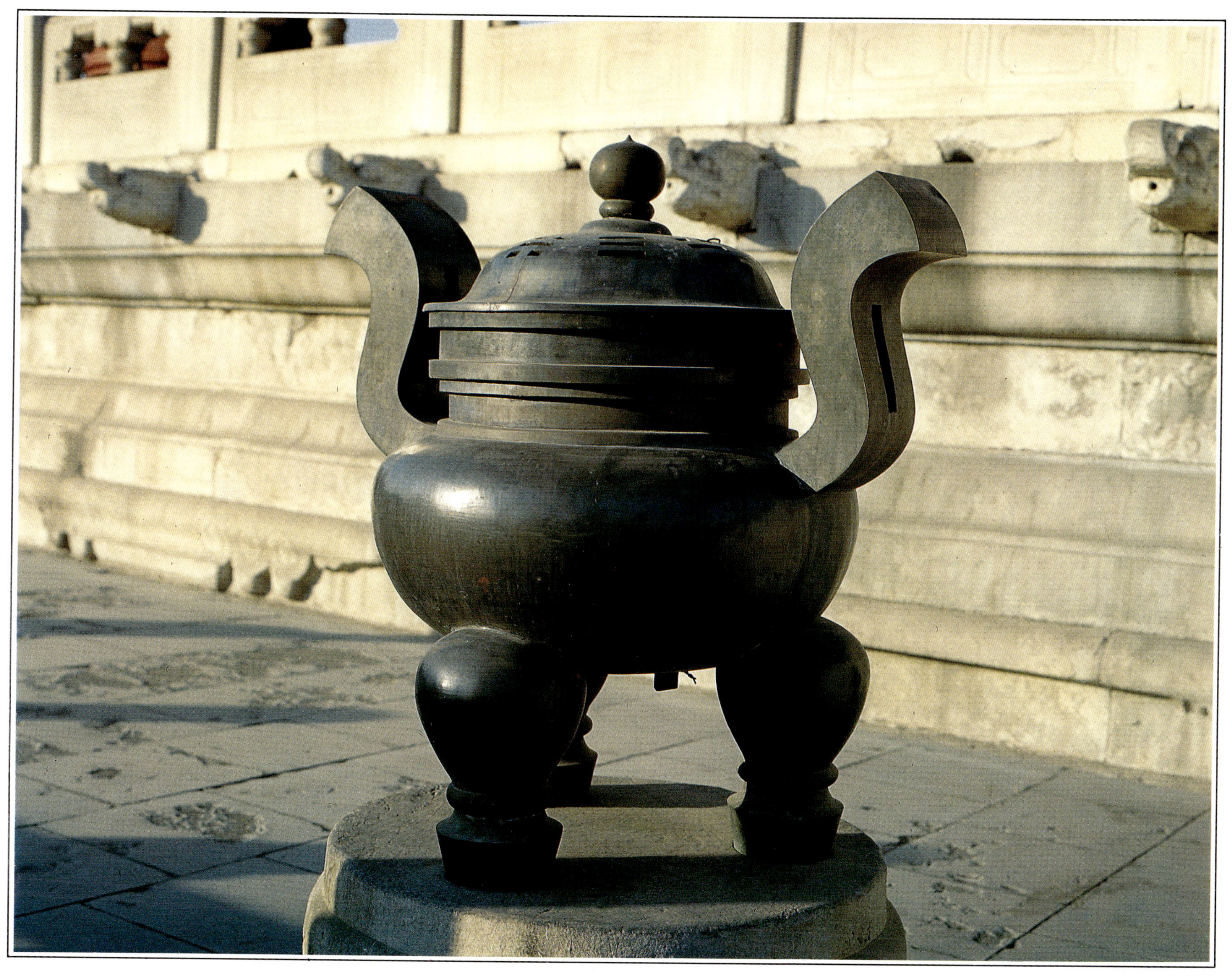

祭壇上台階兩側陳設有鼎爐。天壇鼎爐爲圓形三足，蓋上有鏤空八卦圖案。

On the Altar, incense burners are set on either side of the stairs. They are round-shaped with 3 legs, and hollow out patters of the Eight Diagrams are on the lids.

祭壇の上、階段の両側に、鼎炉がある。天壇の鼎炉は、圓形、三足、ふたの上に、八卦の図案が透し彫りにしている。

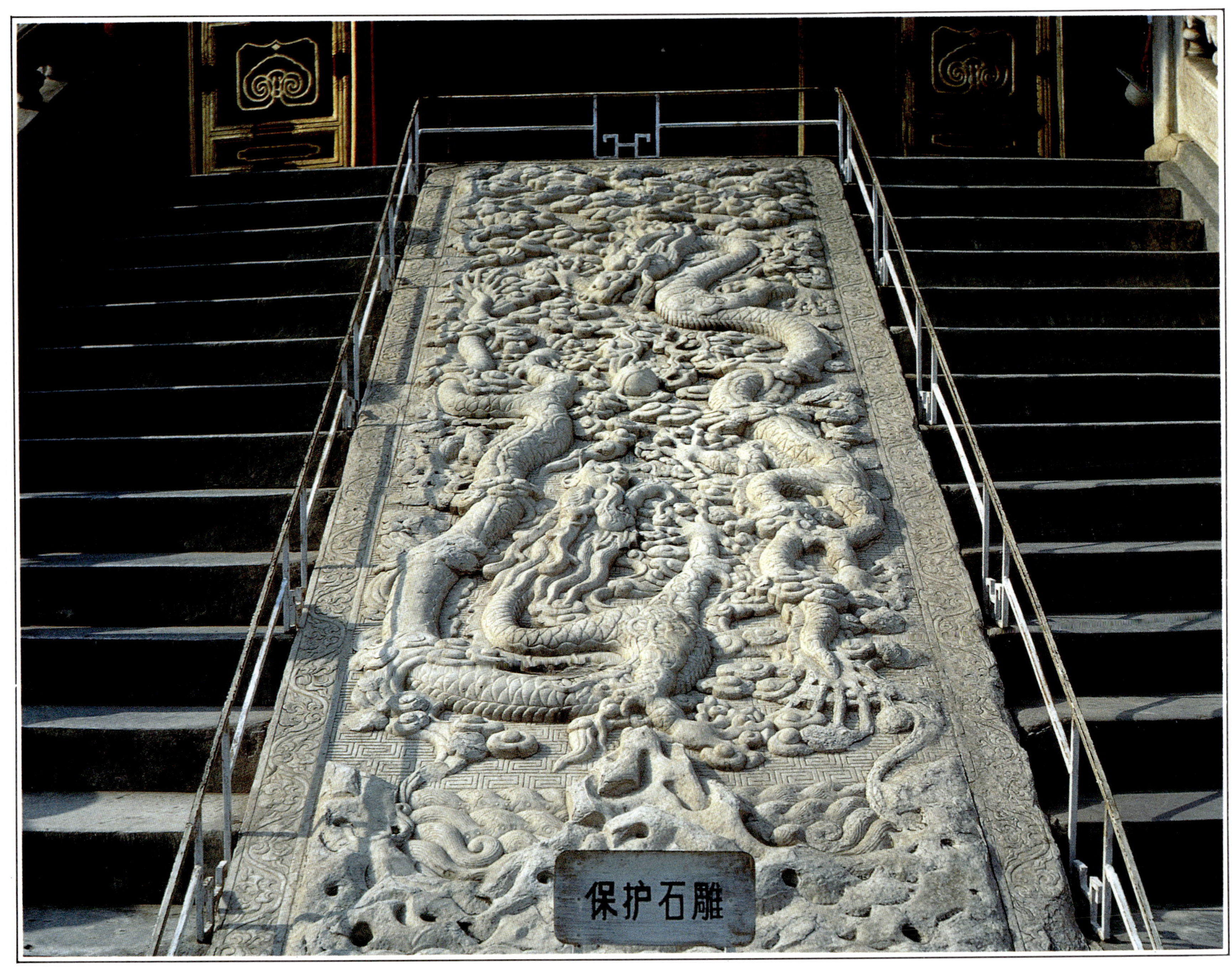

祈谷壇丹墀浮雕　祈年殿坐落在三層石壇一祈谷壇上，祈谷壇從下到上的望柱、出水嘴、丹墀上，都雕刻有吉祥浮雕，依次爲雲紋、鳳紋、龍紋。

Reliefs on the Decoration Stone in Front of the Altar for the God of Grains　The Hall of Prayers for Bumper Harvests is set on the 3-tiered Altar for the God of Grains. On all balustrades, exits of water and decoration stones are carved auspicious reliefs. From the lowest tier up, the pattern of reliefs are clouds, phoenix and dragon in order.

祈穀壇の丹墀の上にある浮彫　祈年殿は、三階建の石壇——祈穀壇の上にある。祈穀壇のあらゆる望柱、水の出口と丹墀の上に、皆縁起がいい浮彫が彫ってある。下からの順序は、雲、鳳と竜の模様である。

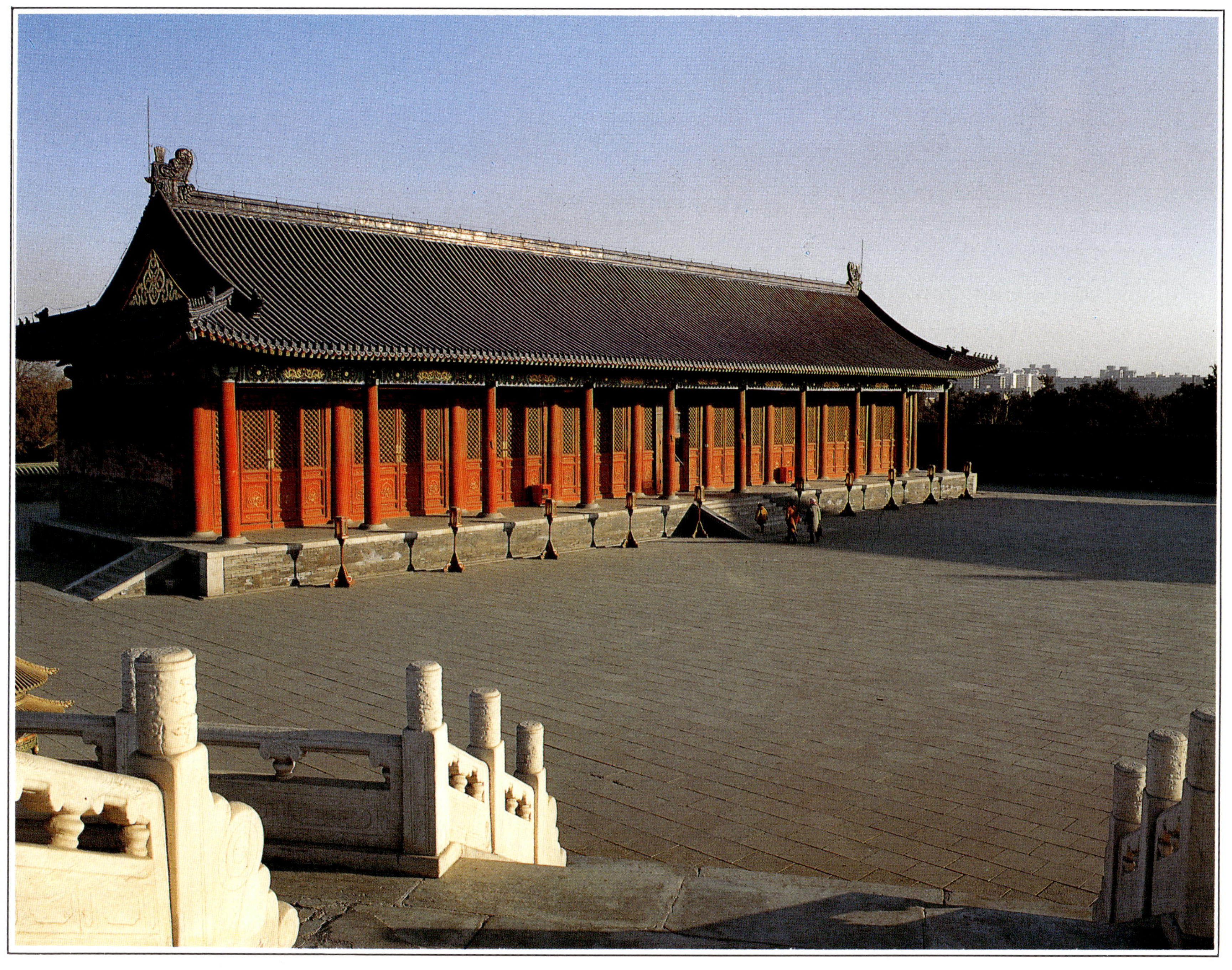

祈年殿東配殿　始建成於明朝永樂十八年(1421年)，九開間，歇山式建築，藍色琉璃瓦頂。內外梁枋飾旋子彩畫。

The Eastern Side Hall of the Hall of Prayers for Bumper Harvests　First completed in 1421 (the 18th year of the reign of Yongle, Ming dynasty), it is a construction 9-bay across, with beams resting on the gable and blue glazed tile roof, and the beams and eaves are decorated by coloured paintings.

祈年殿の東配殿　1421年(明代永楽18年に)にできた、九軒幅、歇山式の建物で、屋根に藍色琉璃瓦が敷きられ、内外の樑枋とともに彩画でかざられている。

天壇由南北兩壇組成，北壇祈谷壇歷史最早，建成於1421年，當時叫天地壇，合祀皇天後土，中心建築爲大祀殿。明朝嘉靖年間四郊分祀，撤大祀殿，在原址建大亨殿。淸朝乾隆年間更大亨殿瓦色，改名爲祈年殿、其制終成。主要建築有祈年殿，皇乾殿，祈年門，七十二長廊，神厨、宰牲亭等。

The Temple of Heaven is composed by the south and north altars. In the northern part, The Altar for the God of Grains is the first built. Being completed in 1421, it was then called the Altar of Heaven and Earth, where both the Heaven and earth were worshipped. The central building is the Great Sacrificial Hall. In Ming Dynasty, sacrificial ceremonies were held separately in the 4 suburbs, thus the Great Sacrificial Hall was removed, and the Daxiang Hall was built on the site. In the reign of Qianlong, Qing Dynasty, the colour of the tiles of the Daxiang Hall was changed, and the Hall was renamed the Hall of Prayers for Bumper Harvests, thus the system was completed at last. The major buildings include the Hall of Prayers for Bumper Harvests, Hall of Imperial Heaven, the Gate of Prayers for Bumper Harvests, the 72-Bayed Corridor, the Sacred Kitchen and Sacrifice-butchering Pavilion.

天壇は、南壇と北壇で組織して作つた。北壇の祈年殿は、1421年に始めてたてられたものだから、一番長い歴史を持つている。できたときに、"天地壇"となつけ、天と地をともに祭りをした。そのあたりの中心建物は、大祀殿であつた。明代嘉靖年間、祭祀は四郊で分別におこなわるとなつたため、大祀殿が撤廃させ、もとのところに大享殿を建てた。清代乾隆年間、大享殿の煉瓦の色をかわって、祈年殿と改名し、完備な形制ができた。主要な建物が祈年殿、皇乾殿、祈年門、七十二長廊、神厨、宰牲亭などである。

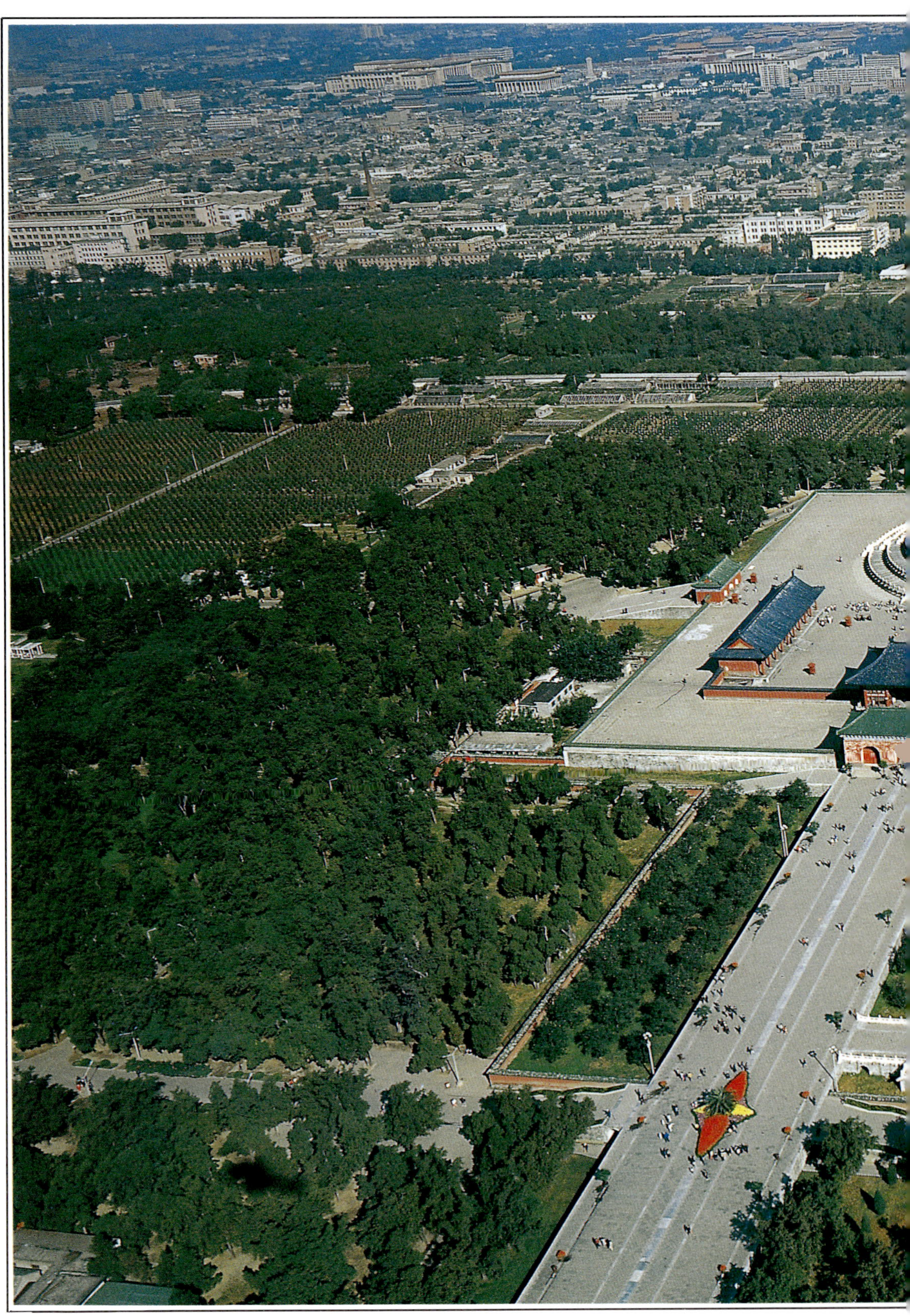

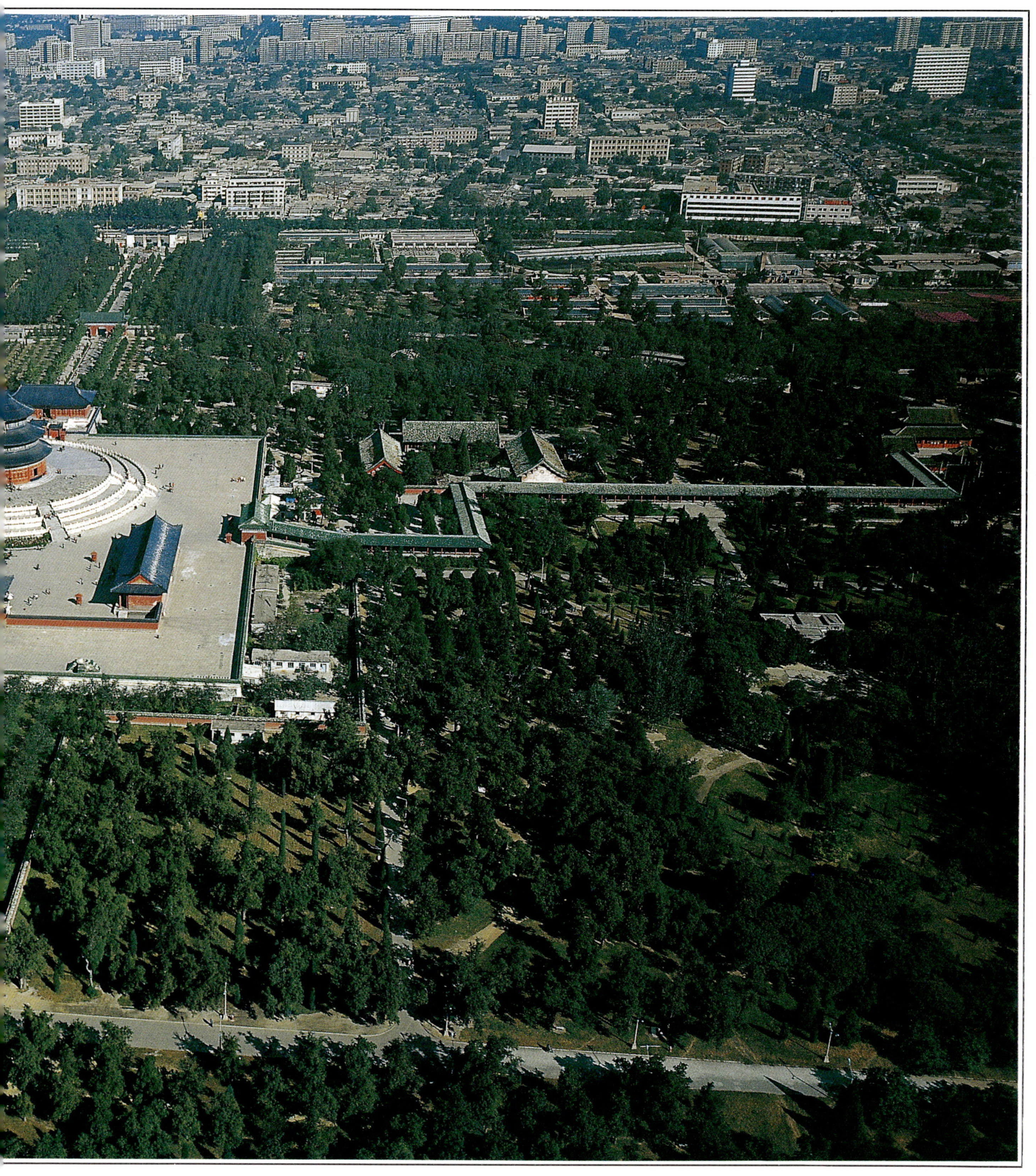

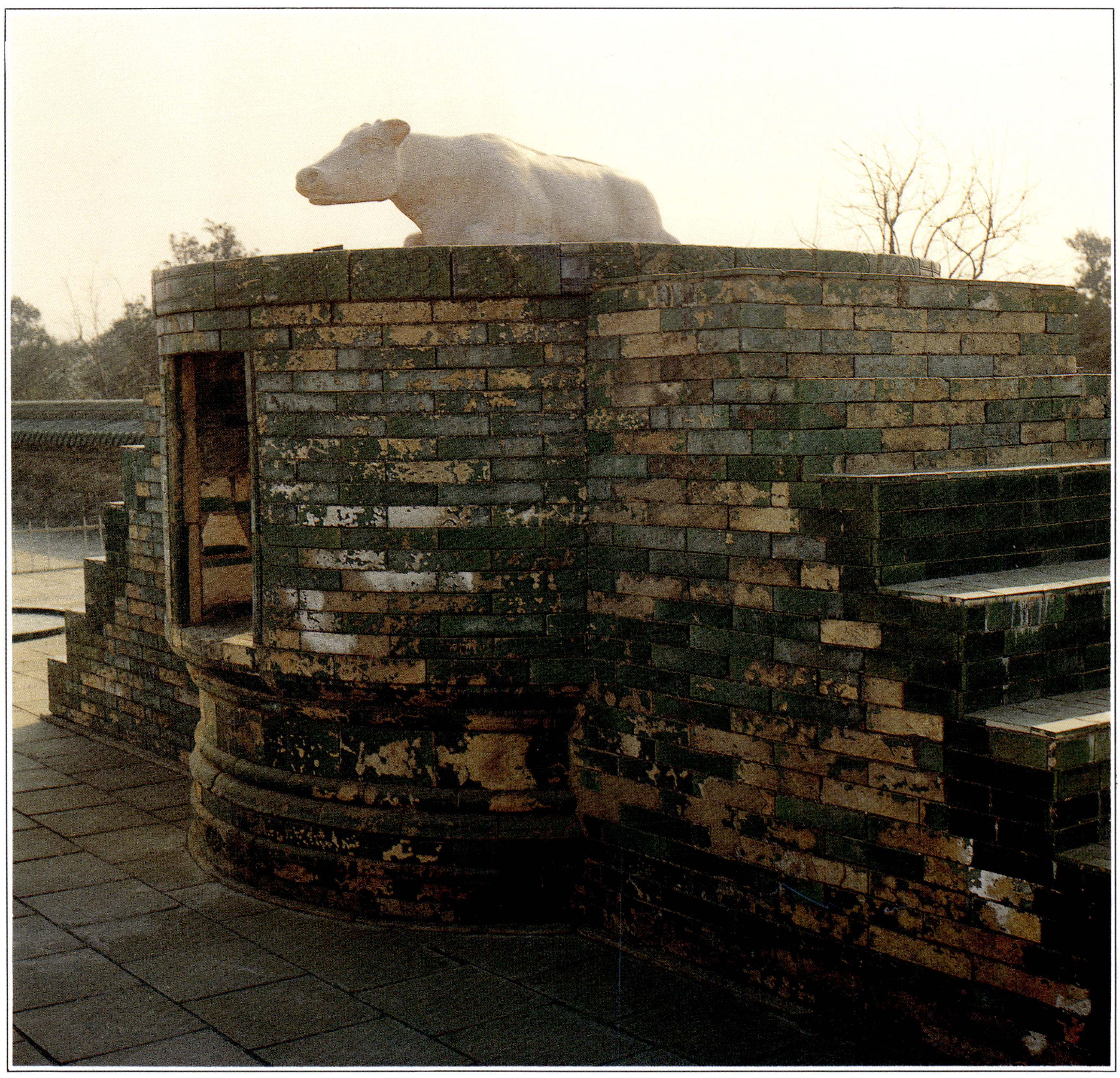

祈年殿

Hall of Prayers for Bumper Harvests

祈年殿

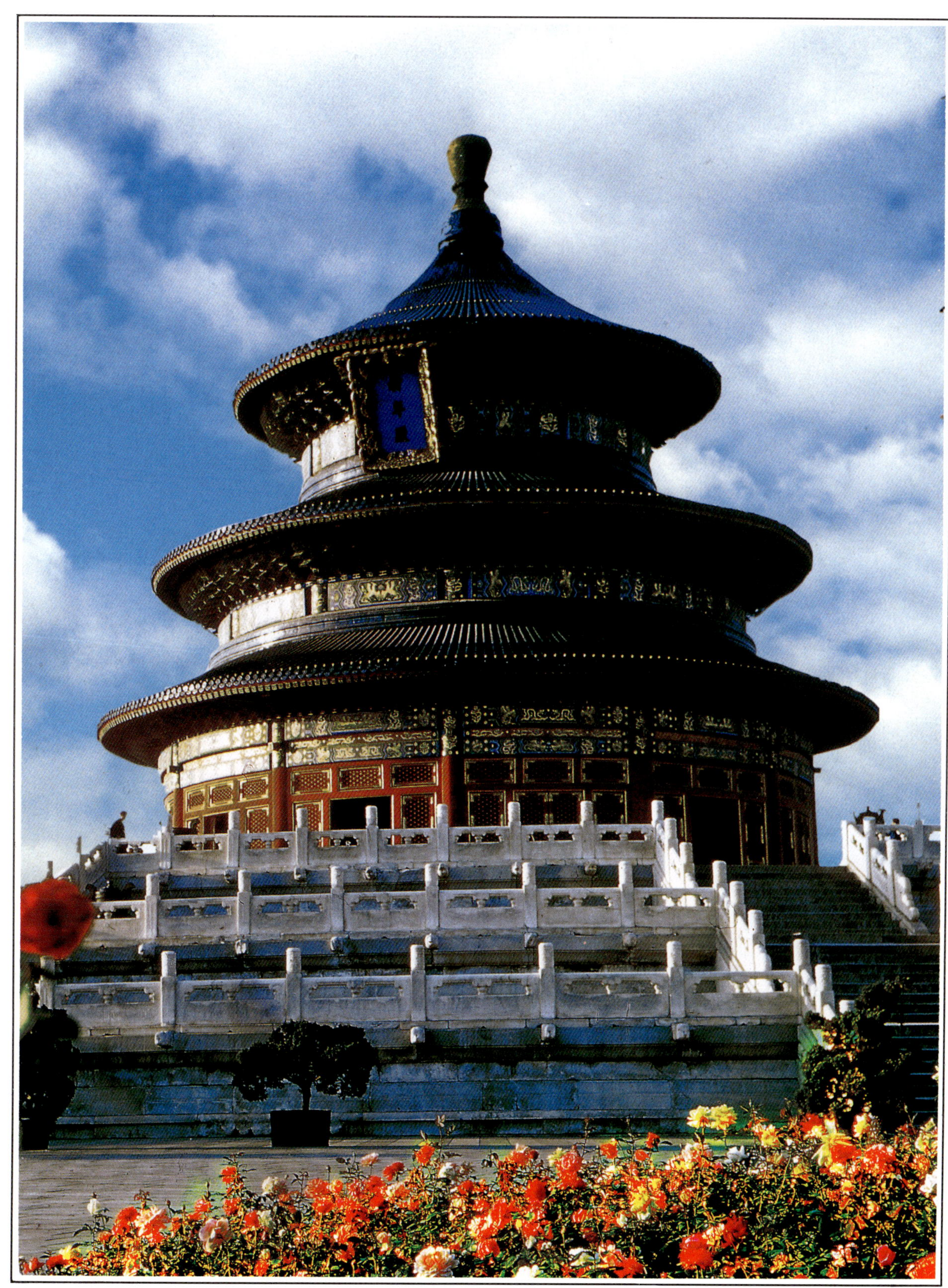

◀燔柴爐

The Stove in the Walls

燔柴炉

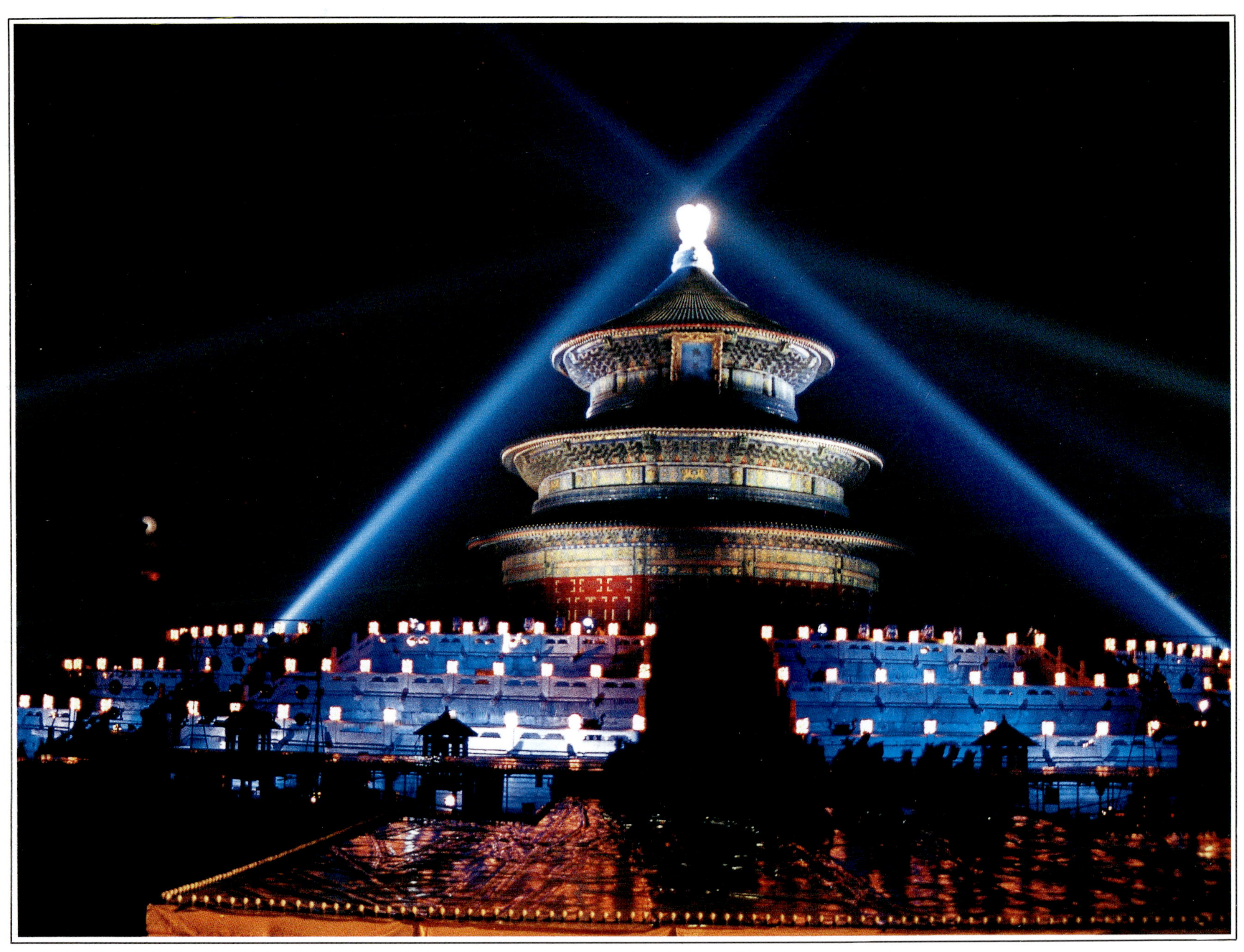

祈年殿之夜

A Night View of the Hall of Prayers for Bumper Harvests.

祈年殿の夜の景色

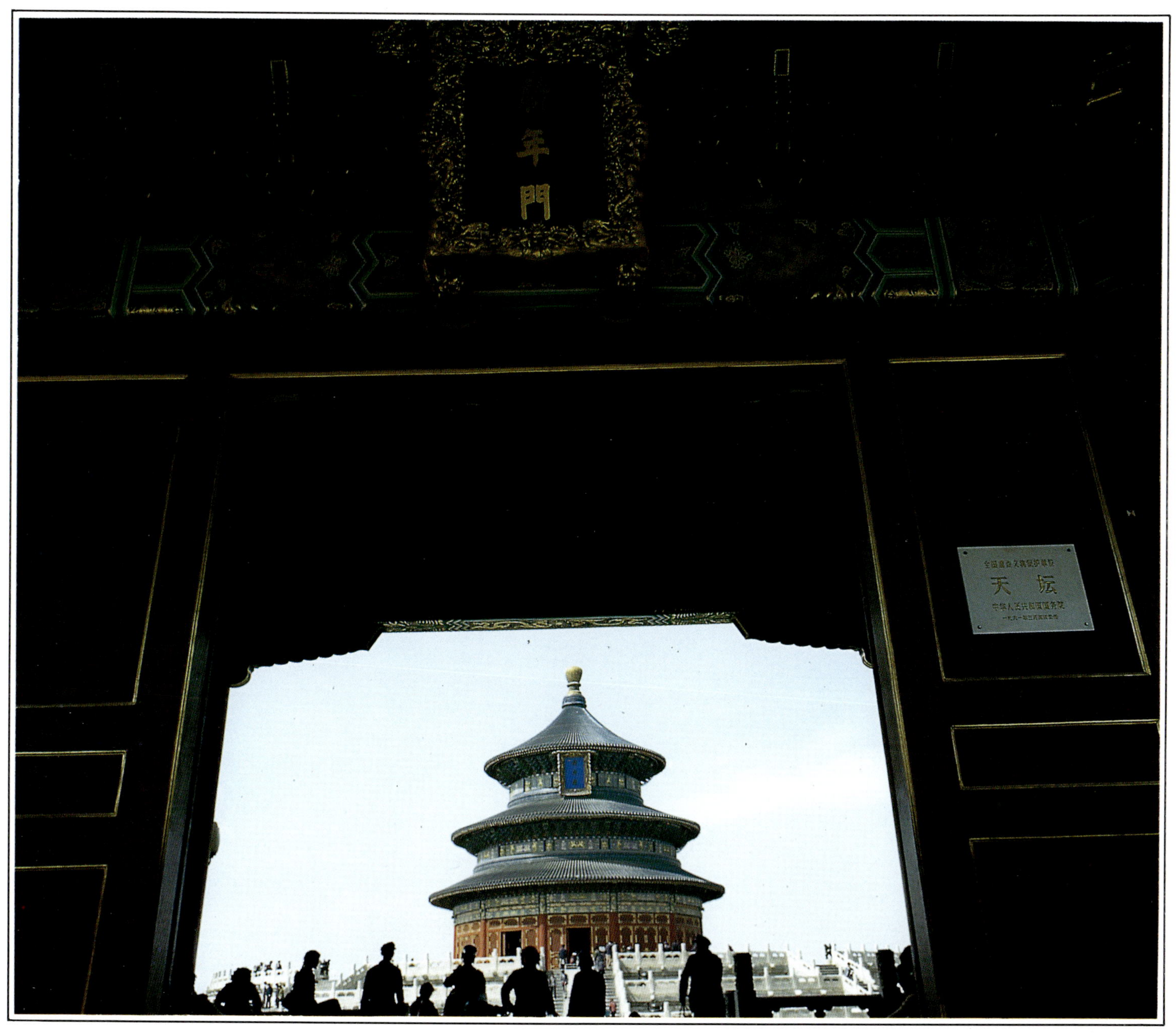

祈年門　位於祈年殿正南，南向五開間，廡殿式建築，藍色琉璃瓦頂，始建成於明朝永樂十八年(1421年)。大門內外滿飾龍鳳和璽彩畫，門內上裝天花。

The Gate of Prayers for Bumper Harvests　Situated at the south of the Hall of Prayers for Bumper Harvests, the Gate is a 5-bay structure facing the south. The roof is covered with blue glazed tiles. The inside and outside of the Gate are decorated by patterns of dragons, phoenixes and golden coloured paintings. Inner side of the Gate is set with caisson above. It was first completed in 1421 (the 18th year of the reign of Yongle, Ming Dynasty).

祈年門　門が祈年殿の真南にあり、南にむかって三軒幅の廡殿式の建物である。1421年(明代永楽18年)に建てはじまり、屋根は藍色琉璃瓦を敷きられ、門の中の上に天花がとりつけられ、門の内外は、竜と鳳と璽の彩画がいっぱいかぢれてある。

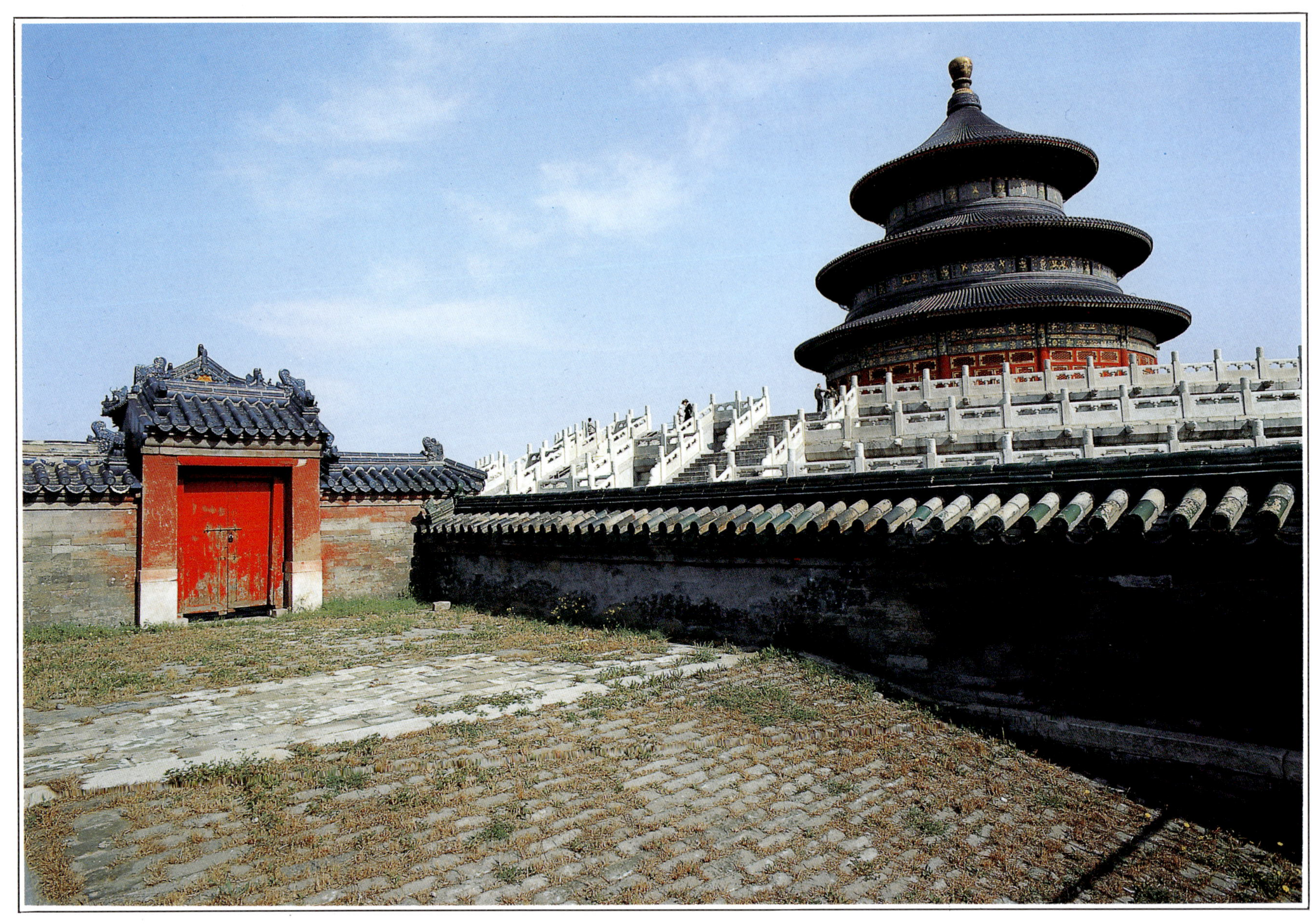

古稀門　位於皇乾殿院西，建於清乾隆朝晚期。乾隆皇帝七十歲時，爲節省步力而建，並下詔其子孫爲皇帝者年屆七旬方可由此門入祈谷壇。天壇歷史上走過此門的皇帝僅乾隆一人。後人稱此門爲“古稀門”。

Guximen (The Gate for 70-year olds)　Situated to the west of the courtyard of the Hall of Imperial Heaven, it was built in the later years of the reign of Qianlong, Qing Dynasty. Emperor Qianlong had the Gate built when he was 70 years old, aiming at saving his strength. He instructed that all ensuing emperors can past through the Gate only when they were 70 years old. In history, only Emperor Qianlong had past through the Gate. Later generations named it the Gate for 70-year olds.

古稀門　皇乾殿の庭の西にあり、清代乾隆皇帝の後期にできたものである。乾隆皇帝が七十歳になった時、体力を節約するために、この門を建てさせ、また、後裔に“皇帝になった人は、七十歳にならないときに、この門をはいるなあ”という詔書をやった。歴史からみれば、この門をとった皇帝は、わずかに乾隆皇帝一人だけだった。後世の人は、この門を“古稀門”とよんでいた。

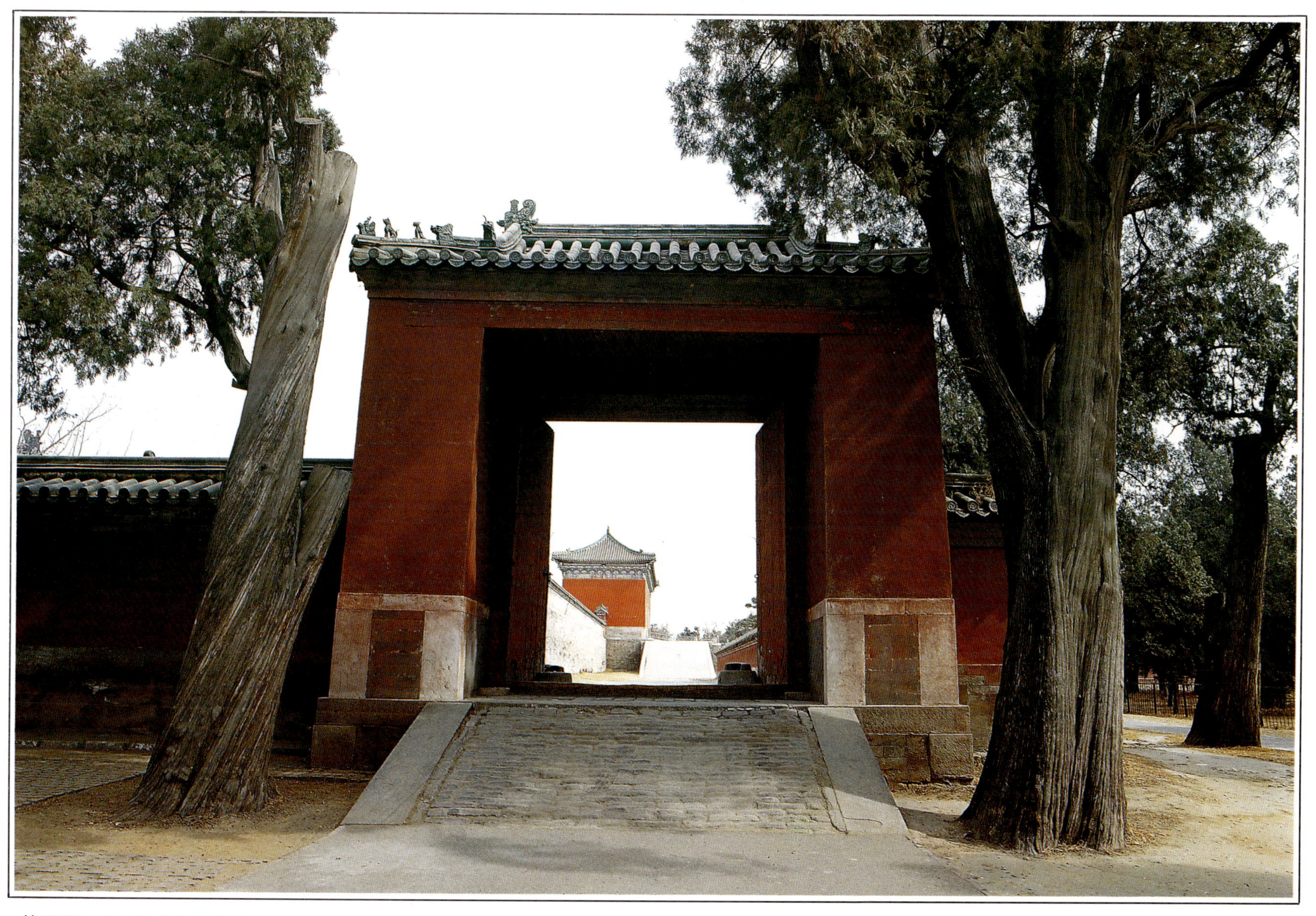

花甲門　位於祈谷壇外壝西南角，由此可達祈年殿院正門。清乾隆皇帝六十歲時爲節省脚力而建，建成後下詔其子孫爲皇帝者，年屆六旬方可由此門入壇祭祀。天壇歷史上走過此門的皇帝有乾隆、嘉慶父子二人。後人稱之爲“花甲門”。

Huajiamen (The Gate for the 60-year olds)　This is a gate situated at the southwestern corner outside the Altar for The God of Grains, through which people can reach the proper entrance of the Hall of Prayer for Bumper Harvests. Emperor Qianlong had this Gate built when he was 60 years old, aiming to save his energy. He instructed that ensuing emperors can past through the Gate only when they were 60 years old. In history, only Emperor Qianlong and Emperor Jiaqing had past through the Gate. Later generations named it “The Gate for the 60-year olds”.

花甲門　祈穀壇外垣西南のかどにある、この門をよって、祈年殿の正門につくる。清代の乾隆皇帝が六十歳になったとき、体力を節約ために、この門をたてさせて、また、後裔に“皇帝になった人は、六十歳にならないときに、この門をはいるなあ”と云う詔書をやった。歴史によれば、この門をとって祈年殿にはえて祭りをする皇帝は、ただ乾隆と嘉慶二人ばかりであった。後世の人は、この門を“花甲門”とよんでいた。

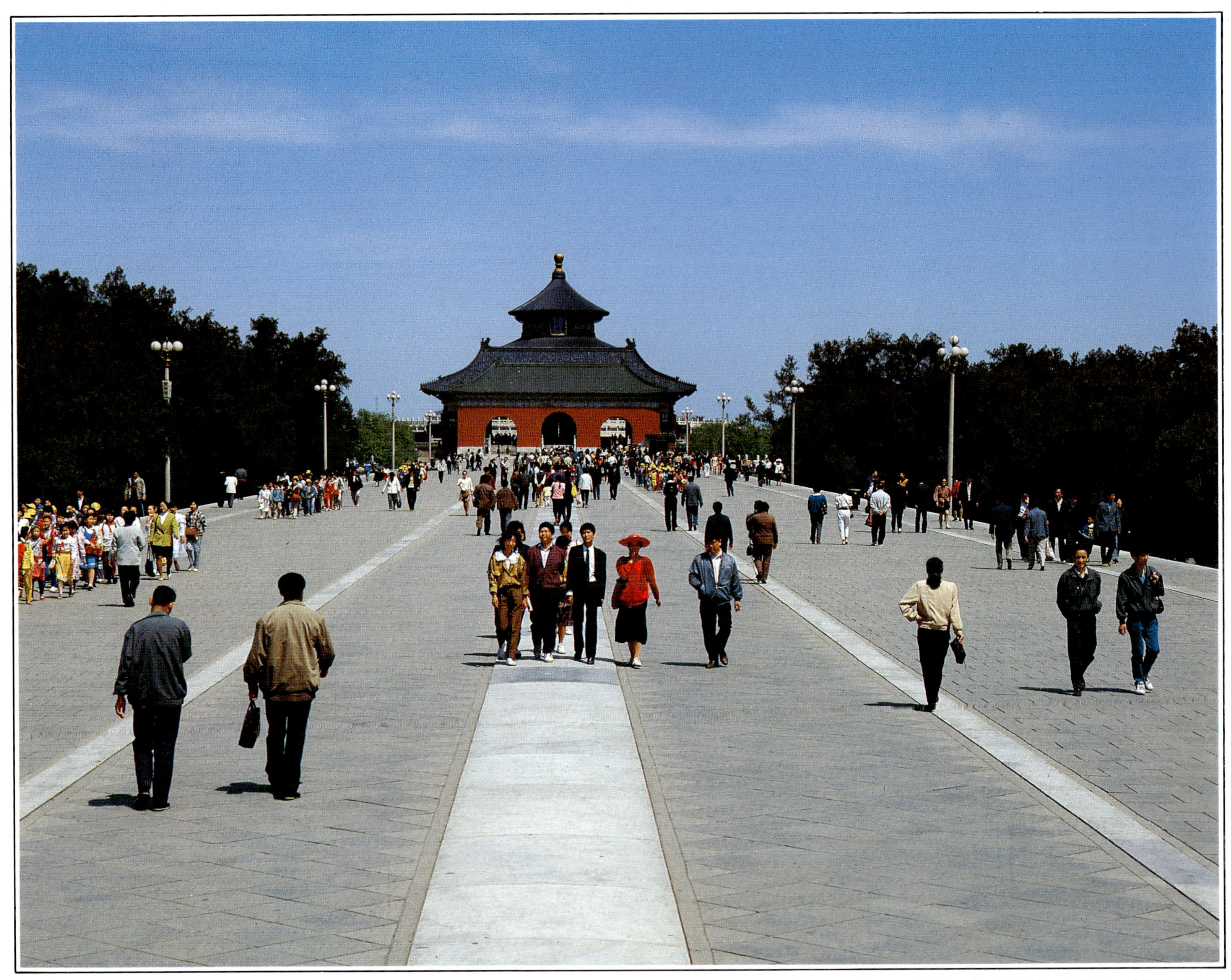

丹陛橋　又叫“海墁大道”或“天橋”。北高南低，長360米，寬30米，中間有三條比道面略高的石質路。中間一條爲神道，東邊一條爲御道，西邊一條爲王道。

Danbiqiao　Also calle “Haiman Road” or “Heavenly Bridge”, this is a long elevated path 360m long and 25m wide. It is higher at the north and lower at the south, with 3 stone-paved roads a litlle higher than other parts of the surface. The one in the middle is the Sacred Way, the one in the east is the Imperial Road, and the western one is the Emperor’s Way.

丹陛橋　“海墁大道”または“天橋”にもよばれている。長さ360メートル、幅25メートル、北のほうが高く、南のほうがひくい、高いみちである。まんなかに、三っの表面よりすこし高くの石路があり、中間のは神道で、東のほうのは御路、西のほうのは王道である。

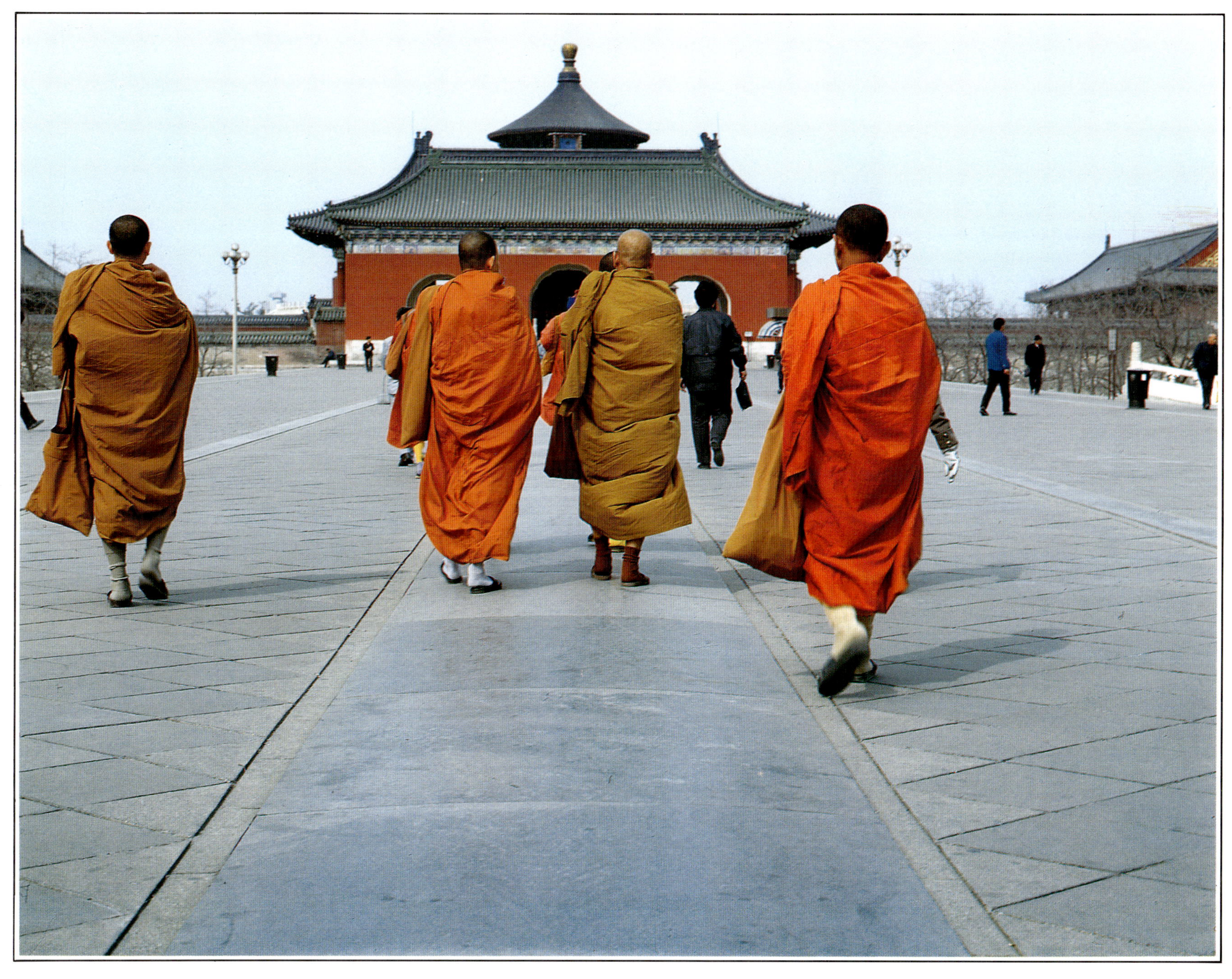

神路　丹陛橋上的石質神道、王道、御道，等級森嚴，不得僭越。中間神道專爲皇天上帝及各種神靈所設，任何人不得涉足。

The Sacred Way　The 3 roads on the Danbiqiao are controlled by sverest ranking system which can not be offended. The one in the middle was set specially for Heaven, God and various fairies, thus no one can trod on it.

神路　丹陛橋の上にある神道と王道と御道は、おきてがきびしいので、わざとふみこむするは、絶対にいけませんだ。まんなかの神道は、専に天や、上帝や、いろいろの神祇のために建てられたので、だれでも、その上にあるくことができませんだ。

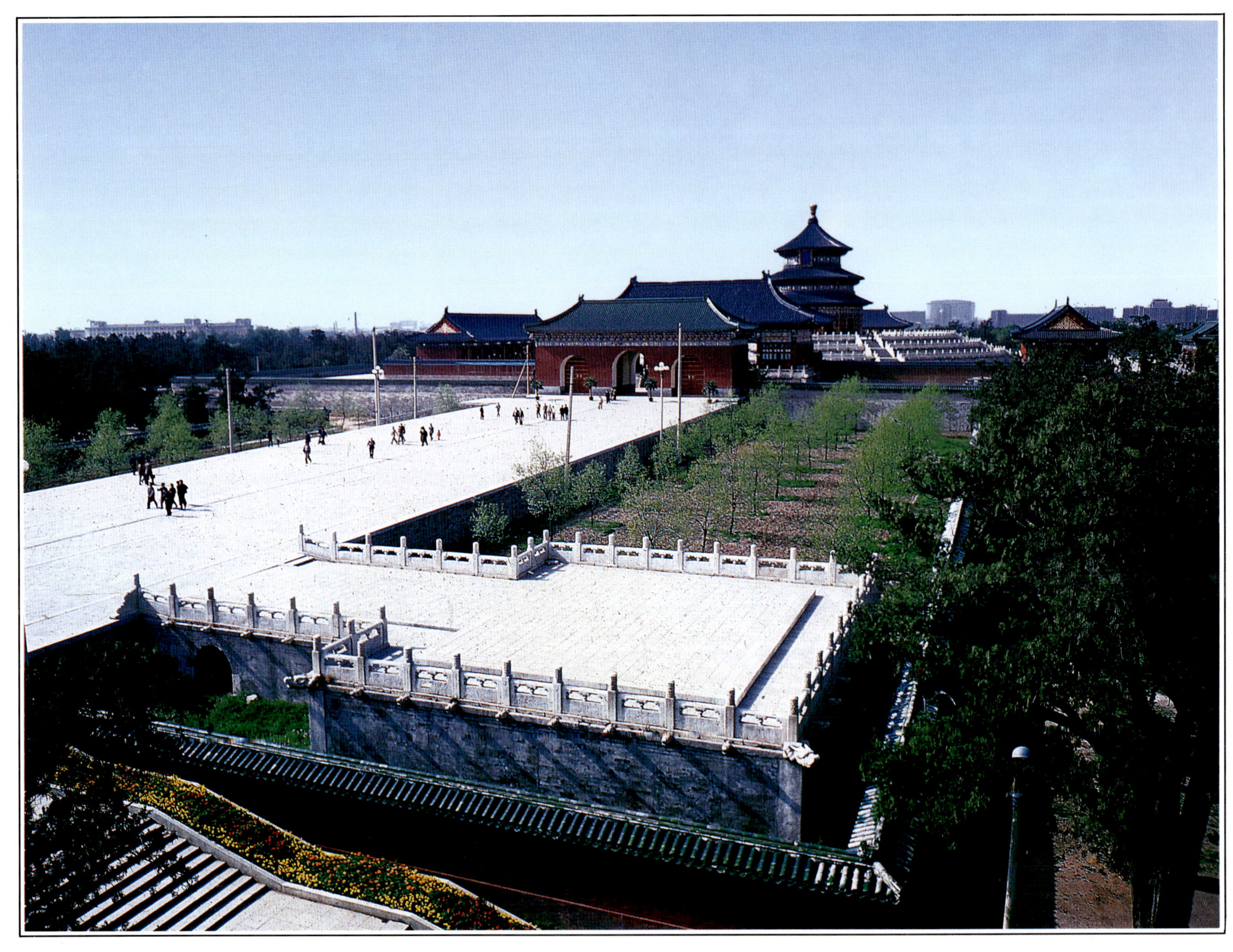

具服台　位於祈年殿外壝南隅，與丹階陛中段相連。祈谷大典時，這裏搭蓋幄次，皇帝由齋宮至這裏更換祭服，做祭祀前的最後准備。

The Changing Terrace　Located to the south of the Hall of Prayers for Bumper Harvests, it is linked to the middle section of danbiqiao. When ceremonies worshipping the God of Grains, tents were set up here, the emperor came from the Southern Palace to take on sacrificial costumes, and made final preparations to attend the ceremonies.

具服台　祈年殿外堺の南かどにあり、丹陛橋の中間とつながっている。祈穀の儀式をするとき，そこでテントを立て，皇帝が斎宮からはなれてから、そのテントで着物をかわって、祭りの最後の準備をする。

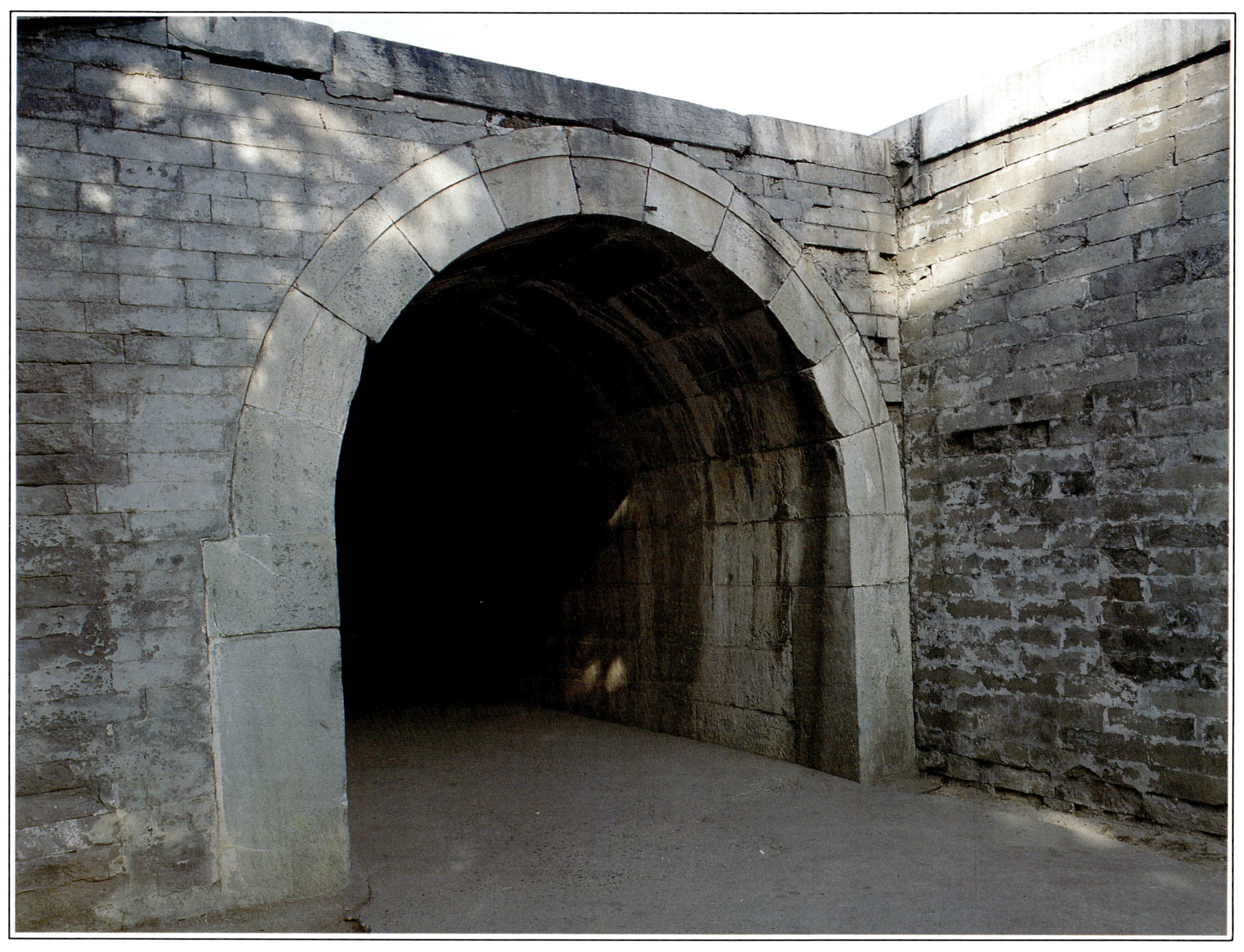

鬼門關　爲丹陛橋之戧橋。位於丹陛橋中段，東西向。歷史上是祈谷壇祭祀的犧牲由犧牲所至宰牲亭的必由之路，犧牲由此出生入死，故稱鬼門關。

"The Gate of Hell"　This is the supporting section of Danbiqiao. It is east-west oriented at the middle part of Danbiqiao. Historically, it had always been the only way by which sacrifices required in the ceremonies held in the altar for the God of Grains were led from the animal farm to the Sacrifice-butchering Pavilion. The sacrifices went dying through this way, hence the name.

鬼門関　これは、丹陛橋の副橋で，丹陛橋の中段とつながれて、東北へむかっている。祈穀壇で祭りをするとき、神前に供えられるいけにえが、かならずこの橋をよって、犠牲所から宰牲亭へゆく。そのいけにえは、いきところから死地へゆくので、そのところを"鬼門関"となづけた。

七十二長廊　由祈年殿東磚門經神厨至宰牲亭，連檐通脊，一共七十二間，爲祭祀時運送祭品的通道，以避風沙雨雪。

The 72-bayed Corridor　It runs from the eastern brick entrance through the Sacred Kitchen and ends at the Sacrifice-butchering Pavilion, with unbroken eaves and ridges, covering 72 bays in all. Sacrificial articles were conveyed through the Corridor when wind, sand, rain and snow came in a ceremony.

七十二長廊　一体になっている廊下は、祈年殿の東の磚門から神厨をよって宰牲亭につく、檐と脊は一線になり、あわせて72軒である。これは、祭りをするとき、祭品をはこぶ、風、沙、雨、雪を避けるために建造したのだ。

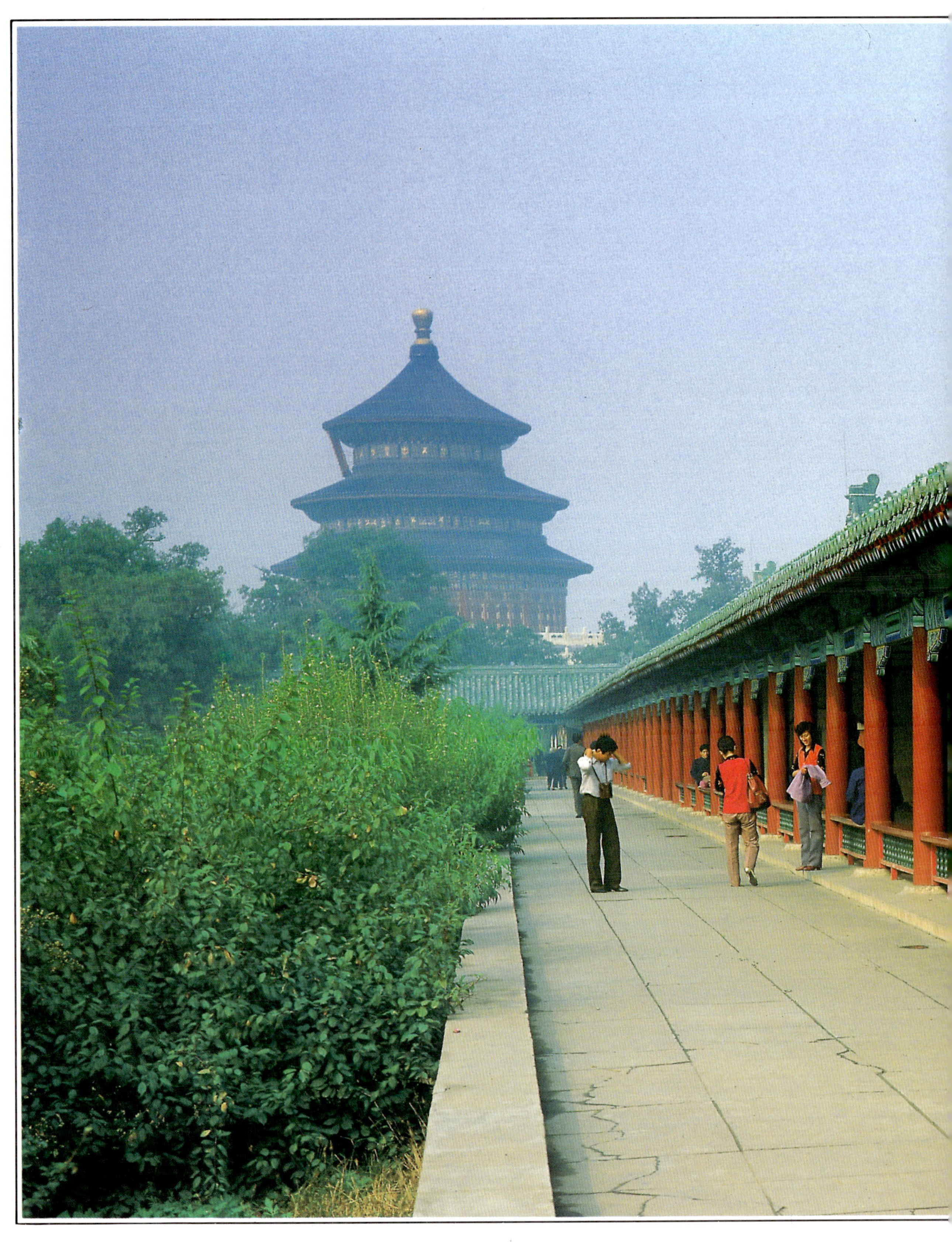

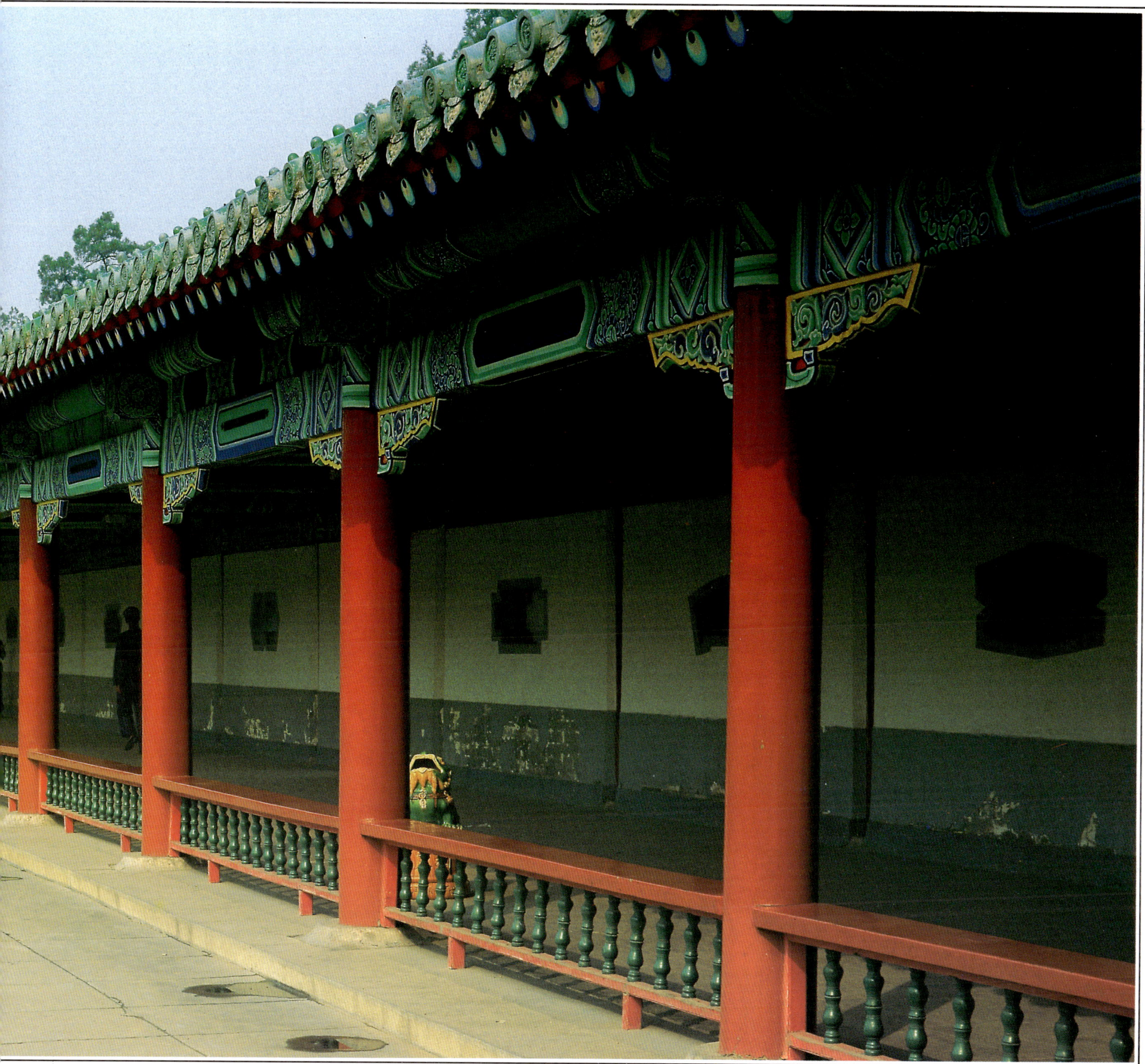

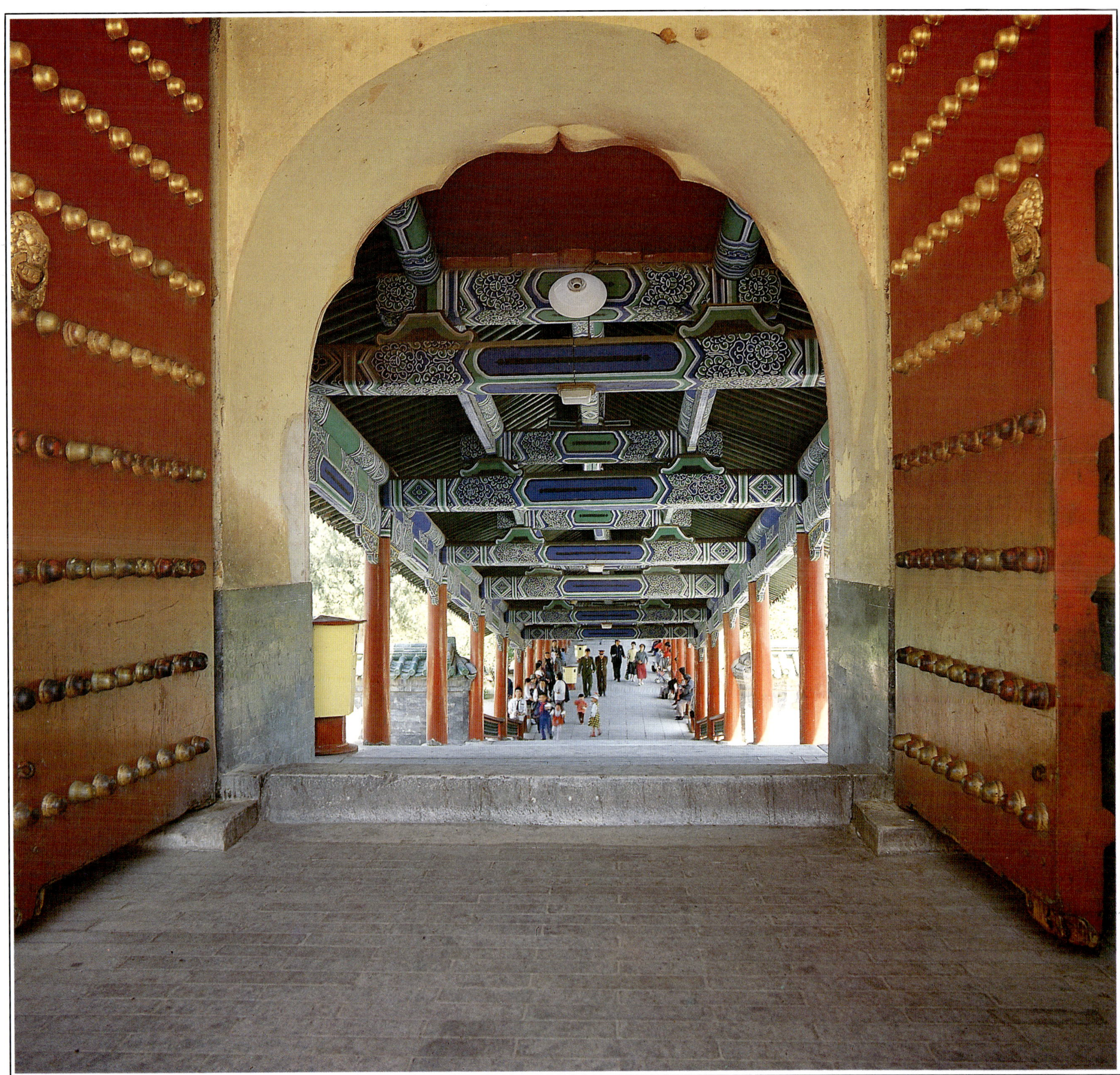

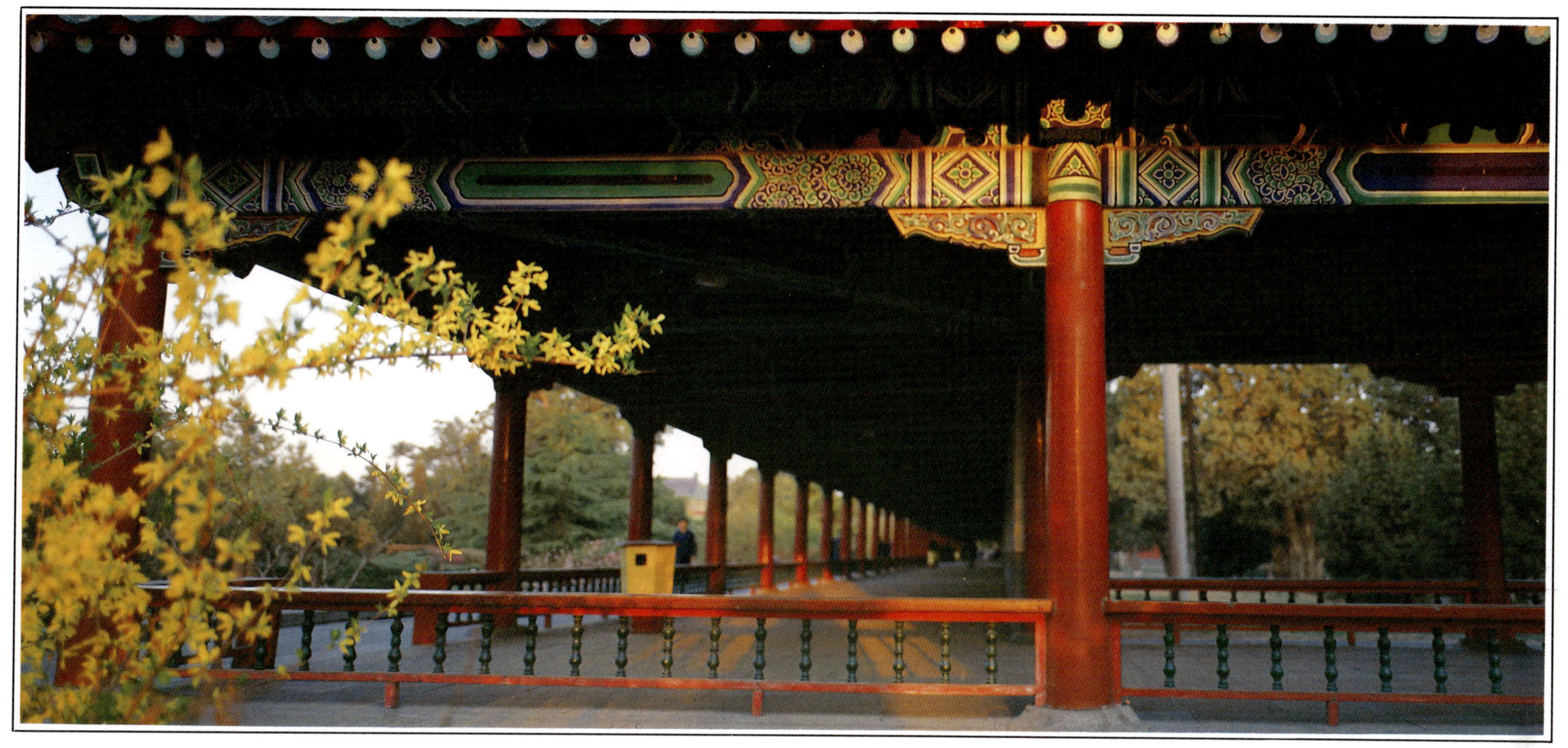

長廊布局呈“W”型，鈎廊縵迴，一步一境。

ɪne Corridor is laid out in the shape of a W. It zigzags and presents a scene almost at every single step.

長廊は、“W”形の仕組みをして，まがりくねった廊下の中でみると、景色がいつでもかわっているようだ。

◀長廊內外梁坊滿飾雅伍墨旋子彩畫，這種彩畫古雅大方，朴素自然，一字枋心寓意“一統江山”。

Wooden constructions inside and outside the Corridor are all painted with coloured pictures which look elegant, natural and unsophisticated. The single-line central supporting pillars implied the meaning of “A Unified Country”.

長廊の內外の樑と枋の上に、彩色絵画がいっぱい、古めかしくて優雅、質素で飾り気がない。まんなかの“一字枋”は、“天下を統一する”という意味を持っている。

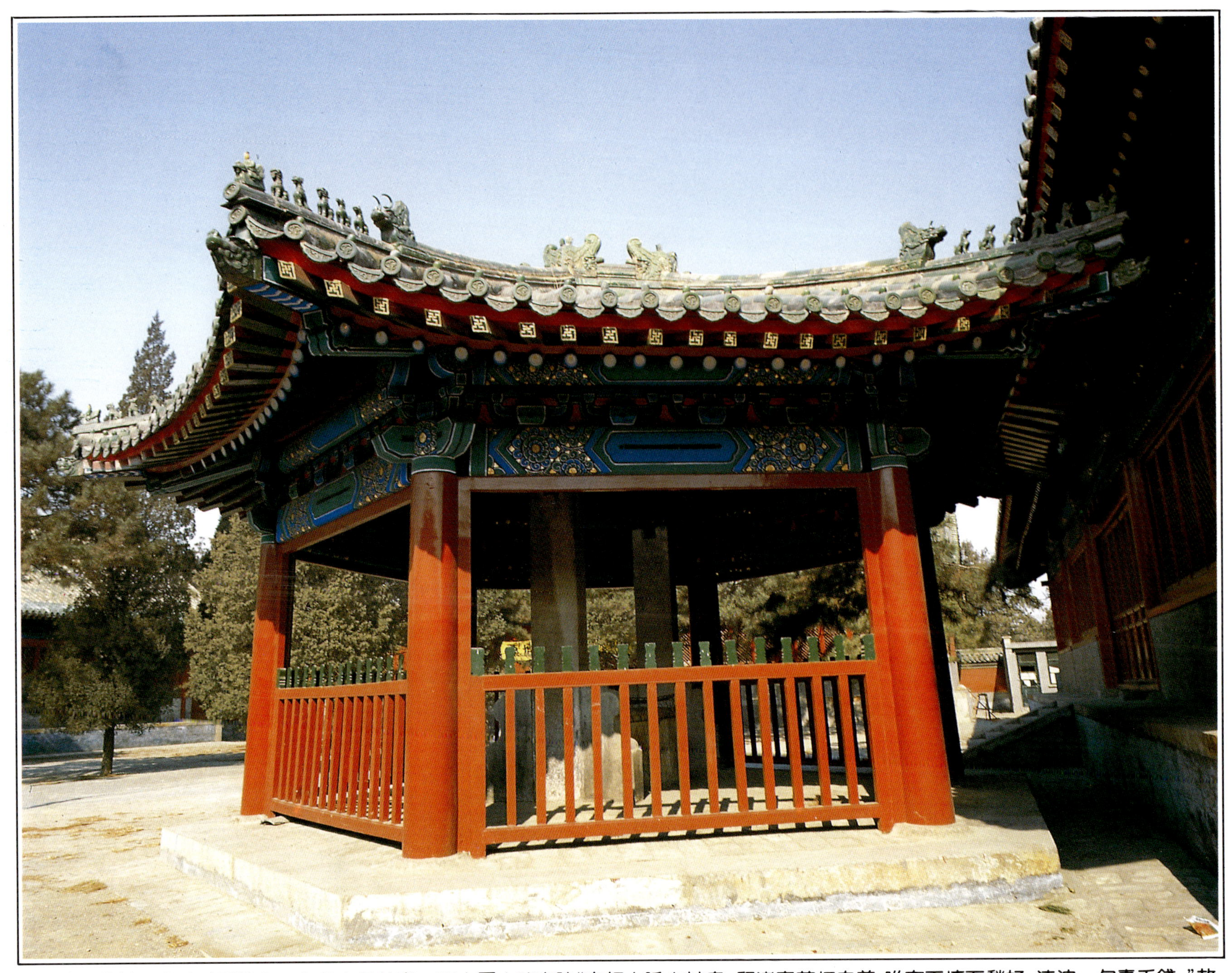

甘泉井　位於祈谷壇神厨院內，上有六角井亭。明人王士禎有詩“京師士脈少甘泉，顧渚春芽枉自煎，唯有天壇石甃好，清波一勺賣千錢。”故得名“甘泉井”。

Ganquan Well (The Well of Sweet Water)　Situated in the courtyard of the Sacred Kitchen in the Altar for the God of Grains, the Well is topped by a hexagonal pavilion. Wang Shizhen, a Ming scholar, had a poem narrating that sweet well was rare in Beijing, that the water in the well in the Temple of Heaven was valuable. Thus it is called The Well of Sweet Water.

甘泉井　これは、祈穀壇の神厨の庭におり、上に六角井亭がある。明代の人王士禎は詩を作って、“北京には、甘泉が少ないだが、この井の水は甘い”という意味を表示した。この井は、“甘泉井”となづけた。

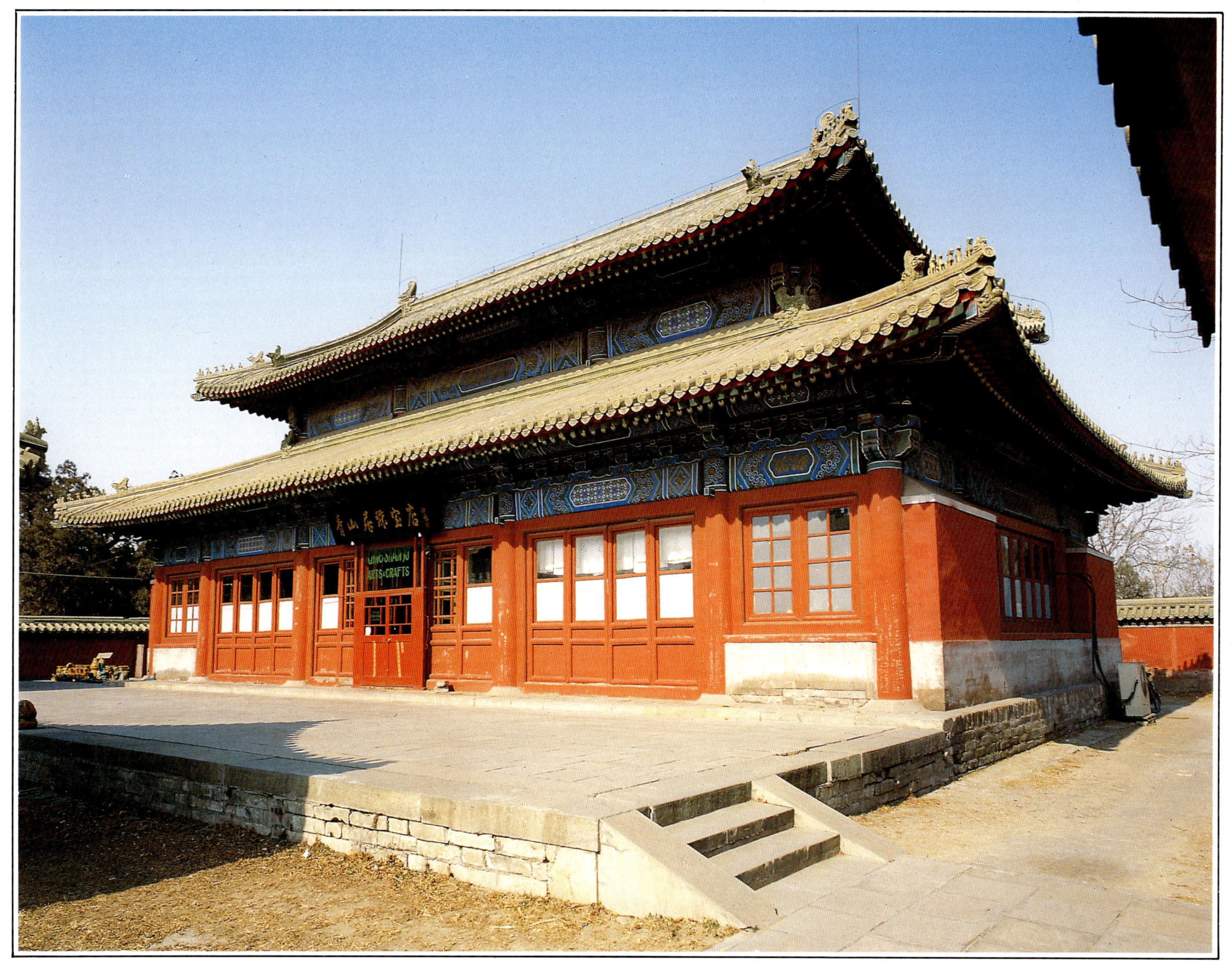

宰牲亭　重檐歇山式建築，五開間，內外梁枋滿飾旋子彩畫，爲祭祀前宰殺犧牲的場所。

Sacrifice-butchering Pavilion　This is a 5-bay across construction with doubled eaves and beams resting on the gables. Wooden pieces inside and outside are all decorated by coloured paintings. It is the site where sacrifices were butchered before the ceremony.

宰牲亭　これは、二重檐、五軒幅の歇山式建物で、内外の樑枋が彩色絵画がいっぱい。祭りをする前に、いけにえをころすところである。

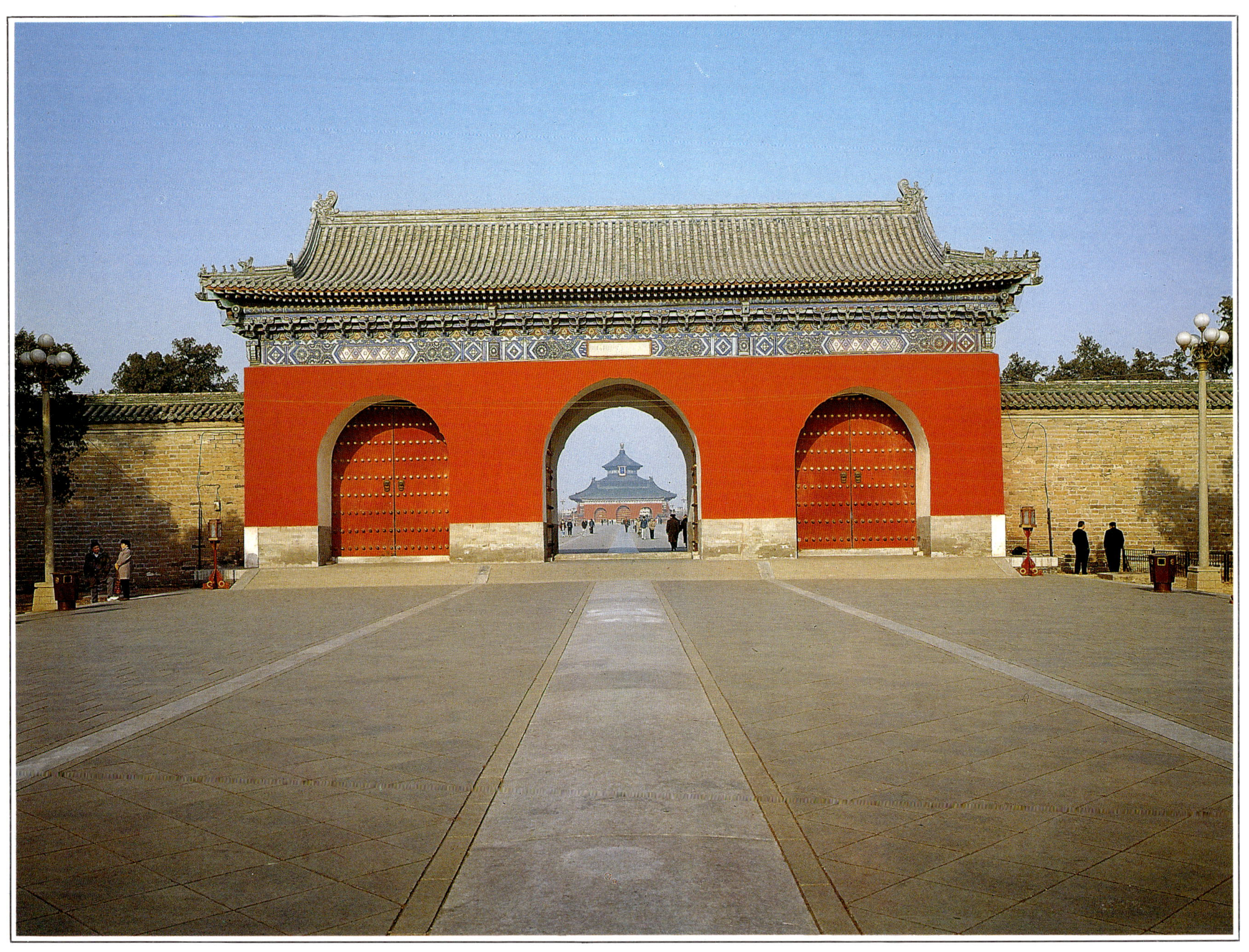

成貞門　圜丘壇內壇牆上有四道天門、按《周易》"元亨利貞"取意爲泰元門、昭亨門，廣利門、成貞門。成貞門是祈谷、圜丘兩壇的交界點，旣是祈谷壇的南天門，又是圜丘壇的北天門。

Chengzhen Gate　4 gates were open on the walls of the inner altar of the Circular Mound Altar. According to《Zhou Yi》, they were separately named as Taiyuan Gate, Zhaoheng Gate,Guangli Gate and Chengzhen Gate. The Chengzhen Gate is at the juncture of the Altar for the God of Grains and the Circular Mound Altar, the southern entrance of the Altar for the God of Grains and the northern entrance of the Circular Mound Altar.

圜丘壇の内壇のかべの上には、天門四ヶしょあけている。《周易》によって、分別に泰元門、昭亨門、広利門と成貞門となづけた。成貞門は、祈穀壇と圜丘壇の相接の境にたてて、祈穀殿の南天門であれば、圜丘壇の北天門でもあるだ。

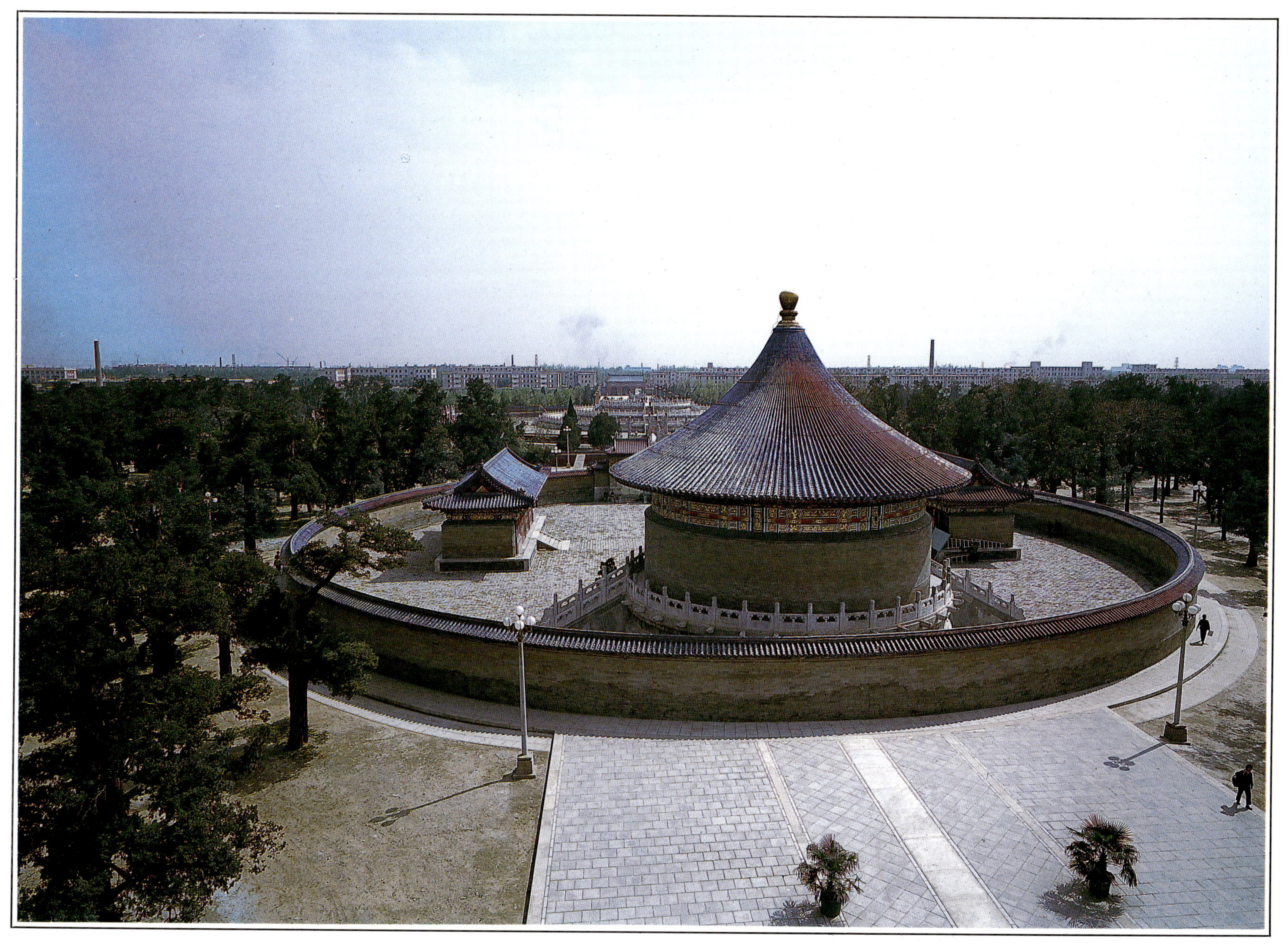

皇穹宇始建於明朝嘉靖九年(1530年)，是圜丘壇貯存神版的地方。內有回音壁、三音石等著名景點。

Started being built in 1503 (the 9th year of the reign of Jiajing, Ming Dynasty), the Imperial Vault of Heaven is the place where sacred tablets were kept. The Echo Wall, Triple Sound Stone and other famous scenic spots are in the site.

紀元1530年(明代嘉靖九年)に建てはじまった皇穹宇は、圜丘壇のなかで神位を保存しているところである。そのなかには、回音壁、三音石などの名所がある。

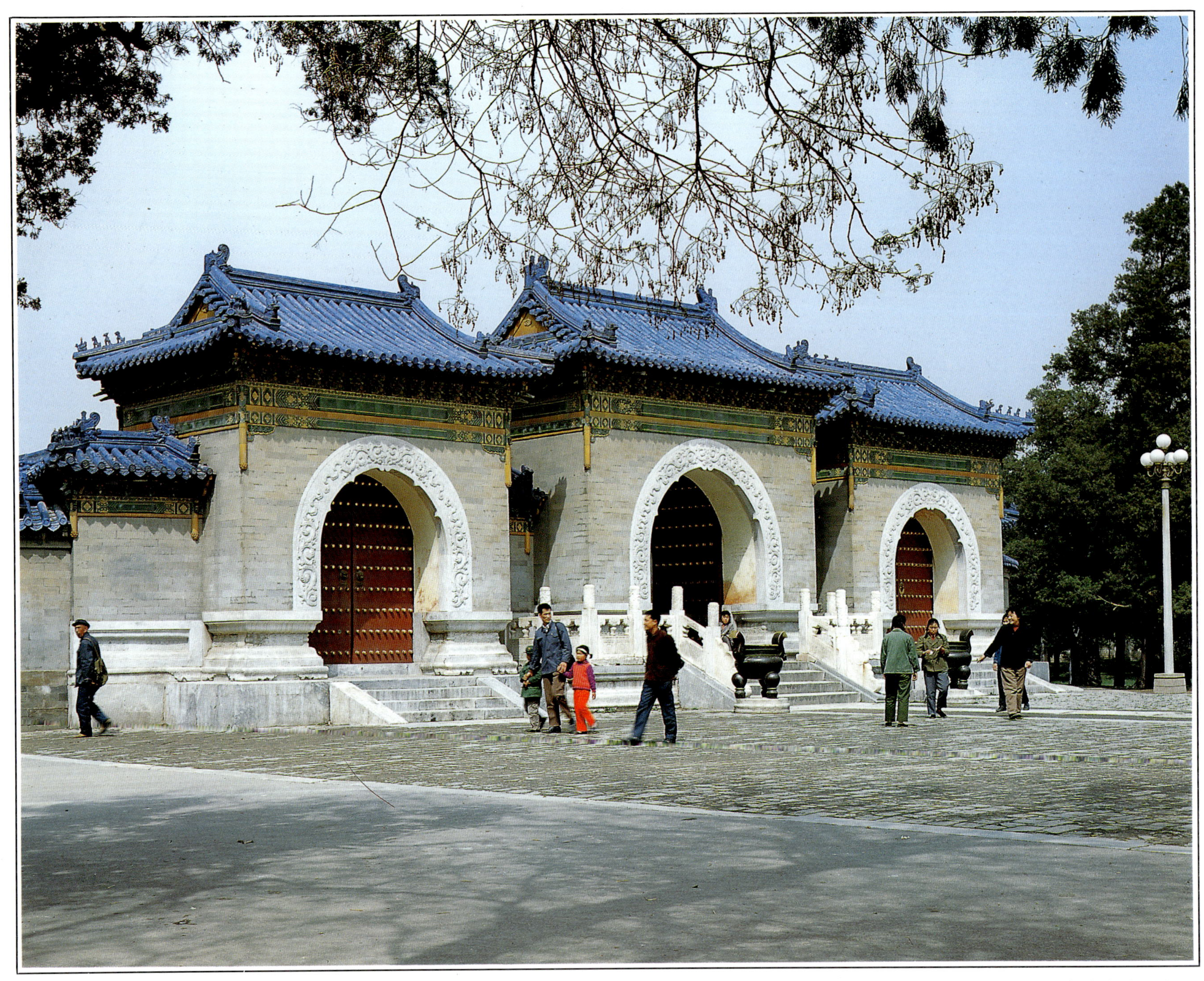

皇穹宇琉璃三座門　爲三座獨立相連的拱券式門洞，下有須彌座，藍色琉璃歇山頂，帶琉璃彩畫及斗拱，是北京僅有的幾座琉璃建築之一。

Glazed 3-bayed Monument　This is a construction with 3 independent but linked arched monuments set on Xumi pedestals, and with blue glazed-tiled Xieshan tops, glazed coloured paintings and brackets. It is one of the few glazed tiles constructions that exist in Beijing.

皇穹宇の琉璃三軒幅門　独立な門だが、互いにつながっている拱券式門の通路である。下には須弥座がある。藍色琉璃煉瓦の歇山式屋根、琉璃彩色絵画と斗拱を持っている。北京にわずかにのこっている琉璃煉瓦建物の一つである。

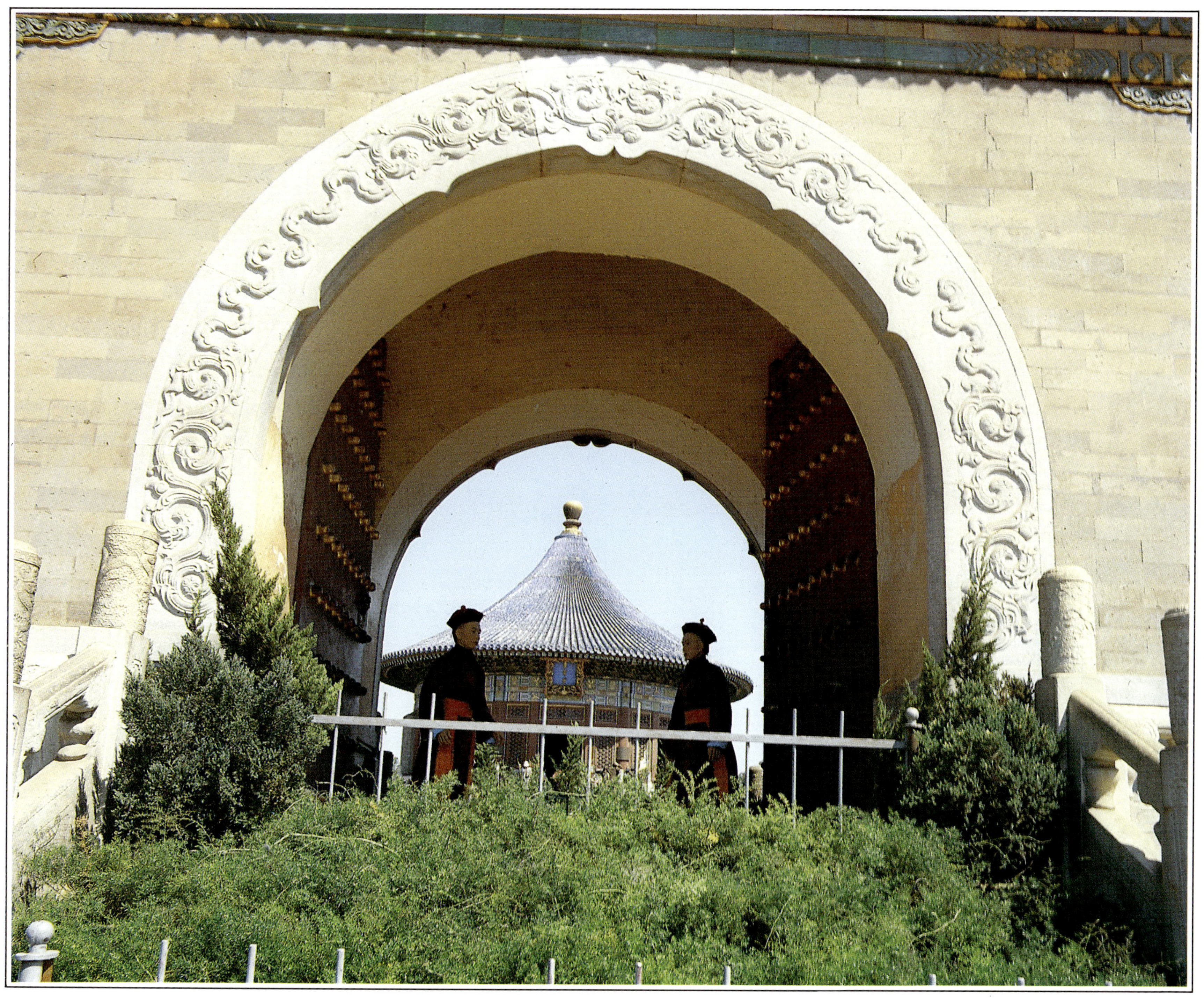

皇穹宇正門　琉璃頂基座帶欄板望柱，拱卷門洞周邊鑲砌石刻浮雕，古朴典雅。

The Main Entrance to Imperial Vault of Heaven　This is a glazed tiles construction on pedestals, and with blocking boards and balustrades. The margins of the arched gate are mounted with carved stone reliefs, looking elegant.

皇穹宇の正門　門が欄板と柱のある基座の上にすえつけて、拱券門の周辺に石刻浮彫がはめこんで，古風で典雅である。

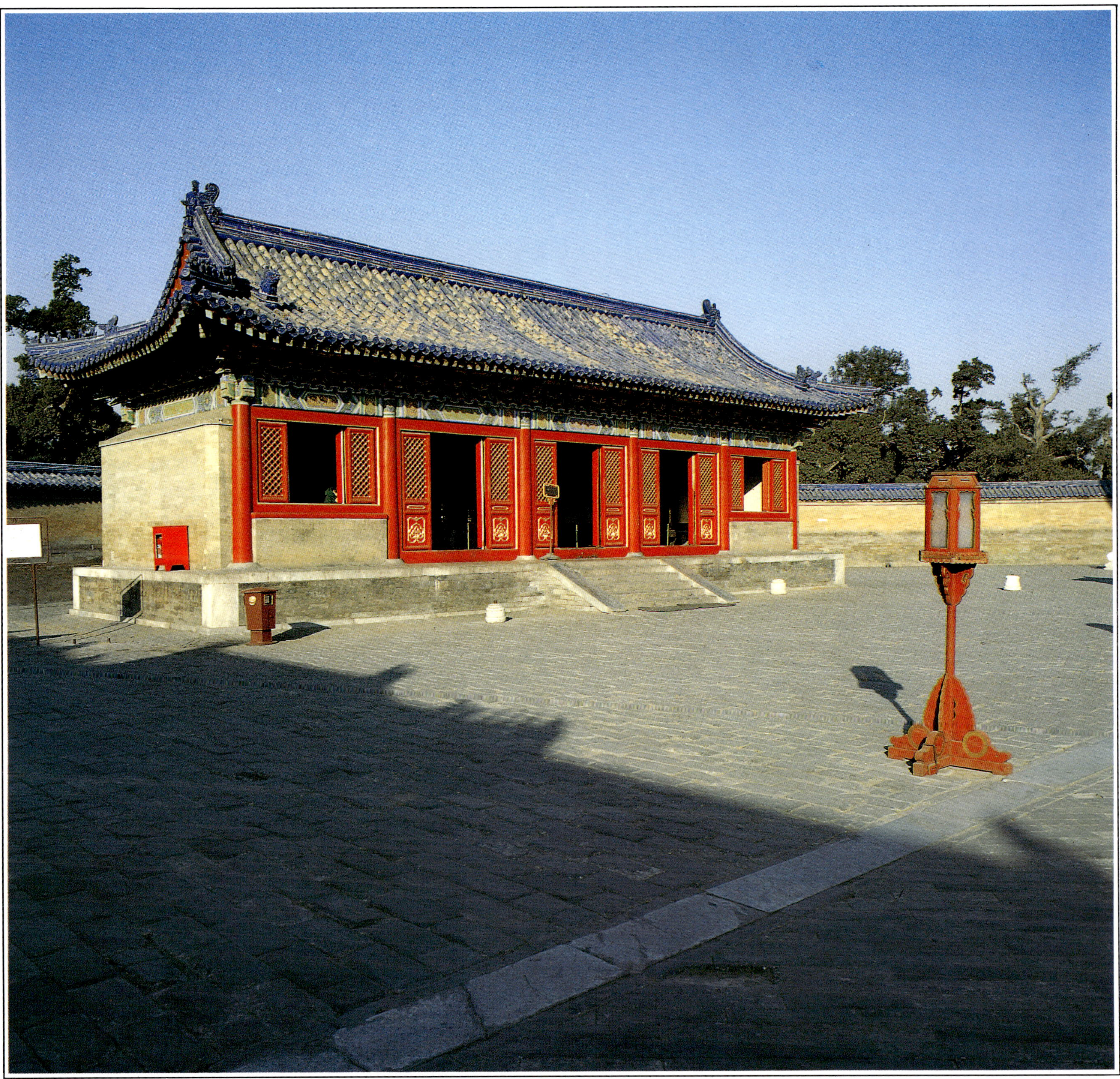

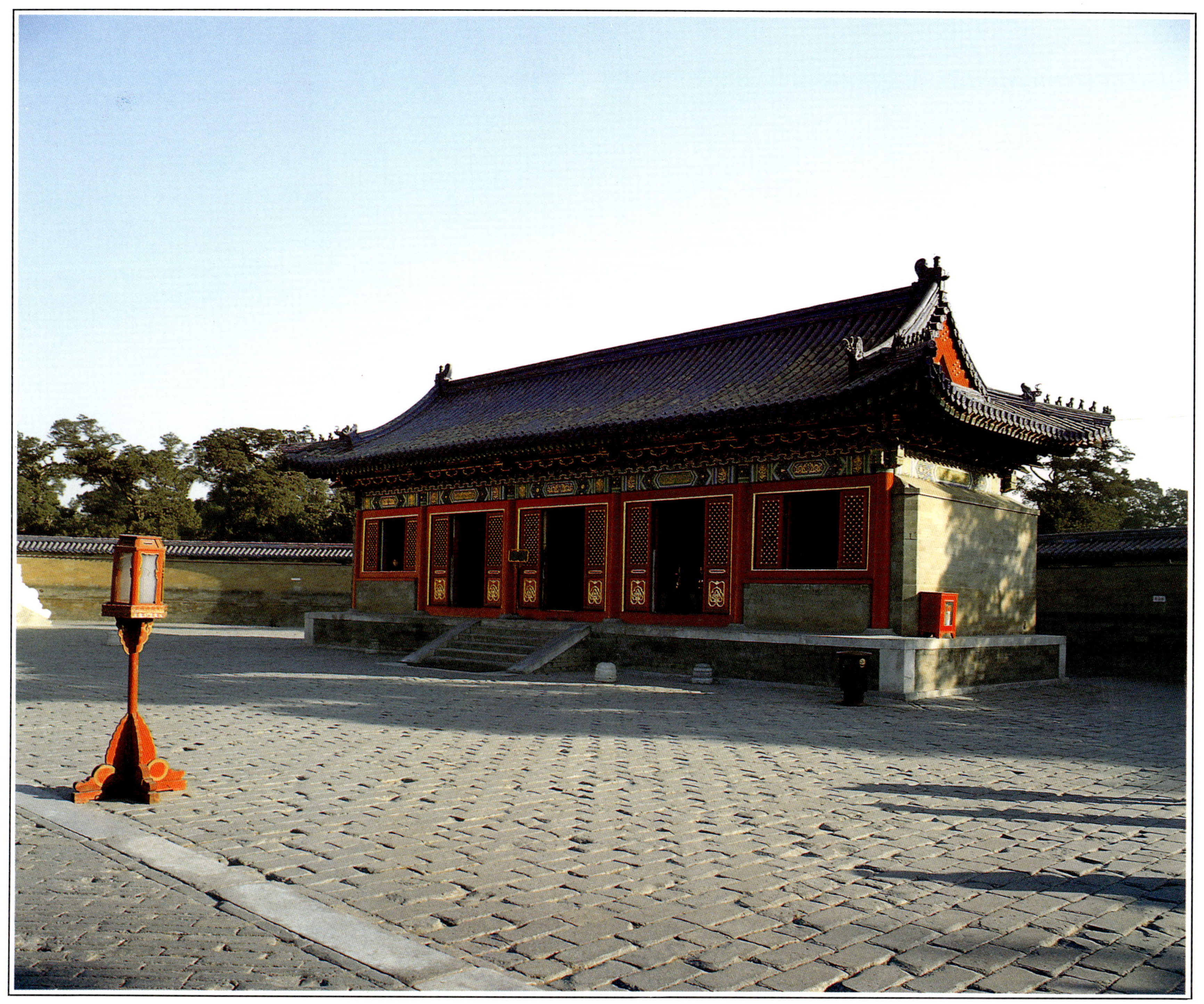

皇穹宇前東西各有一個配殿，五開間，歇山式建築，是存放日、月、山、川等祭祀從位神版的場所。

One each side hall is at the east and west sides of the Imperial Vault of Heaven. They are 5-bay across with beams resting on the gables. Tablets of matching Gods (the sun, the moon, the mountain, the river, etc) were kept there.

皇穹宇の前の東と西のほうに、配殿ひとつつずある。五軒幅歇山式建物で、日、月、山、川など従位神を祭る時つかう神位を保存しているところだ。

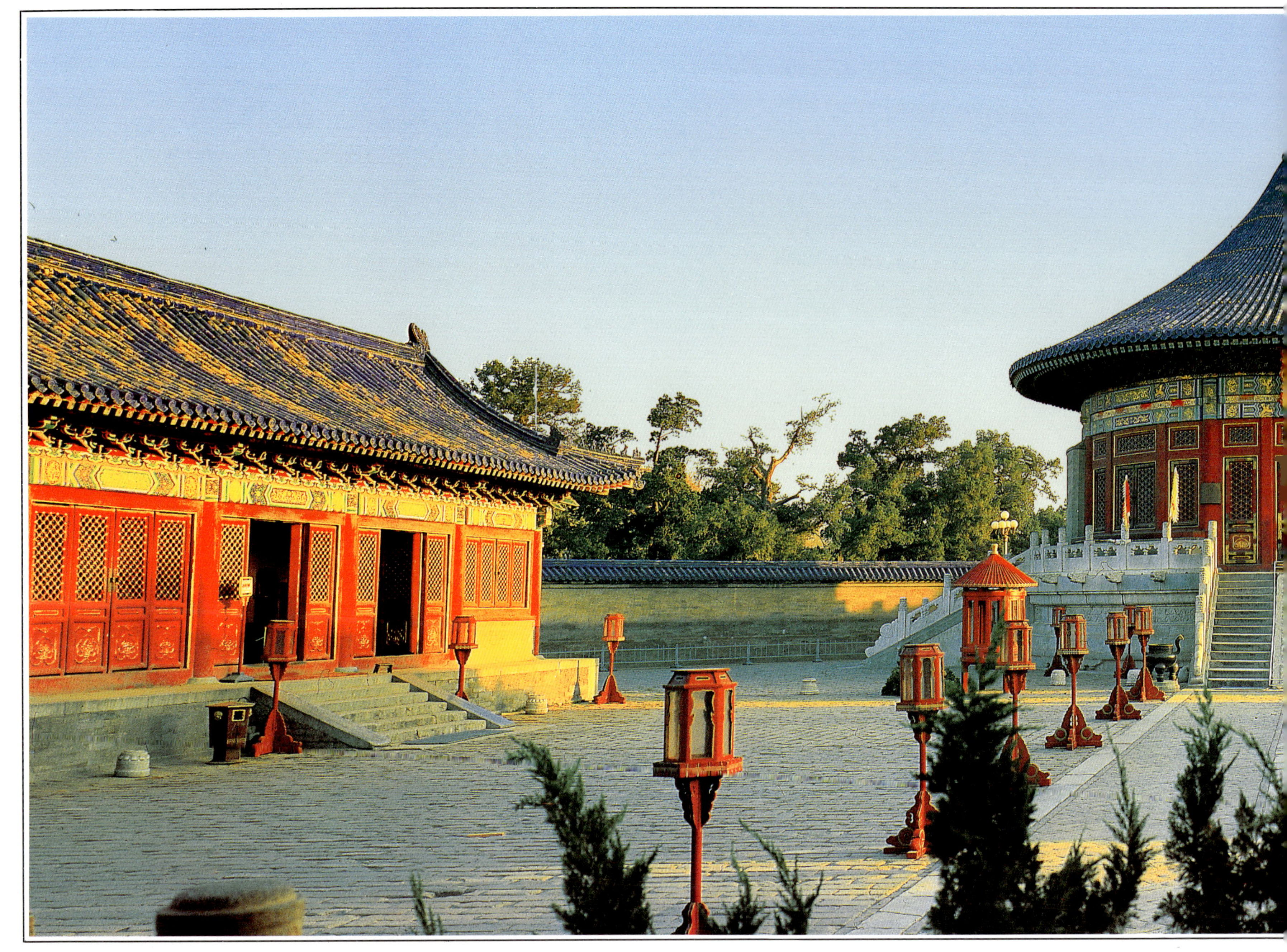

皇穹宇一組建築，方圓結合，藍色殿頂，紅色門窗與白色殿基相互輝映，內外彩畫富麗堂皇，猶如人間仙境。

The Imperial Vault of Heaven Architecture Group combines circular buildings with square ones. Blue roofs and red doors and windows vie with white base of the Hall, plus gorgeous coloured paintings inside and outside, the scene looks like a fairyland in the human world.

皇穹宇の建物が、一組にして、方形のと丸いのと結合して、藍色の屋根、紅色の門とまどは白い殿基に映える。内外の彩色絵画は立派で堂堂たる、人間の仙界に見える。

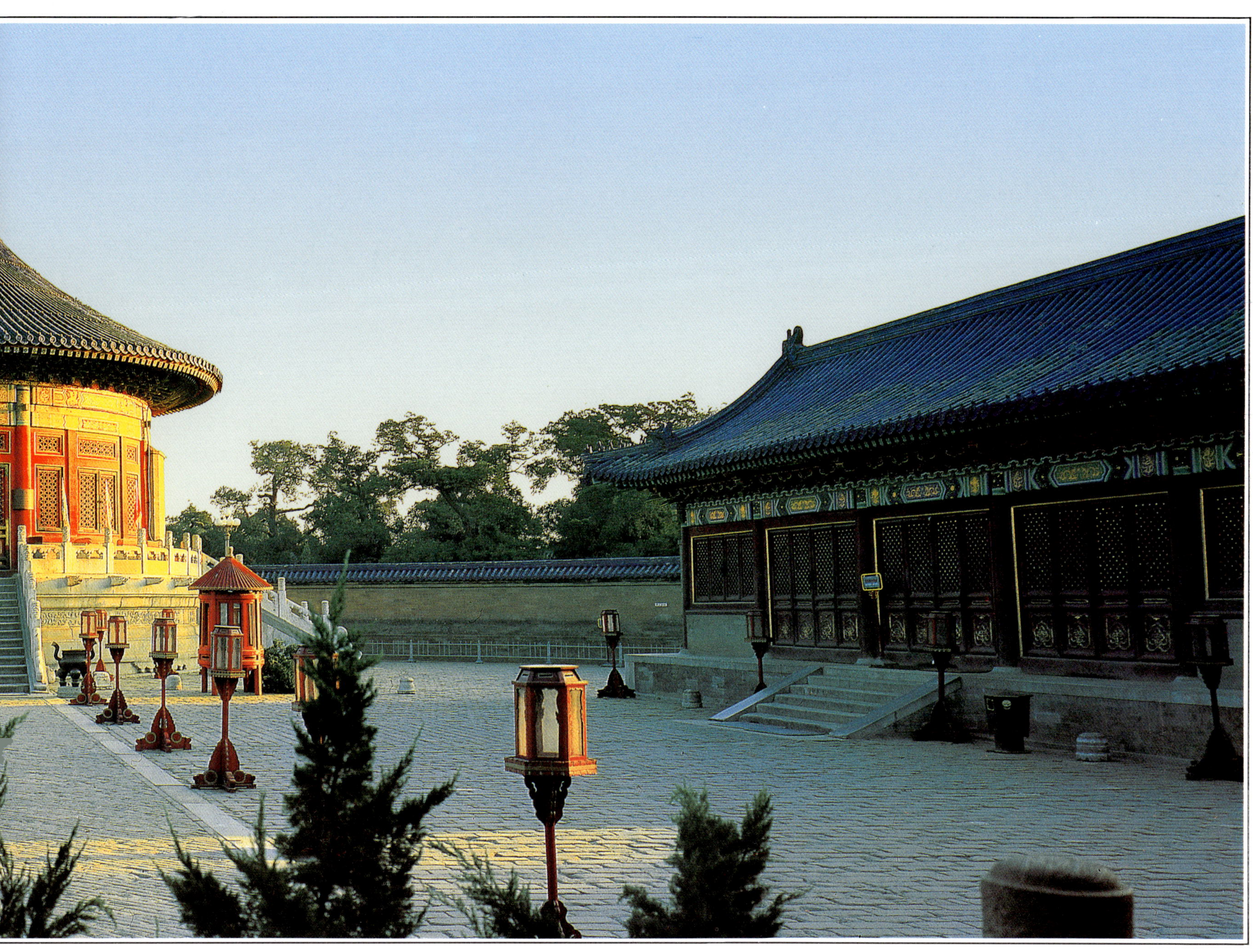

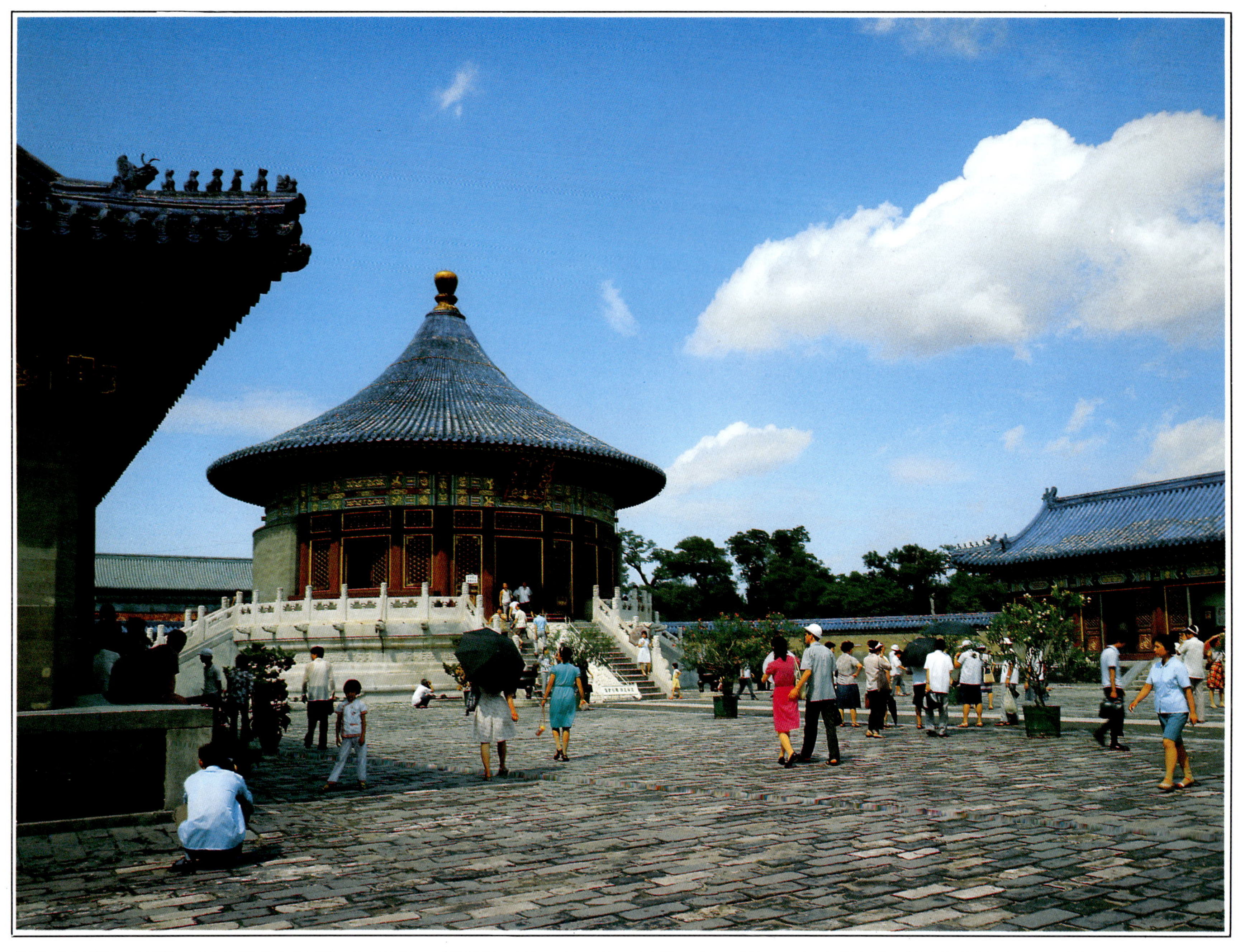

皇穹宇正殿　圓形，單檐攢尖頂建築。下爲白色須彌座，東、西、南共三階，各十四級，內外梁枋飾龍鳳和璽彩畫，是貯存圜丘壇正位、配位神版的場所。

The Major Hall of the Imperial Vault of Heaven　It is a circular, single-eaved construction on white Xumi pedestal, with gradually rising pointed top. Stairs are set in the east, west and south sides, with 14 steps each. Wooden beams and pillars inside and outside are all decorated with coloured paintings of dragon, phoenix and seals. The proper and matching tablets of Gods in the Circular Mount Altar were kept here.

皇穹宇の正殿　これは丸い，一重檐ととがた屋根を持っている建物だ。東、西、南のほうに十四級ある階段がひとつつずある。内外の梁枋が、竜、鳳と璽の形の彩色絵画で飾れている。正殿は、圜丘壇の正位と配位神位を貯蔵するところである。

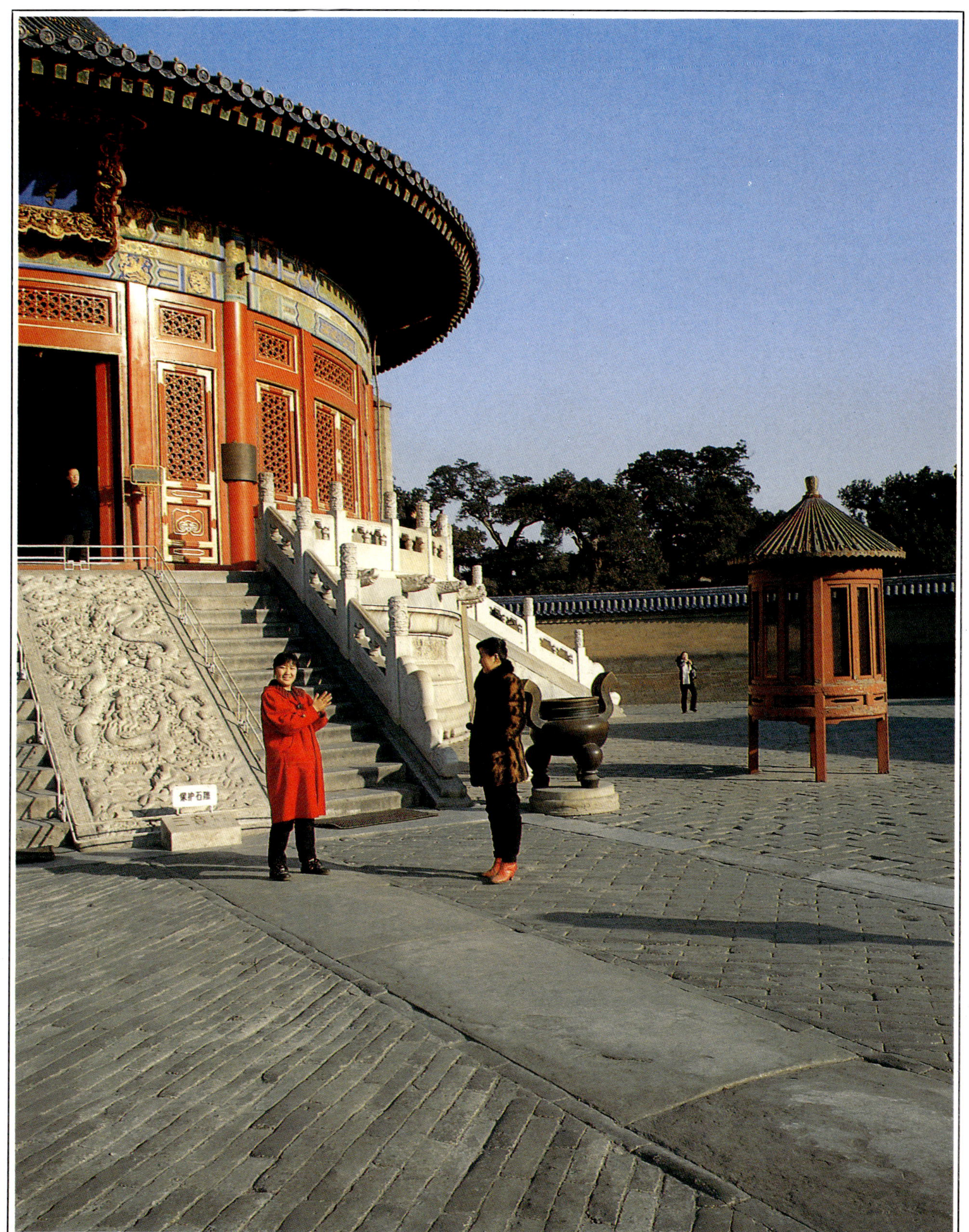

三音石　皇穹宇石階下往南數第三塊石塊處，在此繫掌可聽到連續的三次回聲，這即是著名的三音石。

Triple Sound Stone The 3rd stone slab to the south under the steps of the Imperial Vault of Heaven is the proper place where one can hear 3 echoes if he claps his hand. This is the famous Triple Sound Stone.

三音石　皇穹宇の階段の下から、南のほうにある三番目の石に立って、手をただけと、つづいてくる三度のこだまがきける。これは，有名な三音石である。

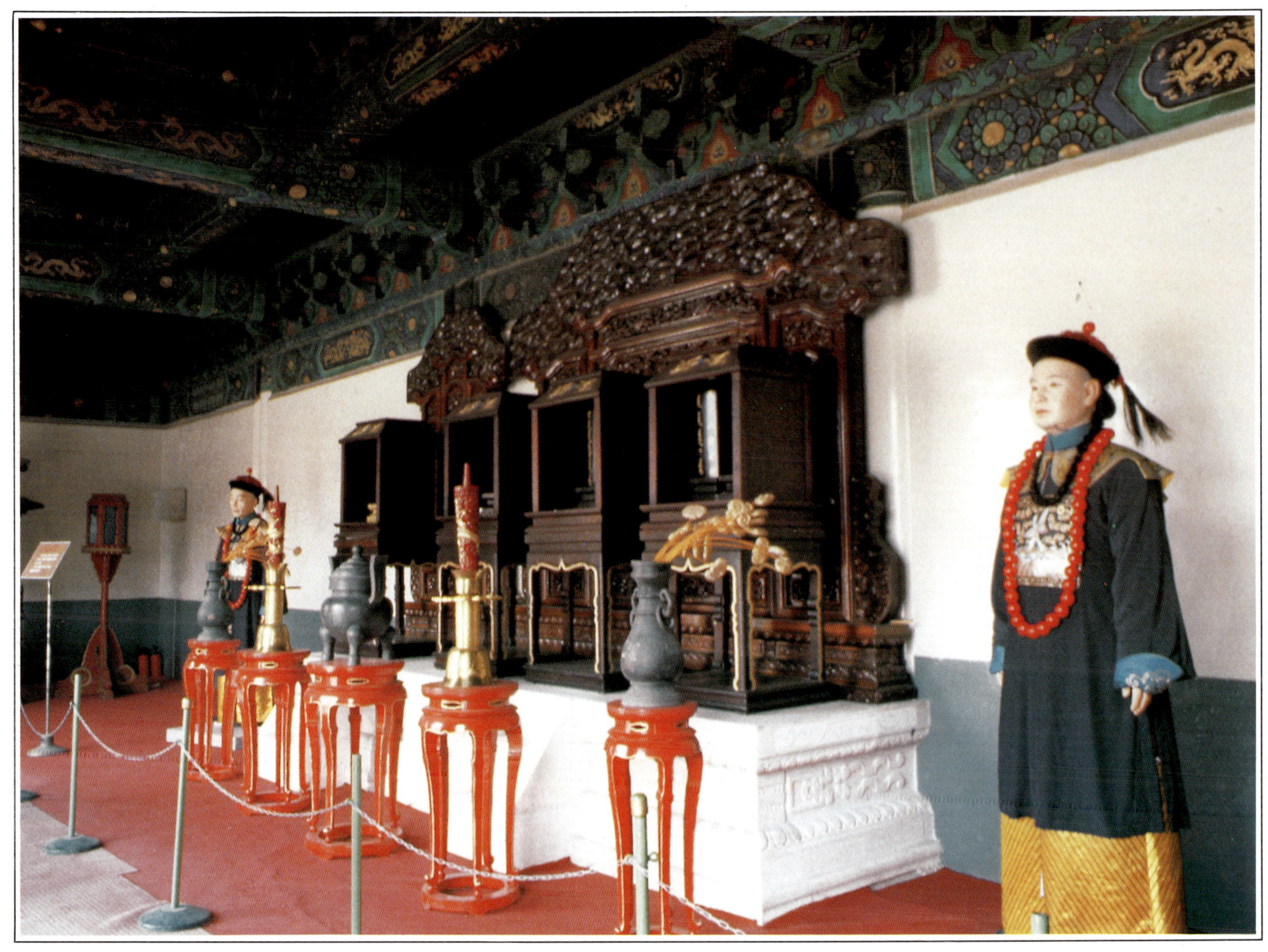

皇穹宇配殿內景　這裏是供奉天壇祭祀從位的地方，從位有日、月、星、辰，山川河瀆，風雲雷雨等神靈的牌位，各種陳設、祭品低於皇穹宇正位、配位。

Interior View of the Sidehall of Imperial Vault of Heaven. This is the place where matching Gods were worshipped, including the tablets of the Gods of the sun, the moon, the stars, the mountains, rivers, streams, wind, cloud, thunder and rain, Various furnishings and sacrificial articles were inferior to those in the Imperial Vault of Heaven.

皇穹宇の配殿の内景　これは、天壇の従位を供するところで、昔、日、月、星辰、山川、河溪、風、雲、雷、雨など神の神位があった。その中の陳列品と祭品の品格と地位が、皇穹宇にあるものより低いである。

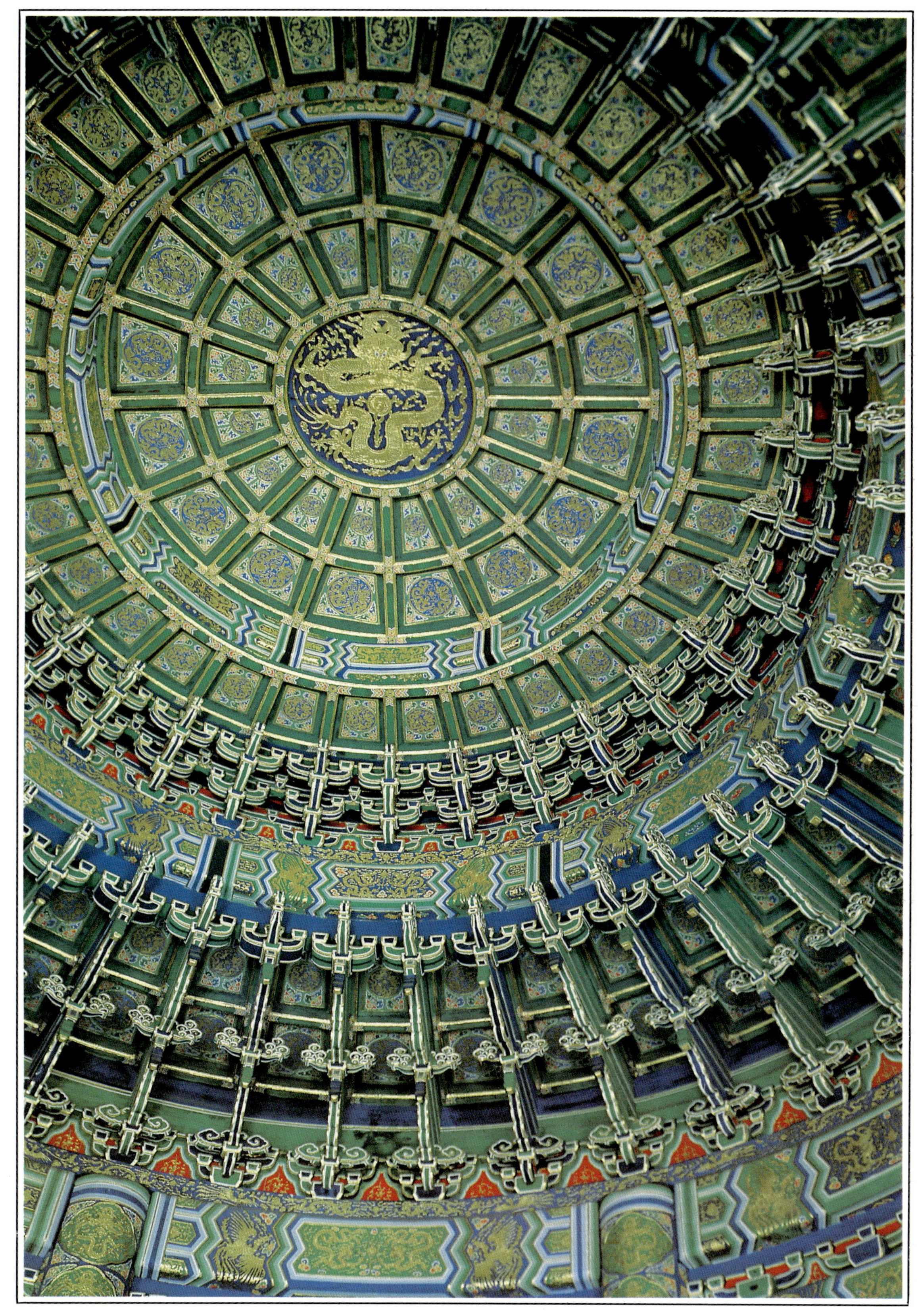

皇穹宇藻井由八根金柱支撑，再由一層鎏金斗拱和一層五踩斗拱逐漸收縮而至井底天花，藻井跨度、結構獨一無二，是此類建築中的珍品。

The caisson ceiling of the Imperial Vault of Heaven is supported by 8 golden columns. A layer of gilded brackets and a layer of multi-coloured brackets, both shrinking gradually, support the ceiling. Both the span and consturction of the caisson are unique, and the caisson ceiling is the masterpiece of constructions of the kind.

皇穹宇の天井が、八枚の金柱にささえられ、または、一重の金斗栱と一重の彩色斗栱が段段と縮小して、天井下の天花につく。天井の直径が唯一無二で、この種類の建物の中の珍しい物である。

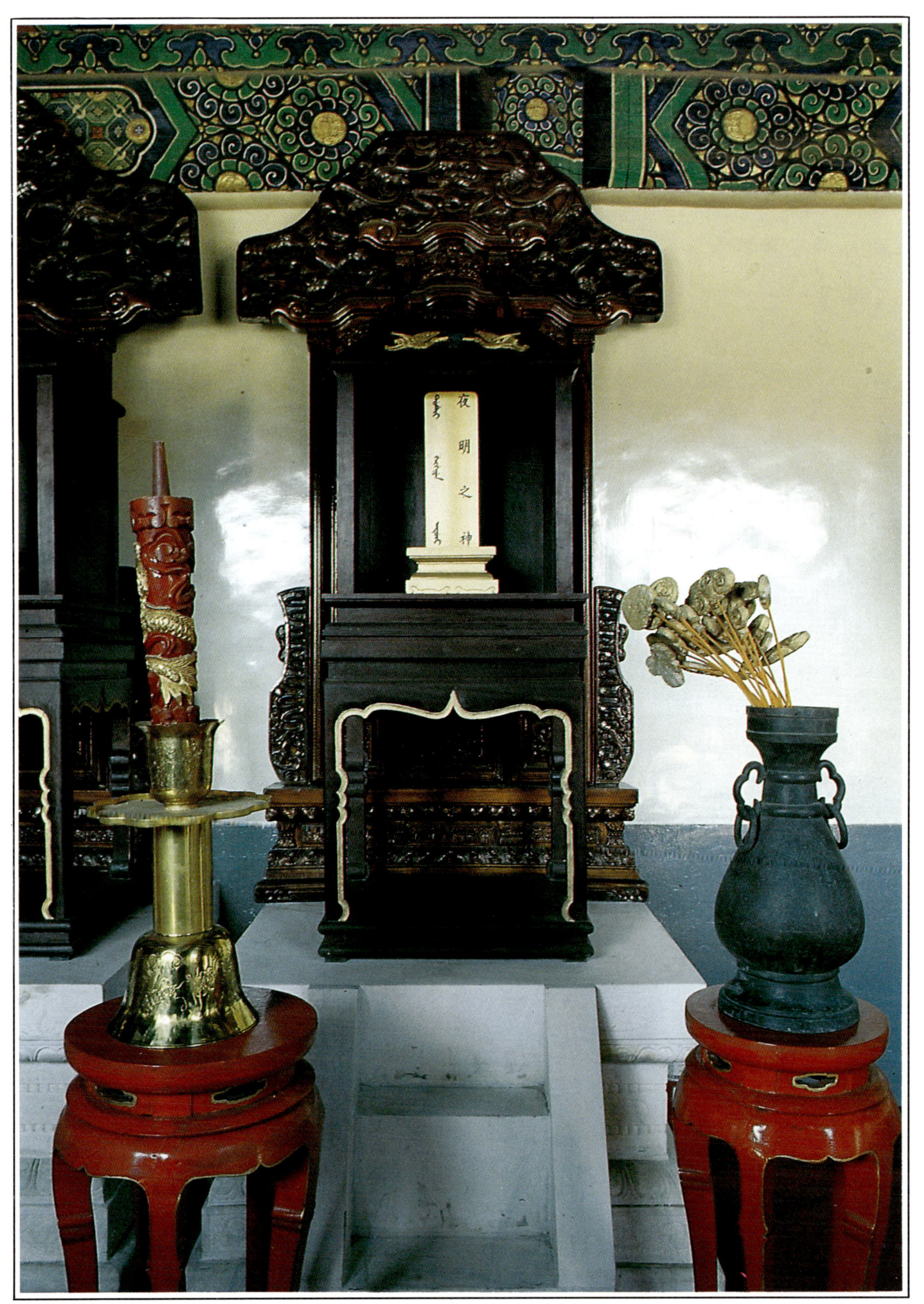

神位　主神位兩側是皇帝列祖列宗的神位。

Tablets of Gods　On either sides of the major tablet are tablets of ancestors of the emperor.

神位　主神位の両側にあるのは、皇帝の祖先の神位だ。

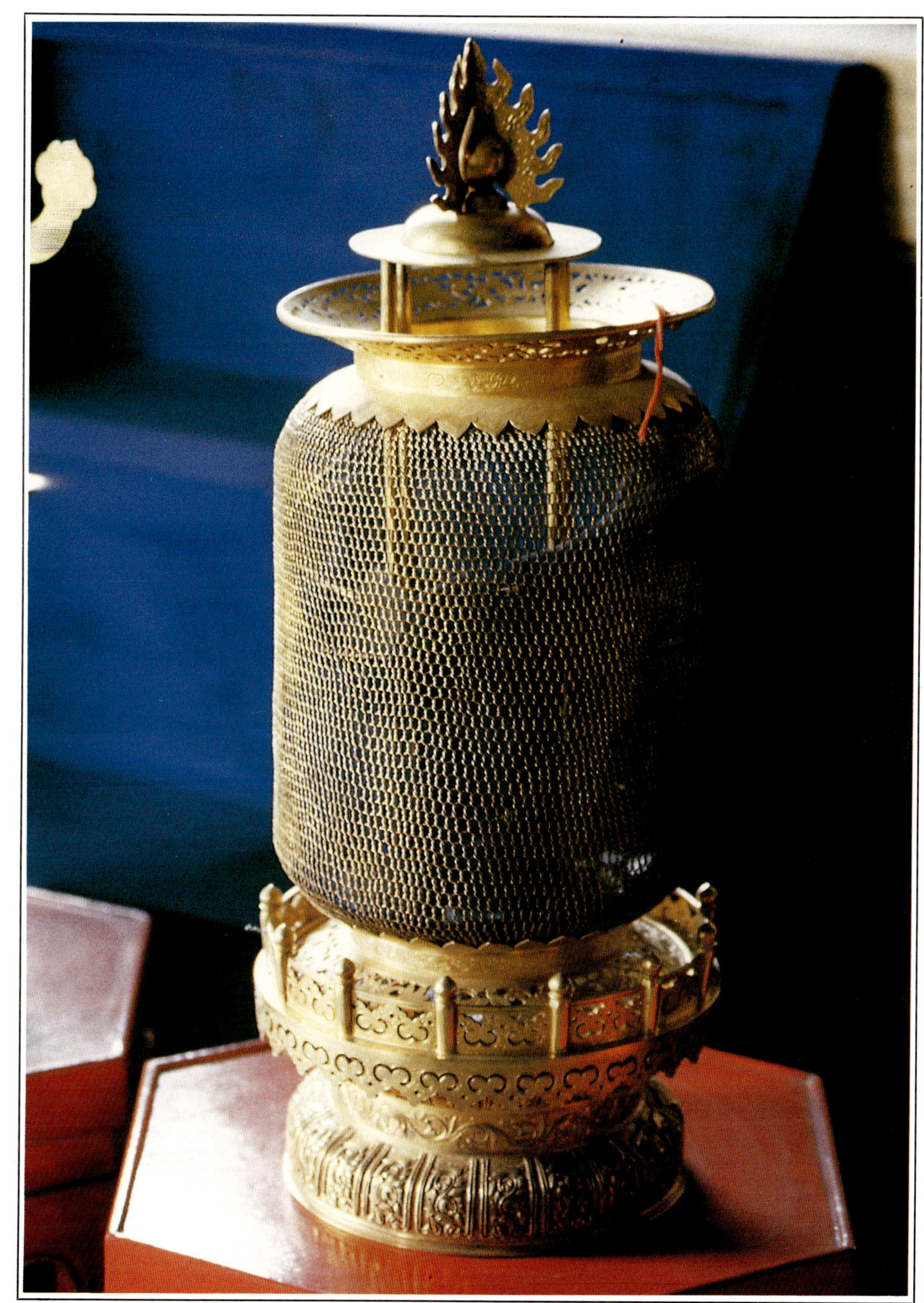

金絲神燈　陳列於皇　祖先神位前，是用於祭祀的神燈。

Golden Thread Sacred Lamp Set in front of the tablets of ancestors of the imperial house, it is the Sacred Lamp used in sacrificial ceremonies.

金糸神燈　皇族祖先の神位の前におけている、祭りをするときつかう神燈である。

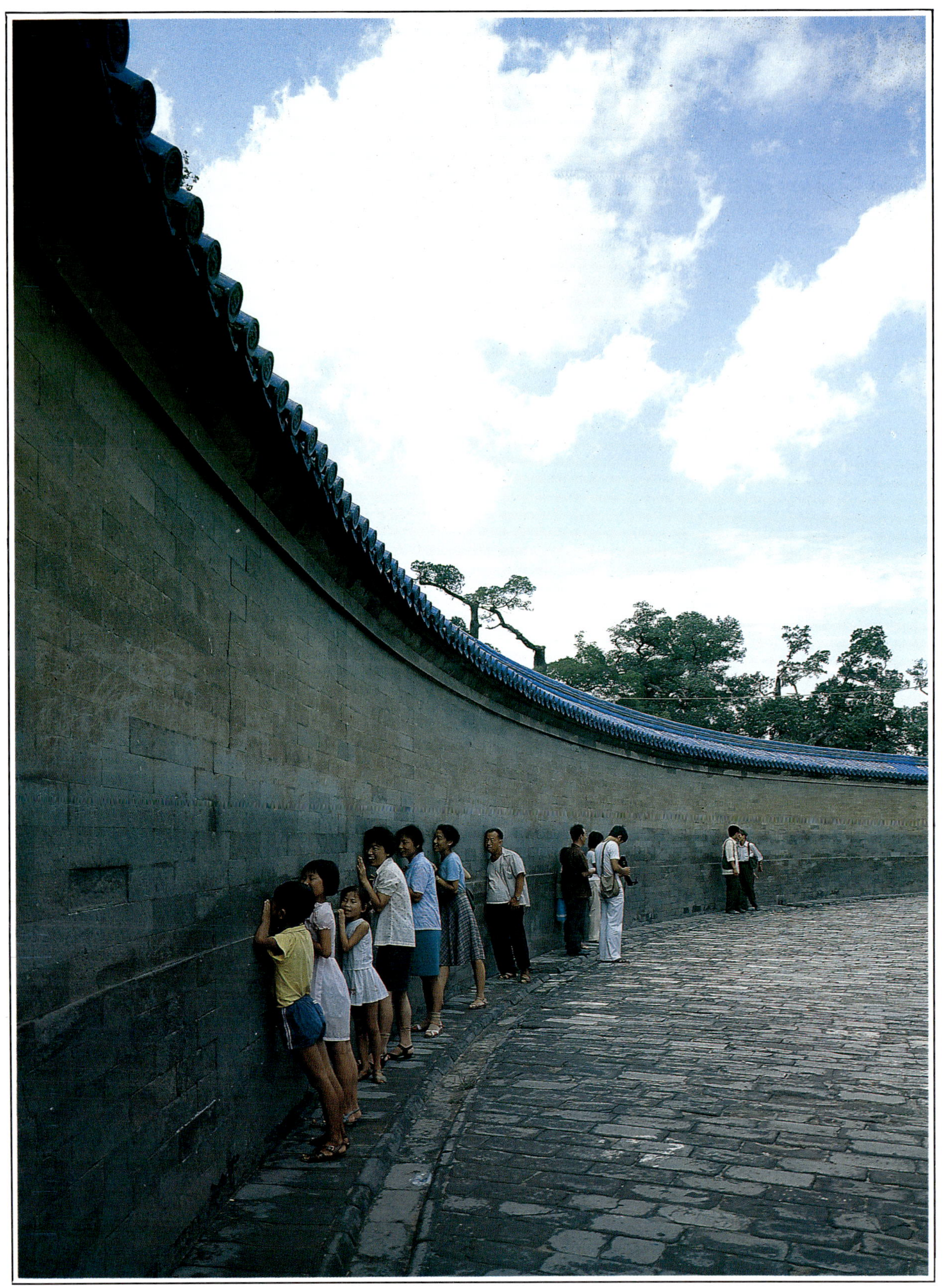

回音壁　皇穹宇圍牆是一道圓形的牆壁，牆體磨磚對縫，異常光滑。在院內東西向靠牆壁面北說話，相互可聽到清晰的回音，人稱“回音壁”。

The Echo Wall The Imperial Vault of Heaven has a circular surrounding wall neatly laid up with polished bricks, forming an extraordinarily smooth surface. 2 persons standing in the east and west separately and speaking to the wall in the north can hear a clear echo. The wall is called “Echo Wall”

回音壁　皇穹宇が一重の丸いかべにとり囲んでいる。塀は煉瓦をすり合わせて目をきっちりにあわせ入念にできた大変すべすべとしているものだ。この庭の中で、東西両側むかって、塀によりかかってはなしをすると、互いにはっきりしたこだまがきかせる。人は、この塀を“回音壁”とよんでいる。

▶九龍柏

The Nine-dragon Cypress

九竜柏

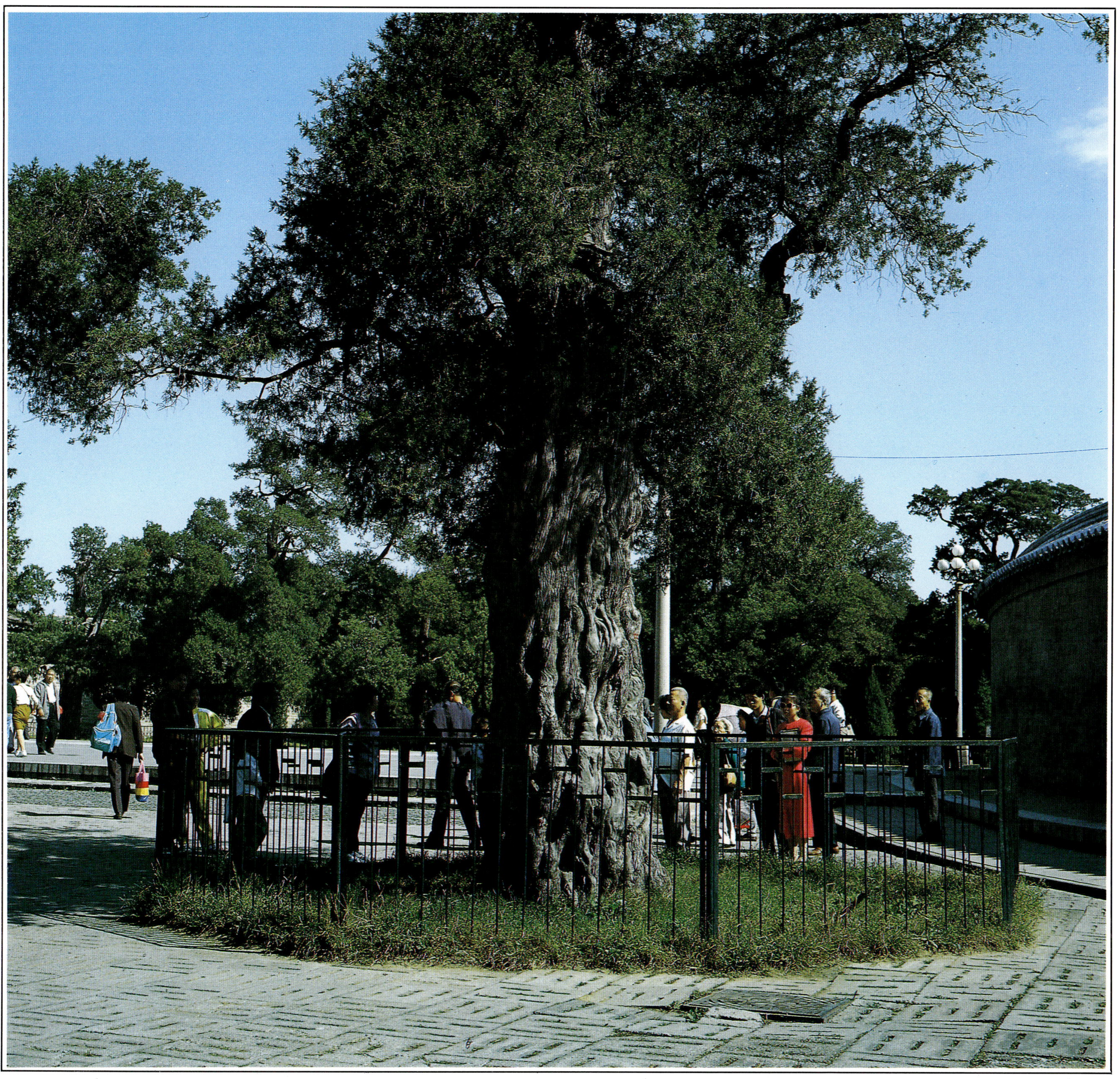

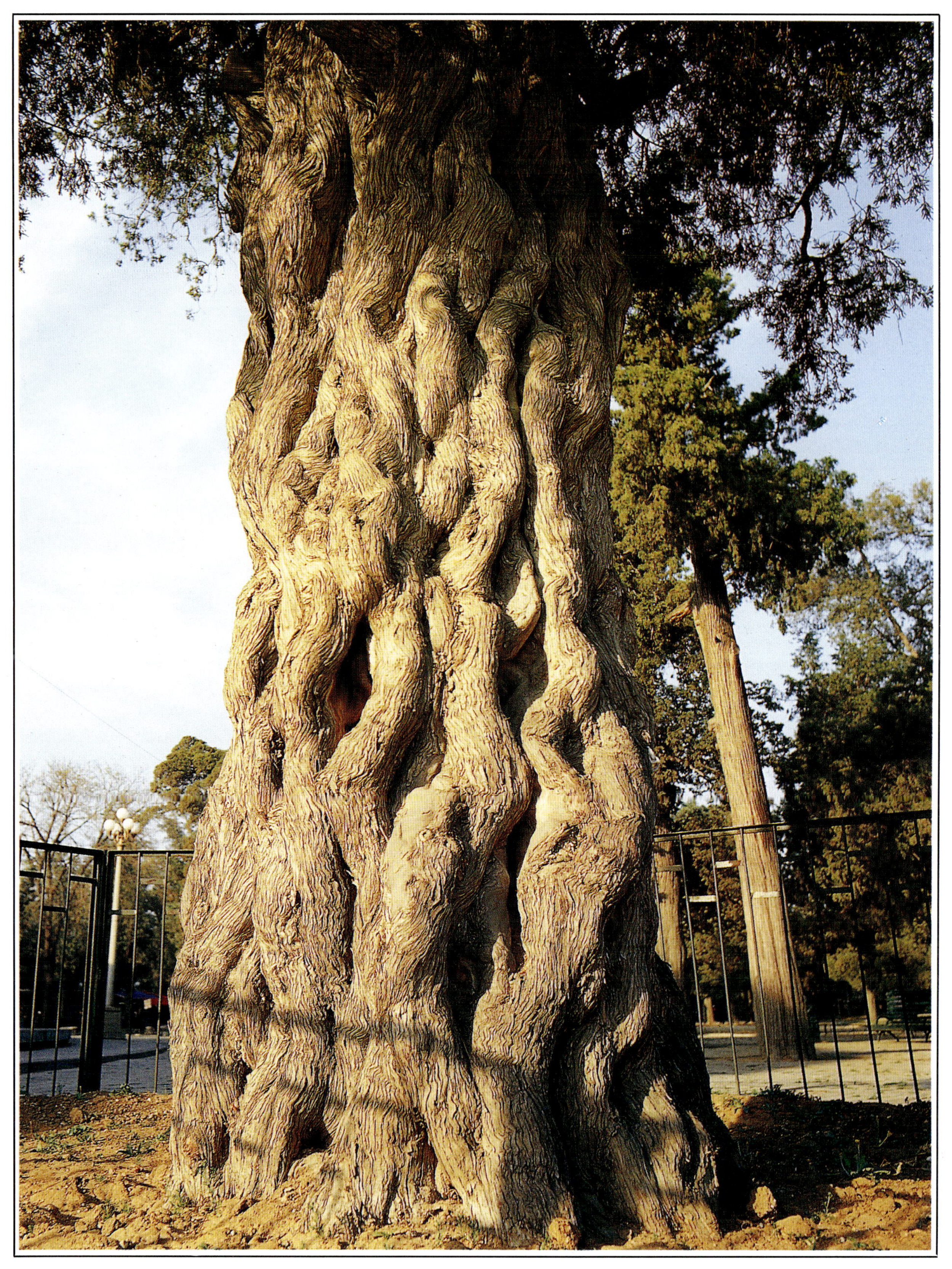

九龍柏　位於皇穹宇院外西北角，爲明代所植。樹干凹凸盤結，似群龍纏身，因稱“九龍柏”。

The Nine-dragon Cypress Situated at the northwestern corner of the courtyard of the Imperial Vault of Heaven, the cypress was planted in Ming Dynasty. The trunk, uneven and coiling, looks like entwined by dragons, hence the name.

九竜柏　この明代に植えた柏の木は、皇穹宇の庭の西北かどにある。樹の節っこが丁度竜が木のうえにつきまとって、だから、“九竜柏”とよんだ。

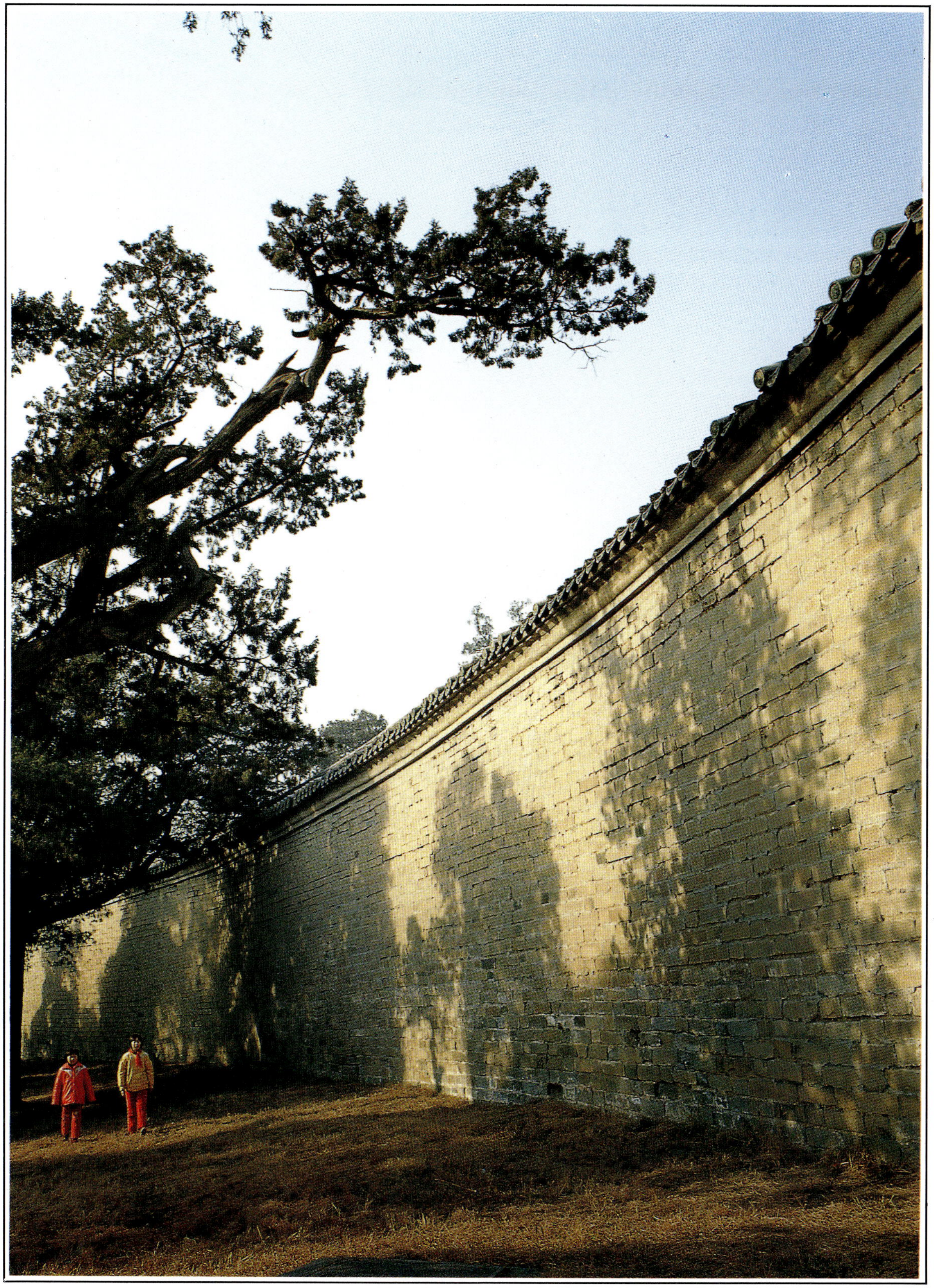

圜形牆　與成貞門相連，半圜形，是圜丘壇北牆，形成圜丘壇北圜南方布局，喩意“天圜地方”。

The Circular Wall Linked to the Chengzhen Gate, it is the semi-circular northern wall of Circular Mound Altar. Thus the Altar presents a layout of circular in the north and square in the south, implicating that the heaven is round and the earth is square.

圓形墻　塀は圜丘壇の北のほうの塀で、半円形になり、成貞門とつながって、壇の“北は丸い、南は方形”の仕組を構成し、“天は丸い、地は方形”の意味を表示している。

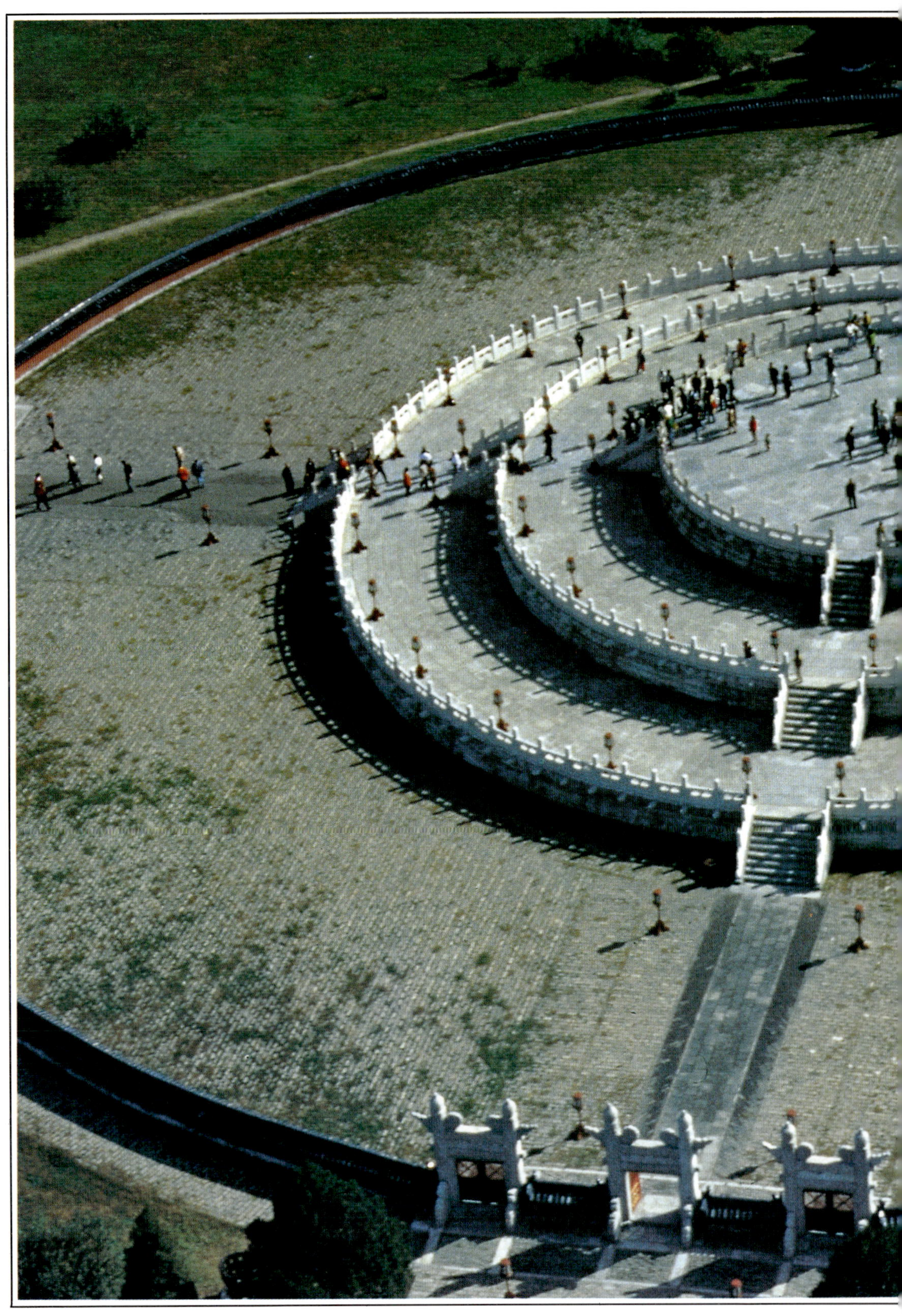

圜丘鳥瞰 圜丘壇始建於明朝嘉靖九年(1530年)，石壇三層，四面出階，內外兩道壝牆，內圓外方，有望燈、燔柴爐等附屬建築。

A Panoramic View of the Circular Mound Altar Beginning being built in 1530 (the 9th year of the reign of Jiajing, Ming Dynasty), the Altar is set on a 3-tiered base with stairs on 4 sides, 2 layers of walls, circular inside and square outside, surround it. There are watching lamps, stove inside the walls and other attaching constructions.

圜丘の鳥瞰　圜丘壇は1530年（明代嘉靖九年）に建てはじまり、四方ともに階段がでている三階建石壇である。内外にふたつの塀が建てられ，内のは丸い，外のは方形になている。望燈、燔柴炉など付属建物があった。

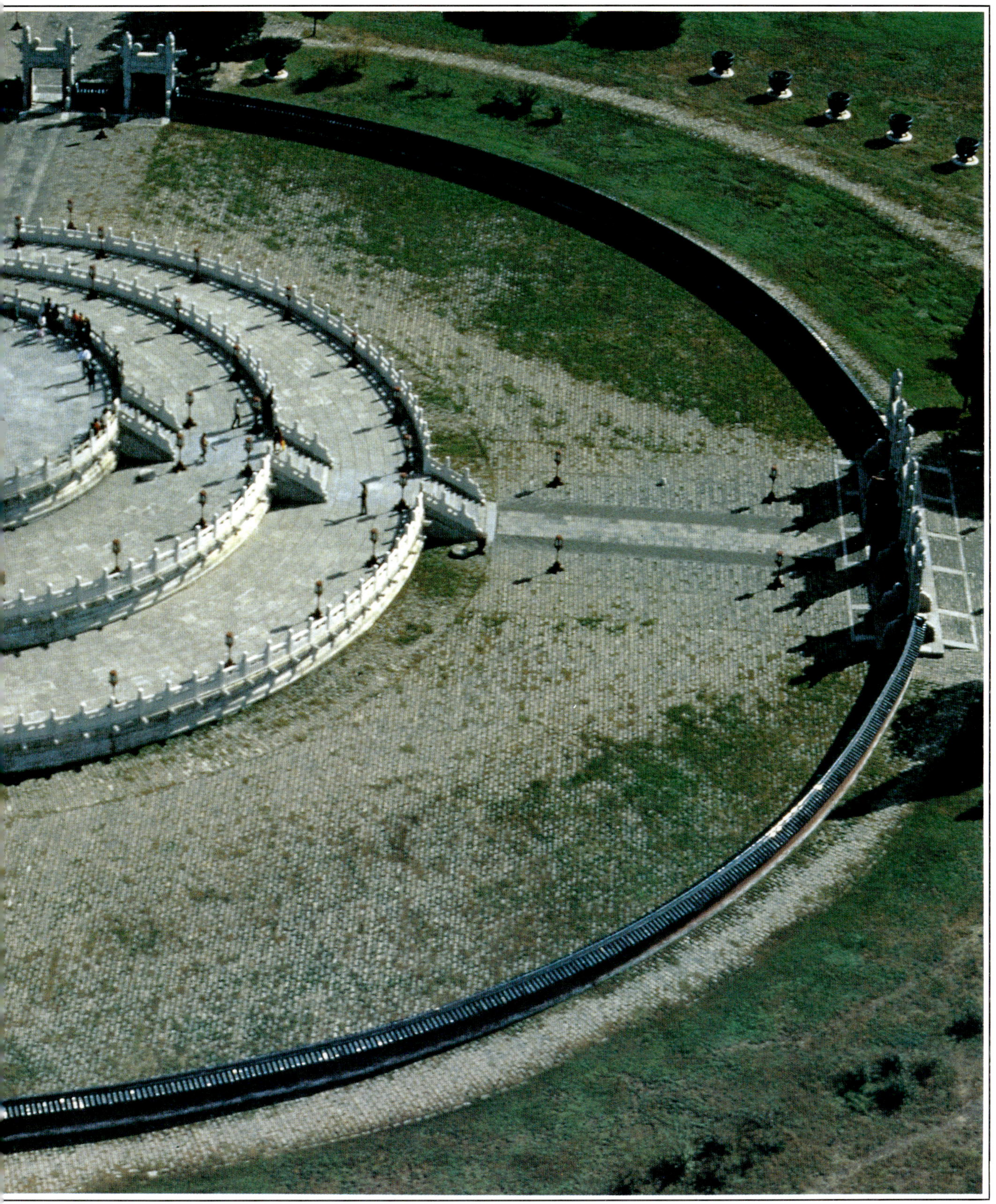

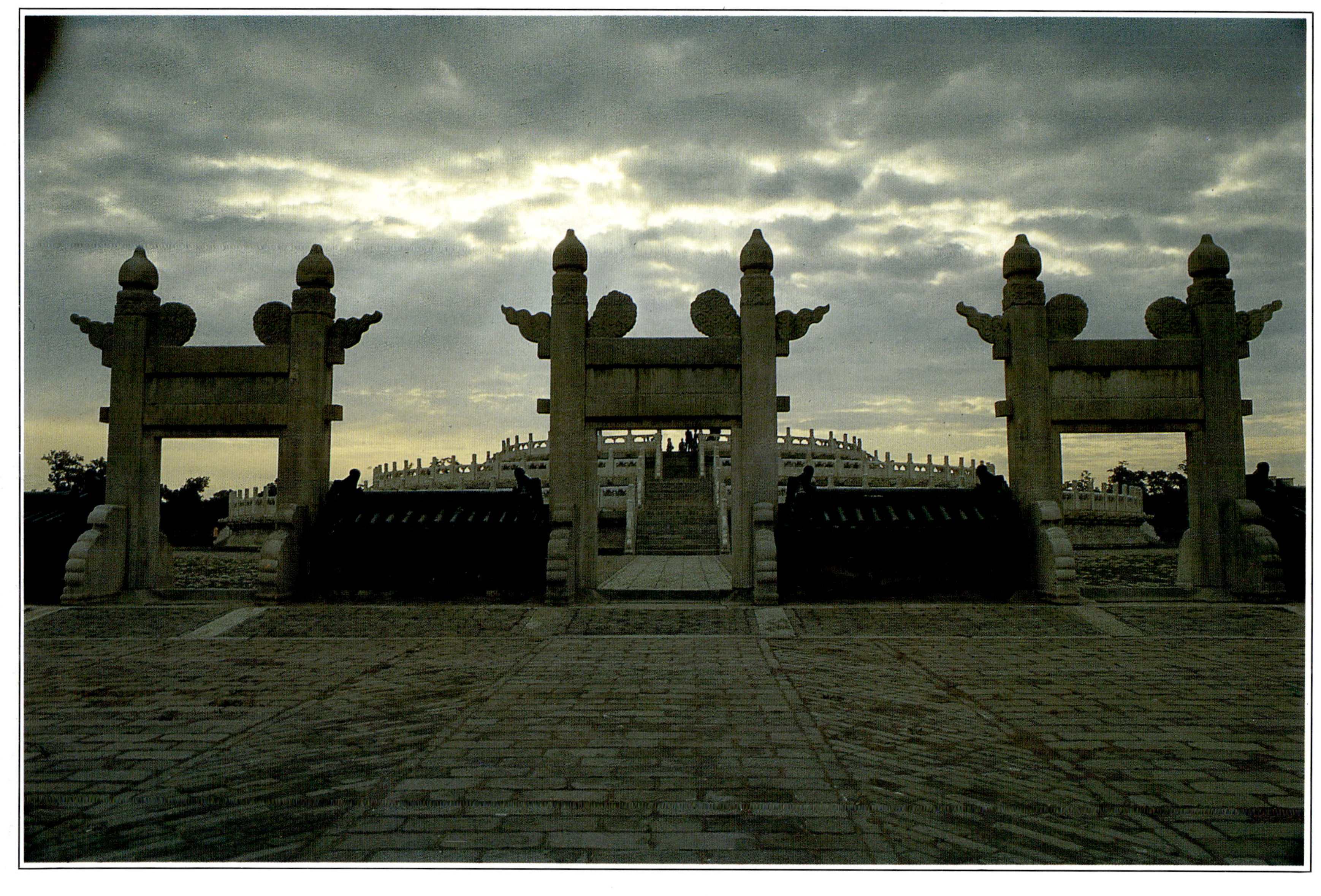

櫺星門　圜丘壇周圍壝牆上共有24道櫺星門，櫺星門是中國祭祀場所的特有建築，石質構件，結構古朴，造型典雅。

Lingxing Gates　On walls surrounding the Circular Mound Altar are 24 Lingxing Gates which are unique construction in Chinese sacrificial sites. They are stone constructions which are unsophisticatedly constructed and elegantly shaped.

櫺星門　圜丘壇まわりの塀の上に、二十四の櫺星門があけていた。こうゆう門が中国の祭壇にある特別なものである。石でできたこんな部材が、構造が古風で飾り気がない、造形が典雅である。

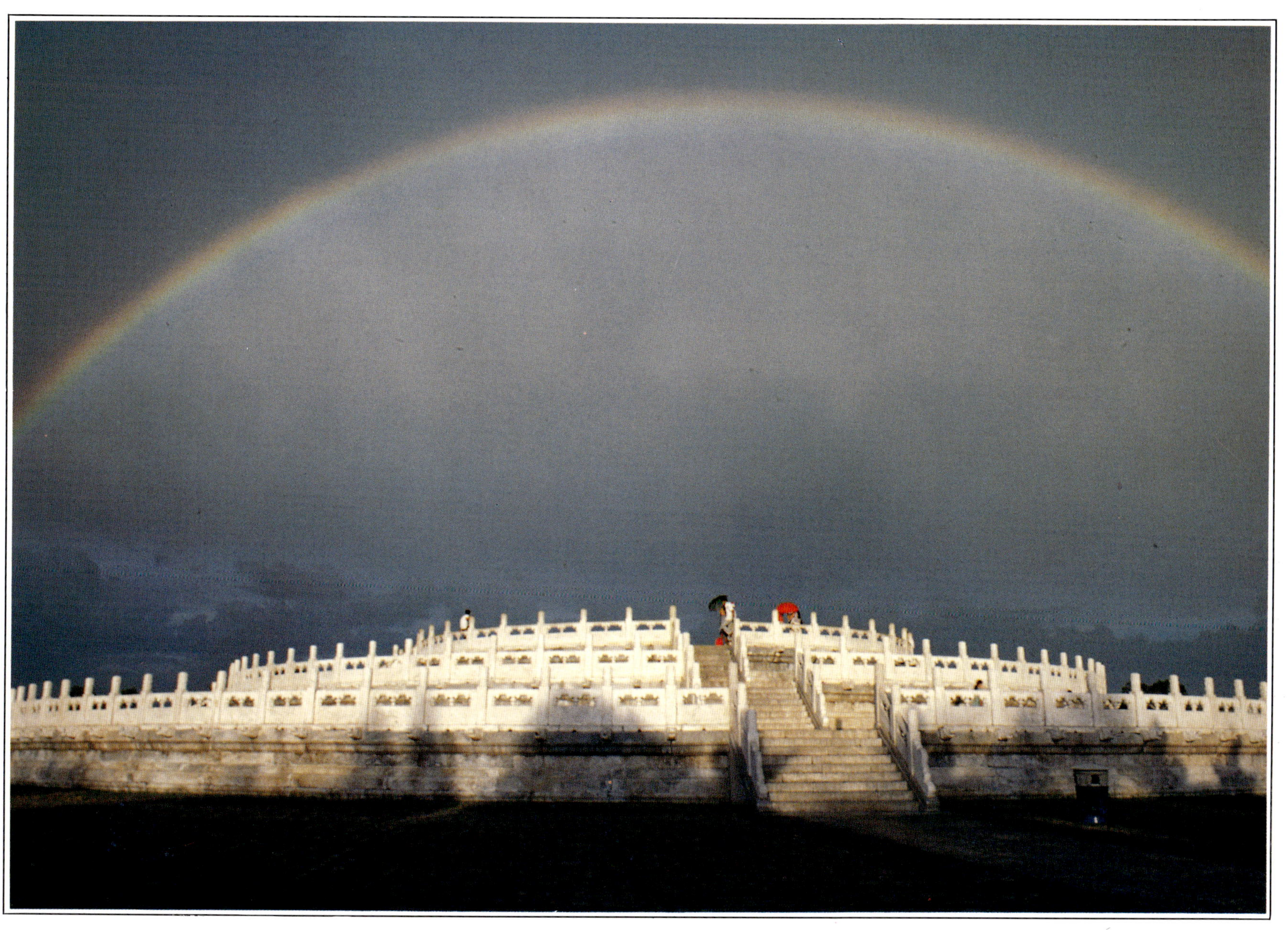

圜丘彩虹

Rainbow over the Circular Mound Altar

圜丘の上の虹

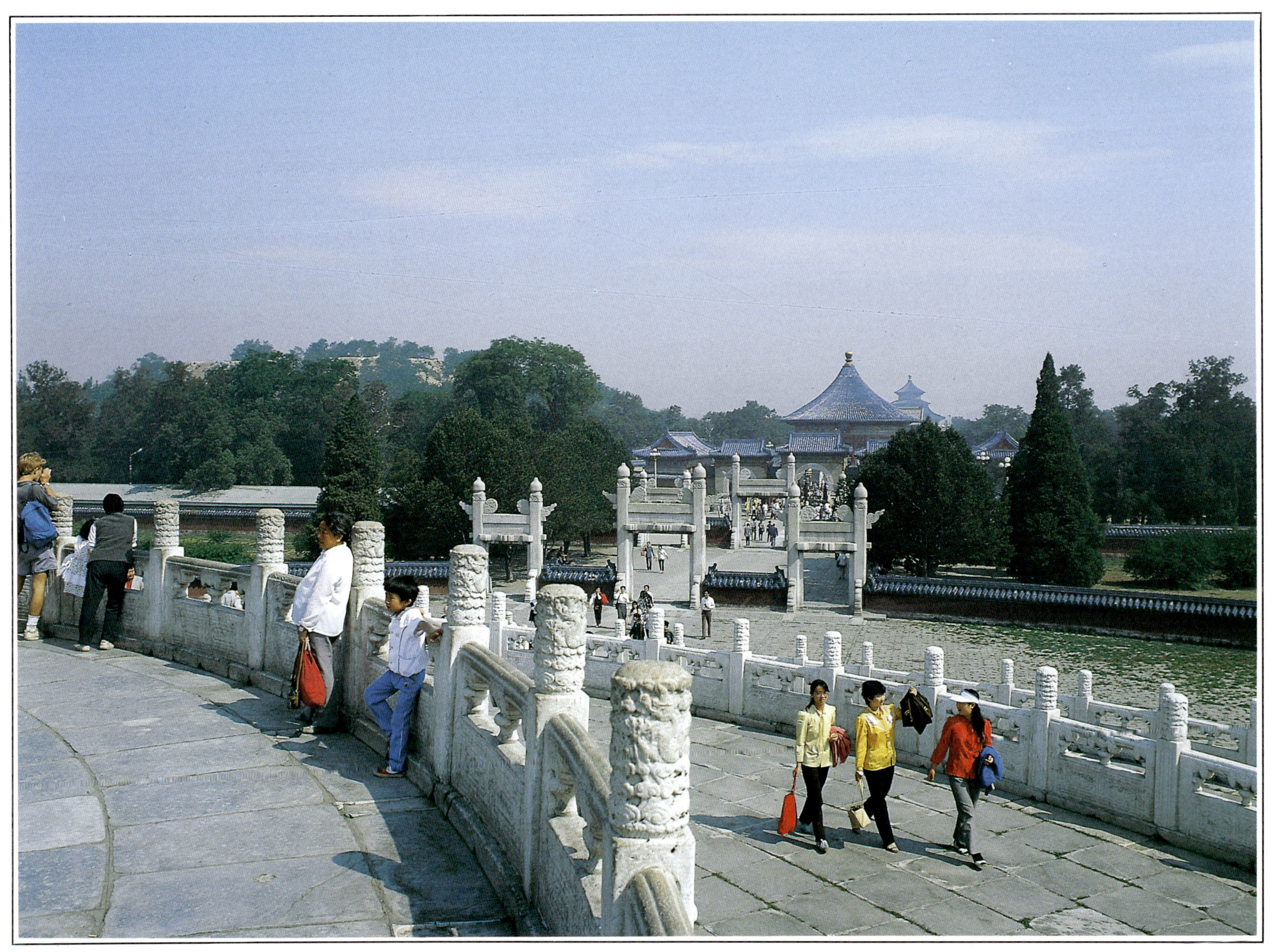

圜丘　爲冬至祭祀皇天上帝的祭壇。四面出階各九級，每層由欄板、望柱圍護，每層爲須彌座，望柱均刻龍紋浮雕。白雲藍天、綠樹紅牆之下，典雅壯麗。

The Circular Mound Altar　This is the altar for offering sacrifices to Heaven and God in the Winter Solstice Day. Stairs are set in 4 sides, with 9 steps each. All layers are surrounded by blocking boards and balustrades. The lower tier is the Xumi base. Balustrades are all carved with reliefs of dragon. Under the blue sky and white clouds, and set off by verdant trees and red walls, the Altar looks elegant and magnificent.

圜丘　これは、冬至のひに天と上帝を祭する祭壇で、四方に九階持つ階段ひとつつずだす、一階から三階まで皆欄板と望柱に囲んで護衛されて、一階は須弥座である。あらゆる望柱は竜の模様の浮彫となっている。白い雲とあおそらは、青い木と赤い塀に映えられて，本当に典雅で壮麗だ。

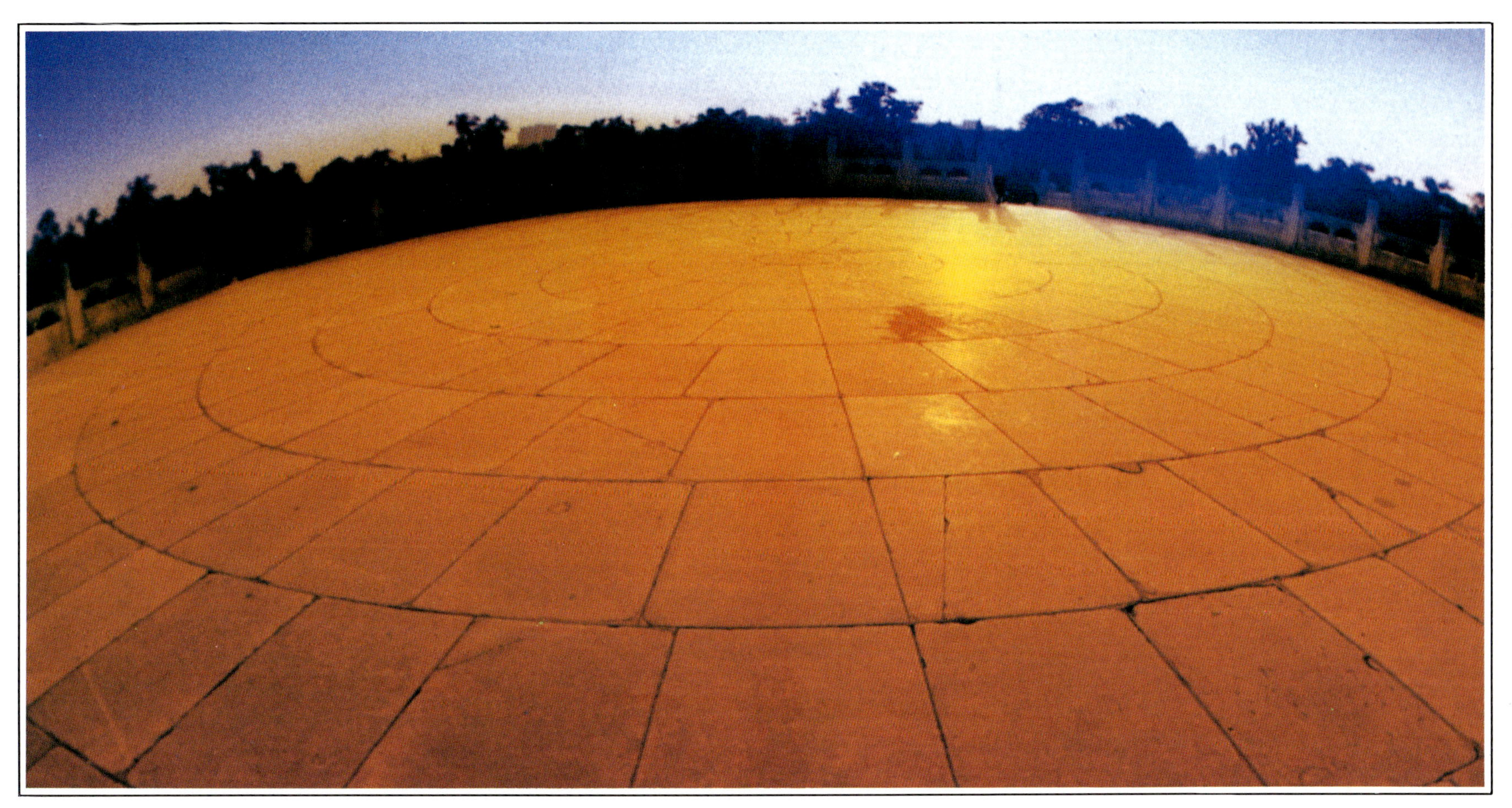

天心石　圜石壇上層壇面中間一塊石板爲圜形，周圍依次有九層扇形石塊，每層石板數均爲九的倍數，取象天意。圖形石板因名天心石，在此處說話，自感聲音渾厚有力。這裏是著名的新北京十六景之一"圜丘清音"。

Tianxin Stone　On the centre of the upper layer of the Circular Mound Altar is a circular stone slab, around which are 9 layers of fan-shaped stone slabs. Slabs on each layer are in the numbers of duplicates of 9, implicating the 9th Heaven, thus the circular slab is called Tianxin Stone. Speaking on the circular stone will make the speaker feel energetic. It is one of the New Beijing 16 scenes "Clear Sounds over Circular Mound Altar".

天心石　圜丘壇の三階の表面のまんなかに、丸い板状石材一枚ある。まわりに順序に九重の扇形塊状石材がある。各重石材の数は皆九、或いは九の倍数で、天意を表示している。丸い板状石材は"天心石"になづけた。そのところではなしをすると、自分でおとが大きくで豊が、力が強い。このところは、"圜丘清音"とよはられて、北京の新しい十六景色のひとつである。

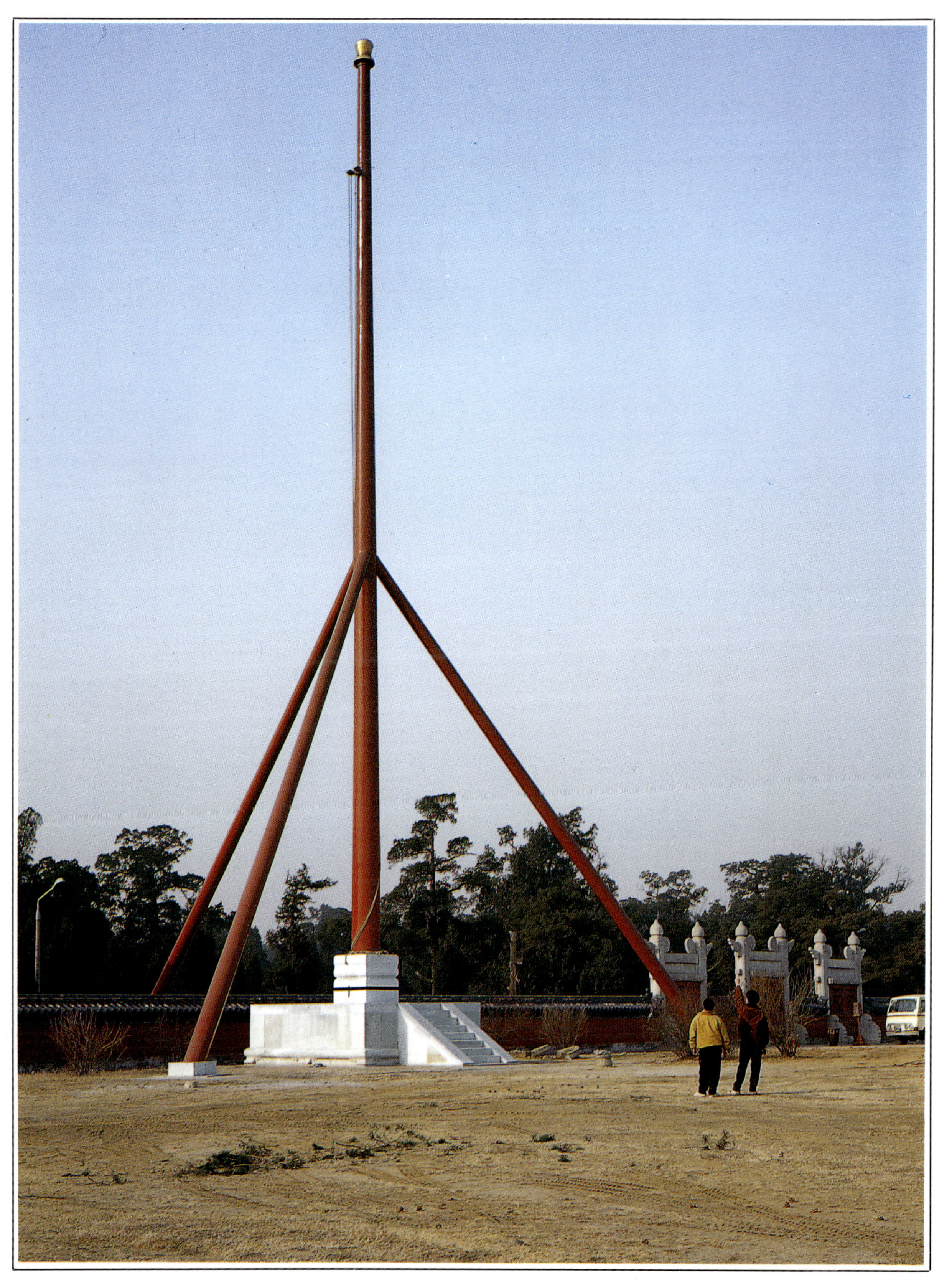

望燈　位於圜丘壇外壝院內西南隅，共三座，現恢復一座，爲祭祀時懸掛天燈之用。

Watching Lamps 3 lamps were in the southwestern corner of the surrounding walls in Circular Mound Altar. Now, one of them has been re-covered. They were used to hang lamps when sacrificial ceremonies were held.

望燈　圜丘壇の庭の西南かどに、望燈三本あった。いま，そのなかの一本を回復した。もと，そのランプは祭りをするときの天燈であった。

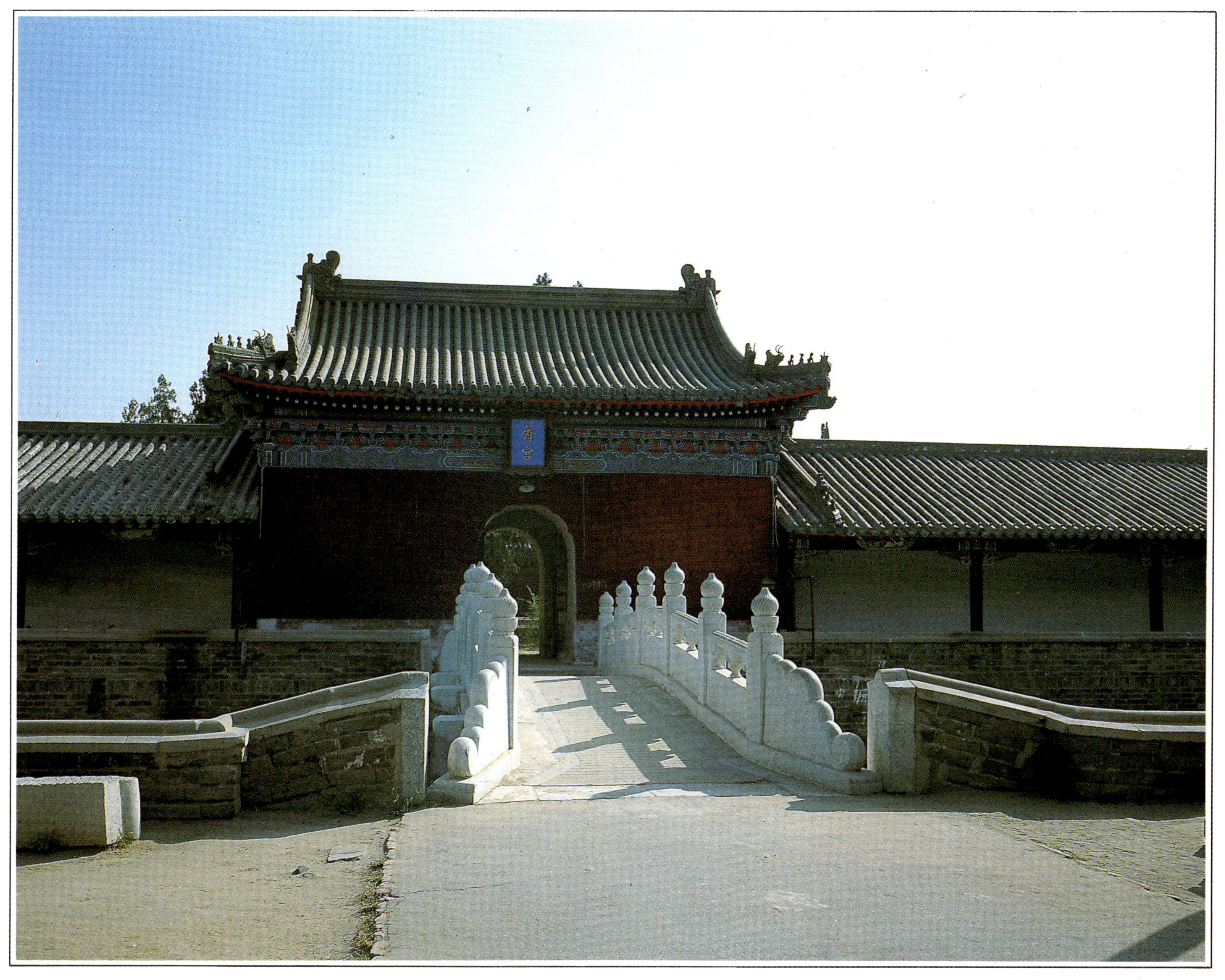

齋宮正門坐西朝東，前跨三道石梁。歇山式綠琉璃瓦頂。其座向、瓦色均取“天子”對天稱臣之意。

The main entrance to the Fasting Palace sits against the west and faces the east. 3 stone beams are set crosswise on the gable, and the roof is covered with green glazed tiles. The orientation and colour of the tiles all implicate that the “Son of Heaven” acknowledges his position of a subject in front of Heaven.

斎宮の正門は東を向って、前のほうに三つの石樑が横に圧って、歇山式緑の琉璃煉瓦房根を持つ建物である。そのむき、煉瓦の色が皆“天子は天を対して、臣として服従する”の意味を表示する。

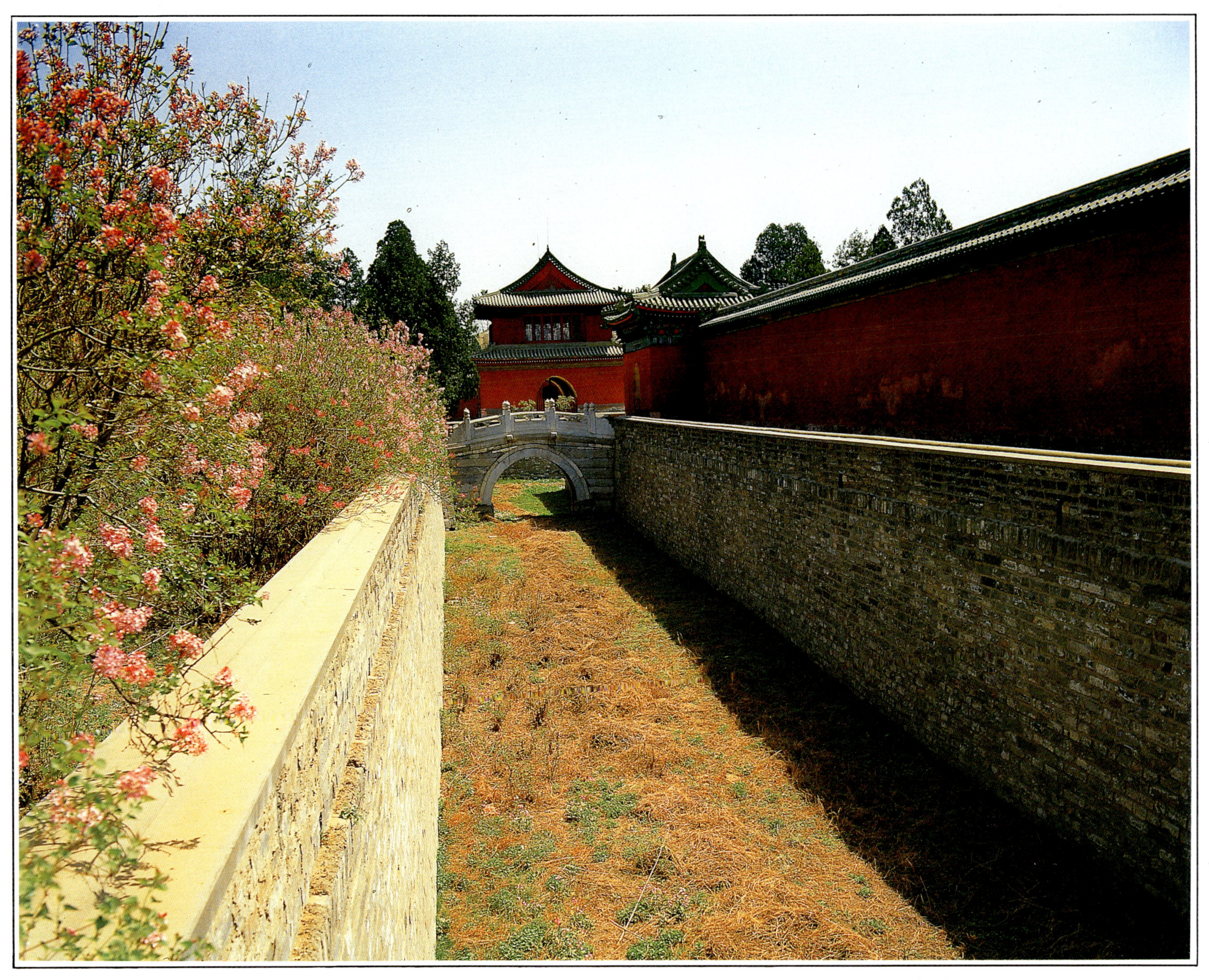

齋宮御溝　齋宮內外兩道宮牆，各有一道御溝。外溝環繞一周，內溝爲“U”形，爲防御之用，圖示爲內層御溝。

Imperial Ditches in the Temporary Palace　One each Imperial Ditch is under the two layers of walls (the inner and the outer ones). The outer ditch runs into a complete circle, while the inner one takes the U shape. They were defending ditches. Picture shows the inner Imperial Ditch.

斎宮の御溝　斎宮には、両線の宮塀と一線つずの御溝がある。外溝は離宮をまわって、内溝は“U”の形とする。防禦するのためで建てた。写真は内溝である。

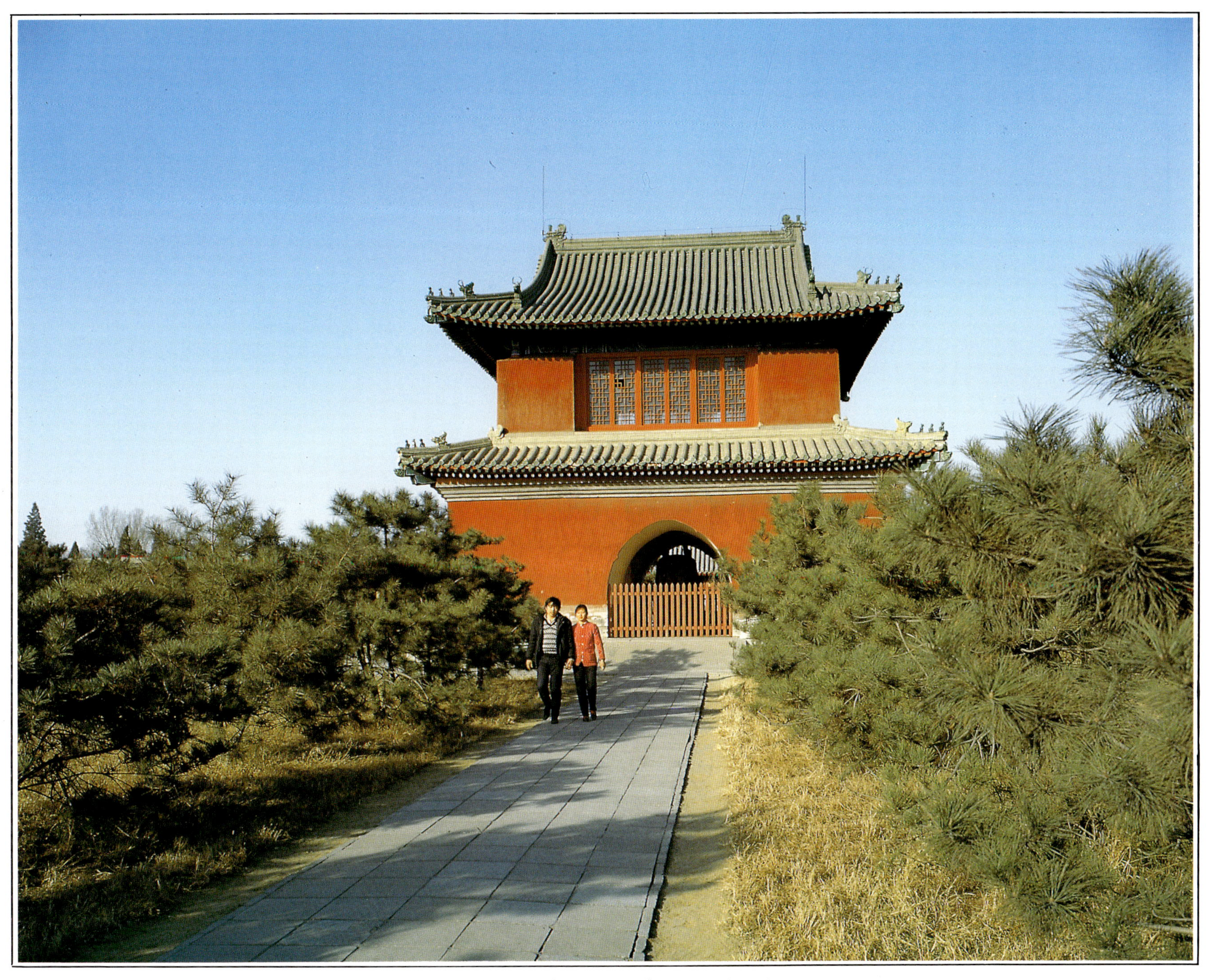

鐘樓　位於齋宮外層東北角，重檐歇山式建築。祭祀時，鐘鳴皇帝出齋宮，至祭壇則鐘止。

The Bell Tower　This is a double-eaved Xieshan construction situated at the northeastern corner in the outer ring of the Fasting Palace. When a sacrificial ceremony started, the bell was sounded and the emperor left the Fasting Palace. The bell stopped ringing when the emperor reached the altar.

鐘楼　斎宮そとの庭にある二重檐歇山式建物がある。祭りをするとき、鐘が鳴ったら、皇帝が斎宮をはなれる、かねなりがやめるのは，皇帝が祭壇についたと示されているだ。

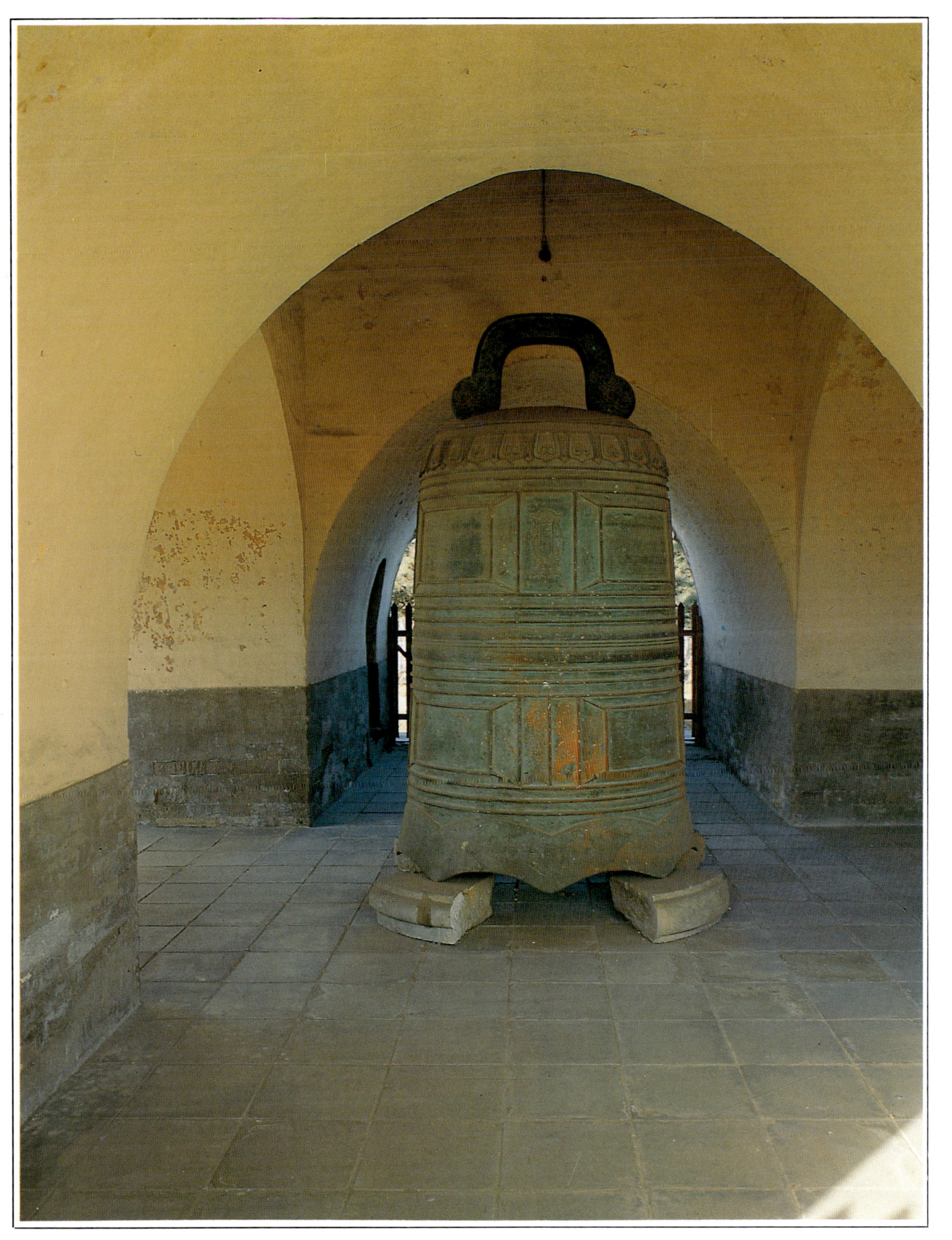

圖中爲鐘樓所懸明朝永樂大鐘。

Picture shows the Yongle Bell from the Ming Dynasty being hanged in the Bell Tower.

鐘楼にかけている明代の永楽大き鐘

▶齋戒銅人石亭　皇帝齋戒時，亭中陳設一銅人，手中持齋戒牌，以示警戒。

The Stone Pavilion Housing A Copper Human Figure When the emperor was fasting, the figure was put into the Pavilion with a “Fasting Plate” in hand, implicating that it was keeping a close watch on the fasting emperor.

斎戒銅人の石亭　皇帝が斎戒するときに、亭の中に銅人ひとりいれる。その銅人が斎戒幌を手にもって、警戒しようの意味だ。

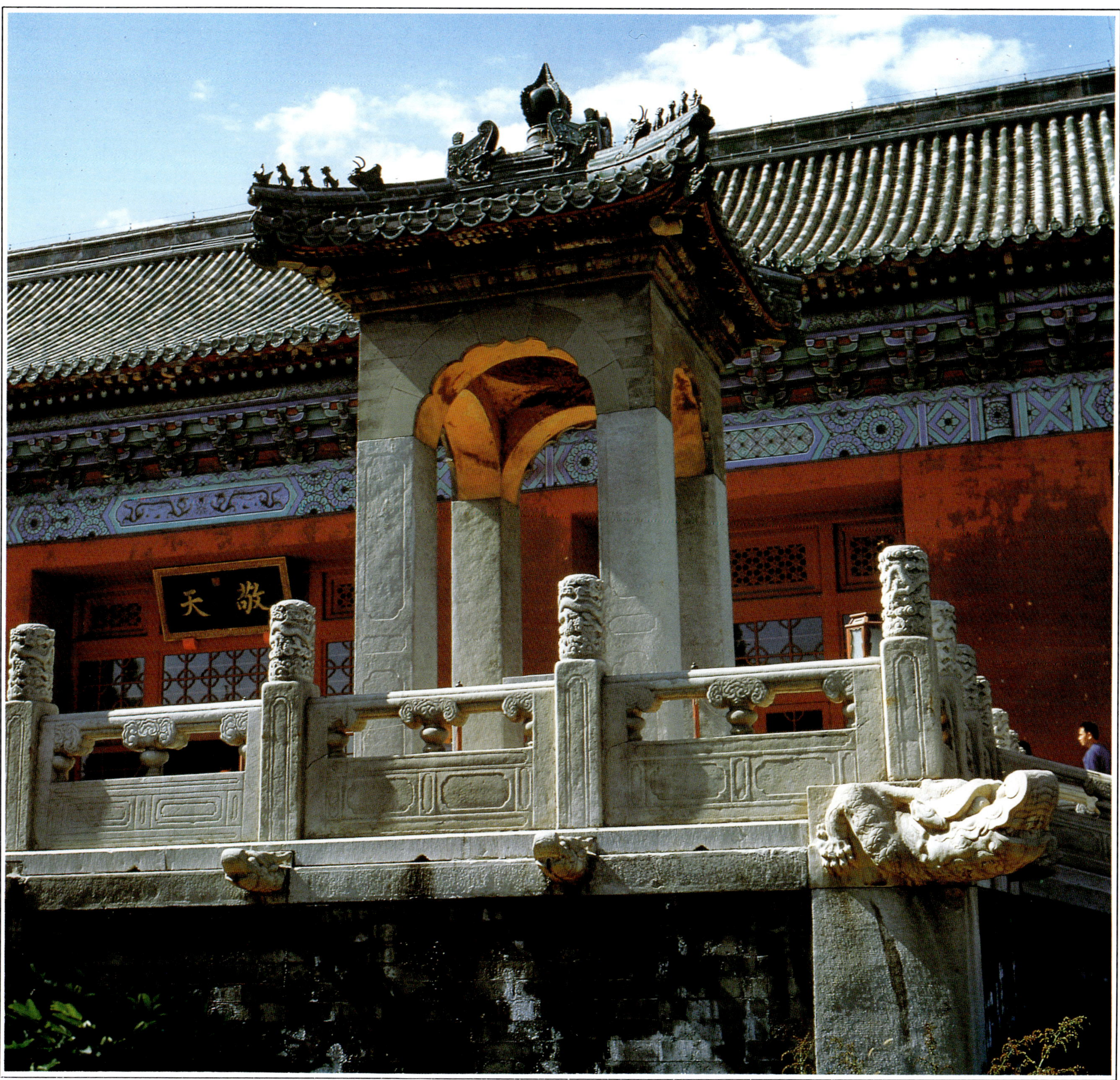
敬天

齋宮位於祈谷壇內壇西南隅，始建於明朝永樂十八年(1421年)整體建築坐西朝東，有無梁殿，寢宮、鐘樓等主要建築。是皇帝在天壇舉行祭祀典禮時齋戒之所。

Situated to the southwest of the inner part of the Altar for the God of Grains, the Fasting Palace was first built in 1421 (the 18th year of the reign of Yongle, Ming Dynasty). The whole group of buildings sits against the west and faces the east, and there are such major buildings as Beamless Hall, Sleeping room, Bell tower, etc. It was the place where the emperor kept fasting when sacrificial ceremonies were held.

斎宮は、1421年(明代永楽18年)に建て始まり、祈穀壇の内壇の西南かどにあり、まったく東をむかっている。主要な建物は無樑殿、寝宮、鐘楼などがある。斎宮は、皇帝が天壇で祭祀するときに、斎戒するところであった。

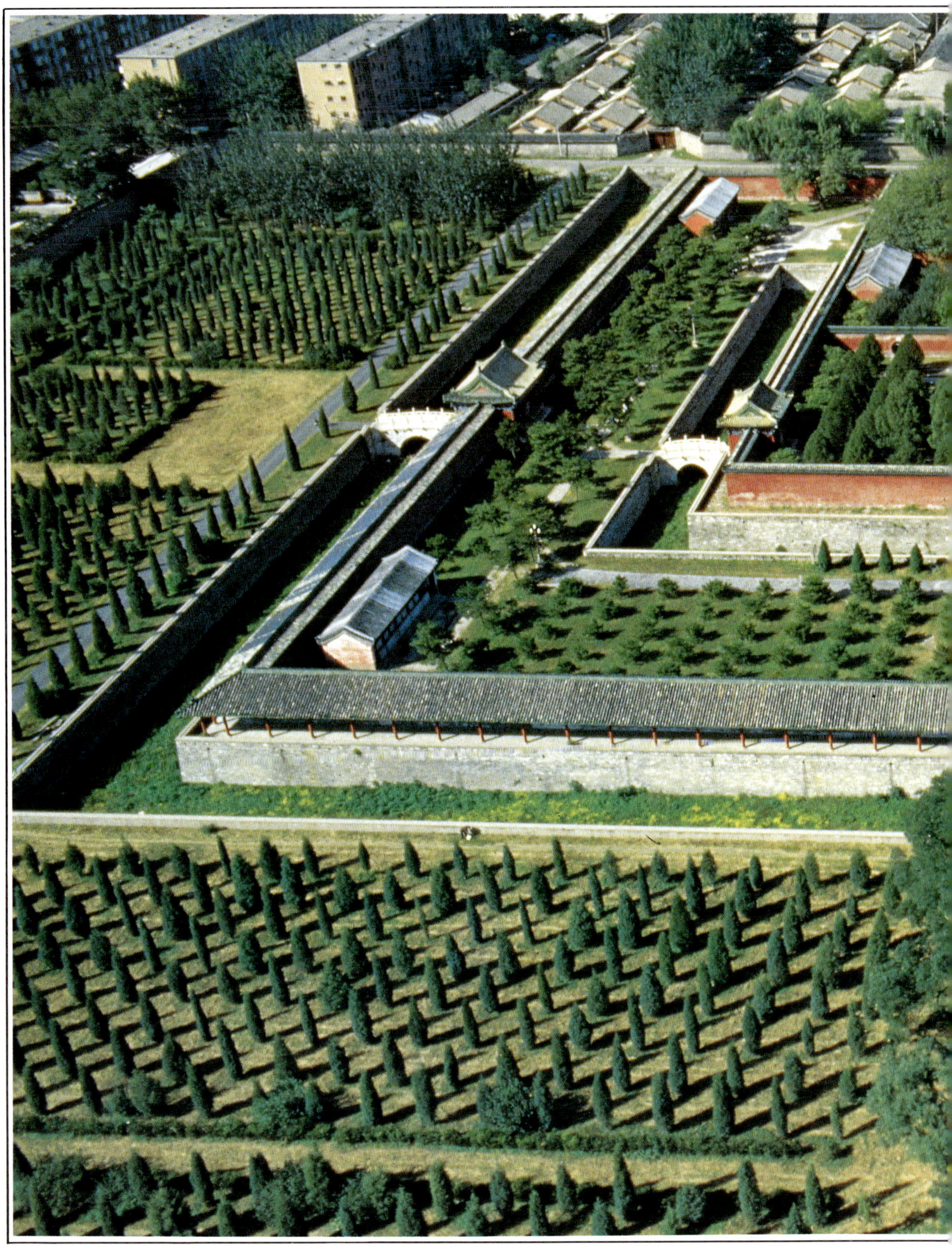

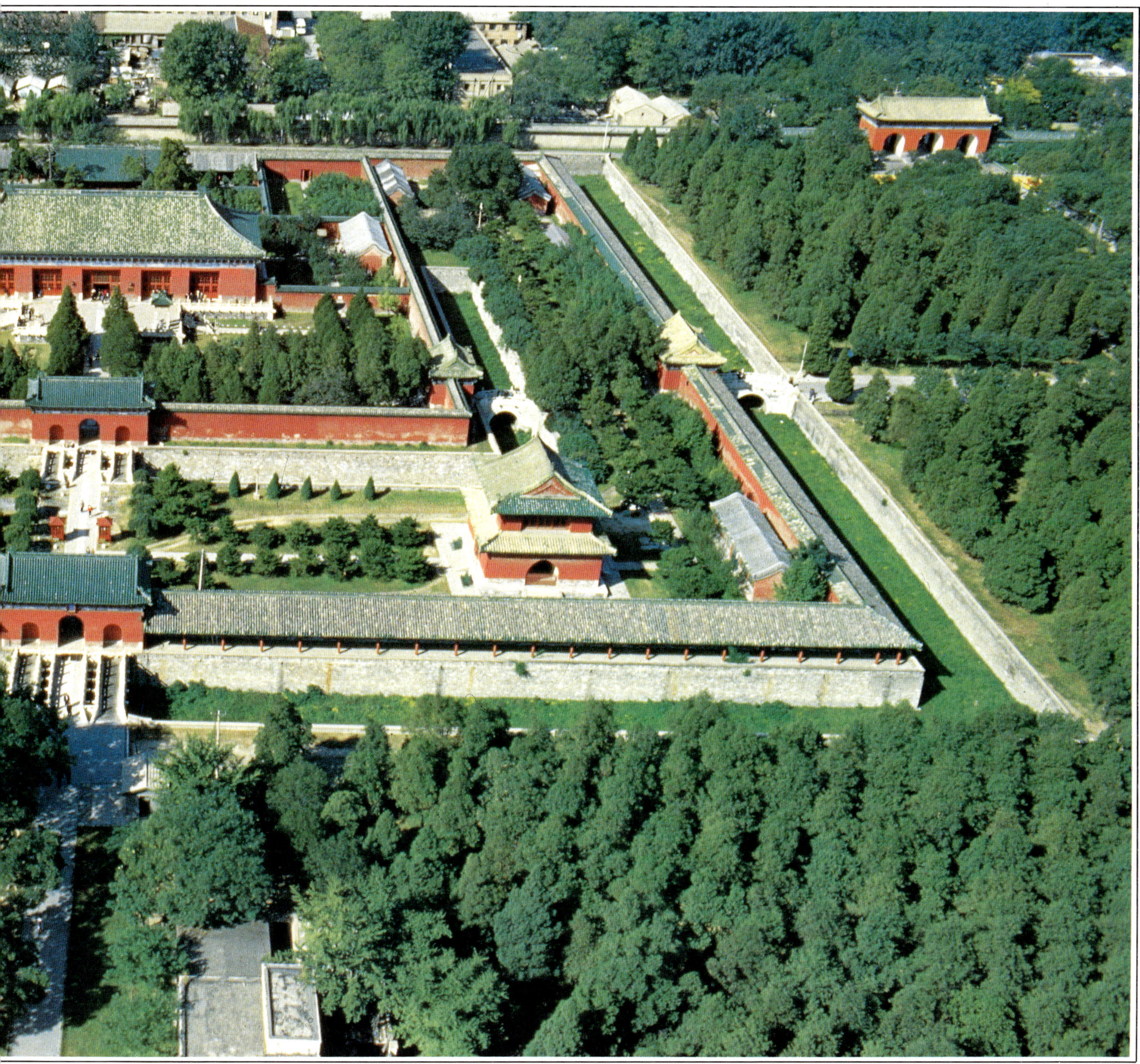

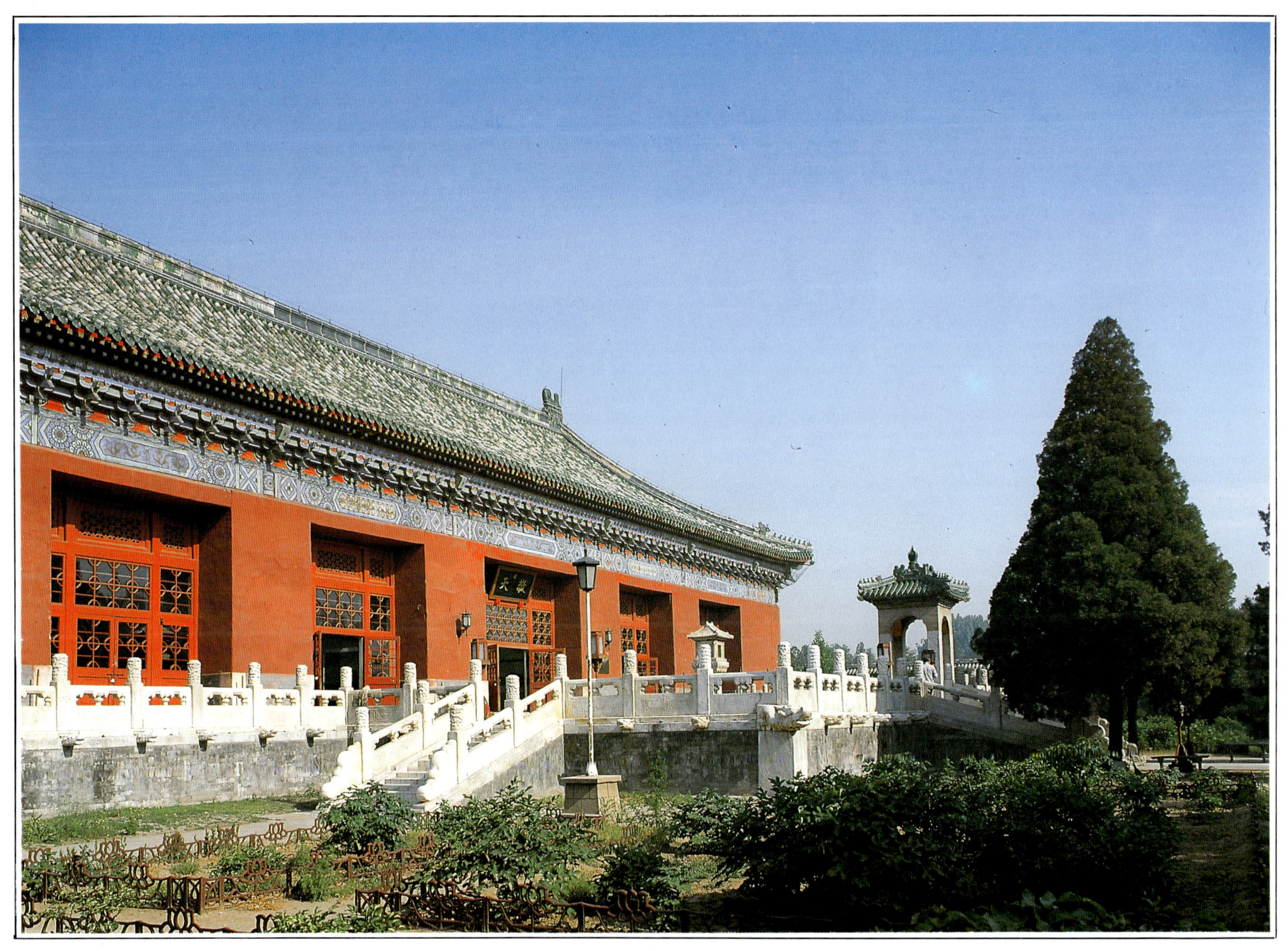

齋宮無梁殿(敬天)　磚砌拱券式建築、無梁枋，故稱無梁殿。綠色琉璃頂，五開間。前月台上有時辰亭，銅人亭等建築，是皇帝齋戒的主要場所。明間門額懸“敬天”一匾。

Beamless Hall in the Fasting Palace (Paying Respects to Heaven)　It is an arched brick construction without beams, hence the name. Originally, the Hall, 5 bays across, was covered with green glazed tiles. On the front terrace are buildings like Time Pavilion, Pavilion Housing Copper Human Figure, etc. The site is the major fasting site for the emperors. In Ming Dynasty, a plaque with the inscription of “Paying Respect to Heaven” was hung above the door.

斎宮の無樑殿(敬天の意味)　この殿は拱券式建物で、樑枋ともないので、無樑殿とよばれていた。後殿は五軒幅、緑の琉璃瓦の屋根を持つ。前の月台には時辰亭や銅人亭などの建物がある。この殿は、皇帝が斎戒するときにつかう主要な場所である。明室の門の上に、“敬天”という額がかけている。

祭天陳設　齋宮無樑殿中陳設的是祭祀時皇天上帝位前的陳設祭器、祭品及各種燈具，五供等情況。

Tablet for Honouring Heaven The furnishings in Beamless Hall, Fasting Palace, include sacrificial utensils set in front of Heaven and God when worshipping, sacrificial offerings, various lamps, etc.

敬天の神位　斎宮の無樑殿の中に陳列しているのは皆、祭祀する時に、皇天上帝神位の前における祭器、祭品、各種類の燈具と"五供"などである。

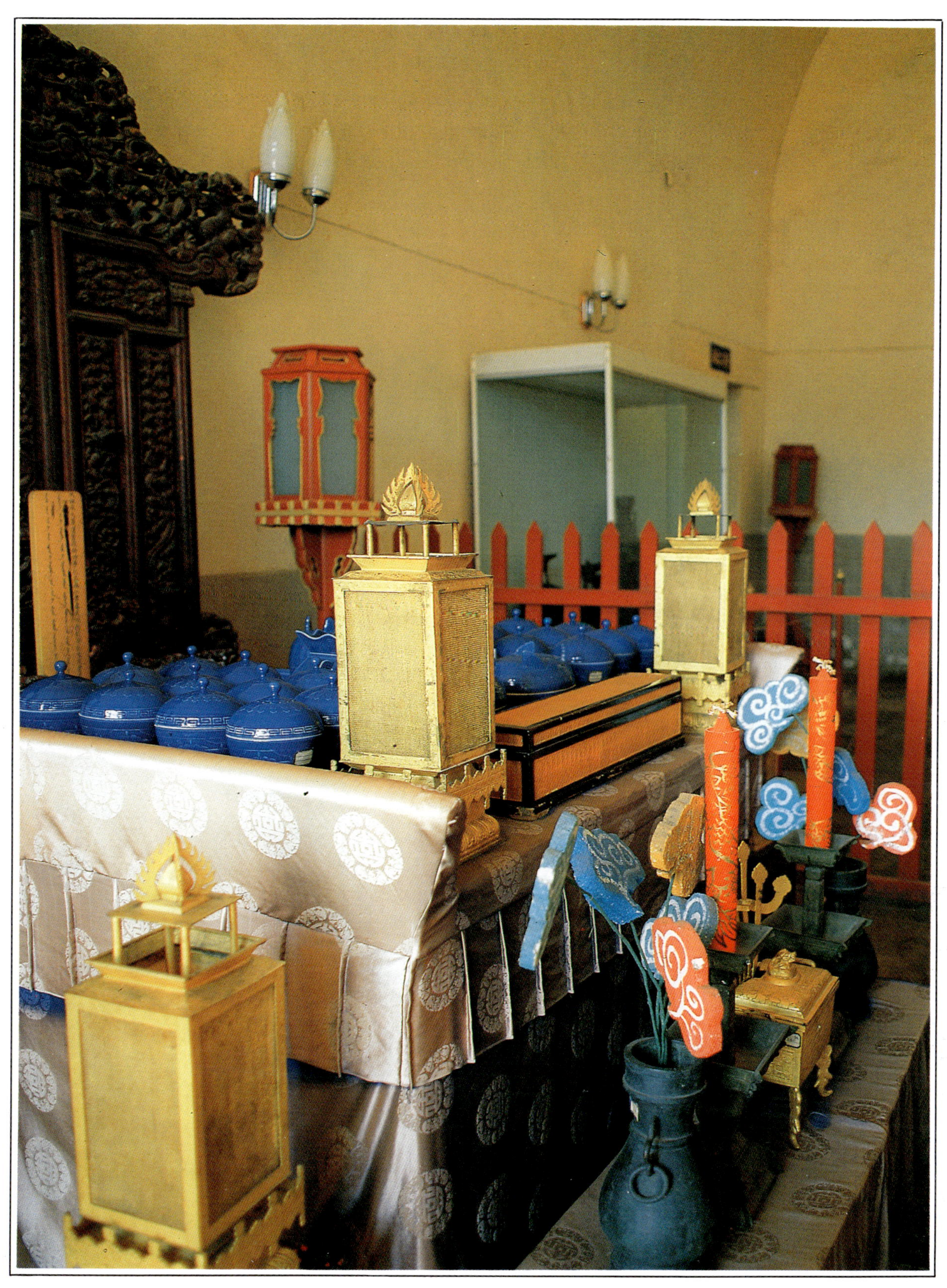

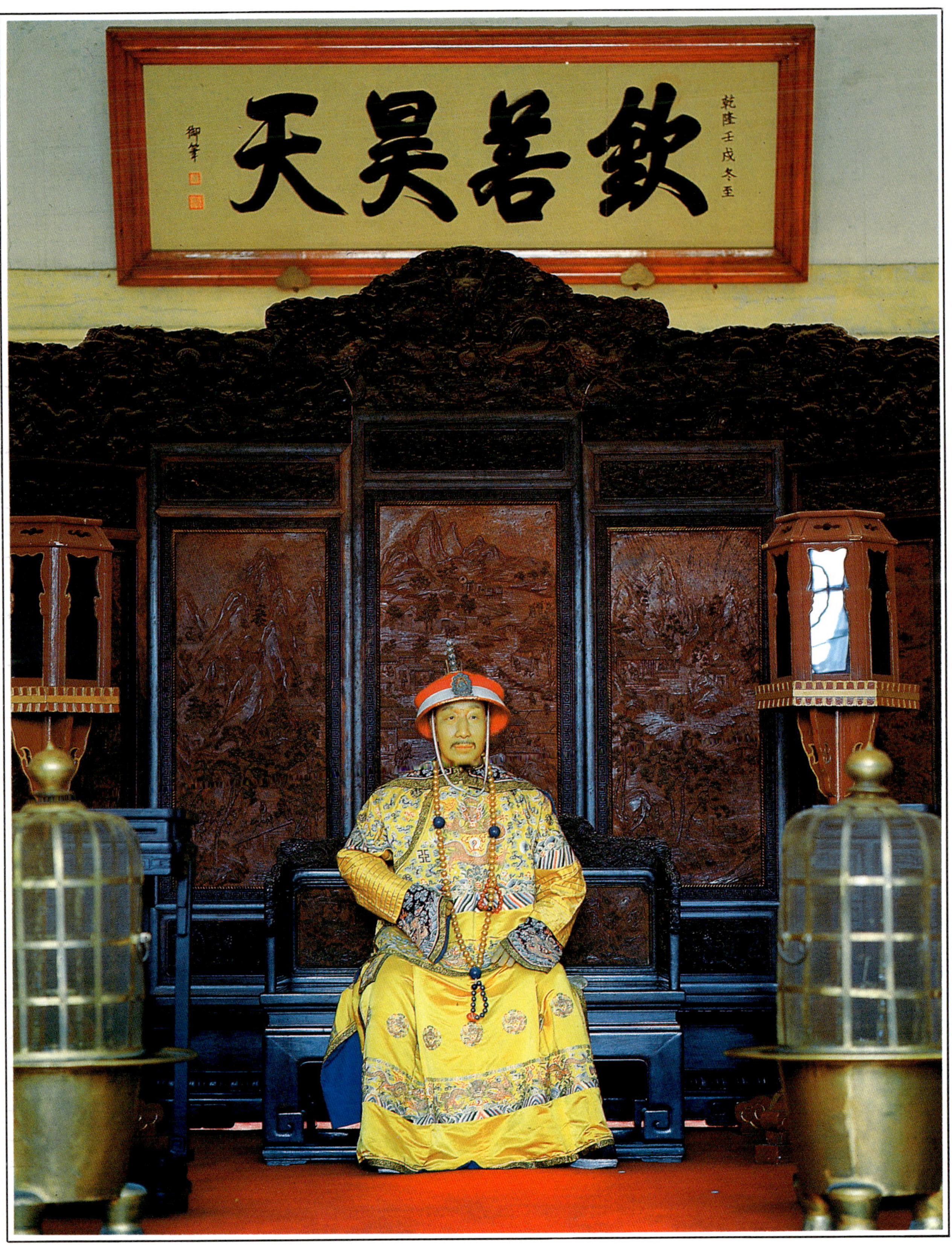

無樑殿明間爲皇帝齋戒期間處理事務之所，懸匾"欽若昊天"爲乾隆御筆，寓意對皇天上帝的尊敬與對"天道"的順從。

The open room in the Beamless Hall was the place where the emperor handled routine affairs when he was fasting. A plaque with the inscription of Emperor Qianlong was hung in the room. The inscription implied that man should honour Heaven and God, and that the emperor is obedient to "Heaven's Ways".

無樑殿の明室は、皇帝が斎戒中事務を処理するところである。そこに、乾隆皇帝手書"欽若昊天"の額がかけられ、皇天上帝を尊敬する、または天道に順従する意味だ。

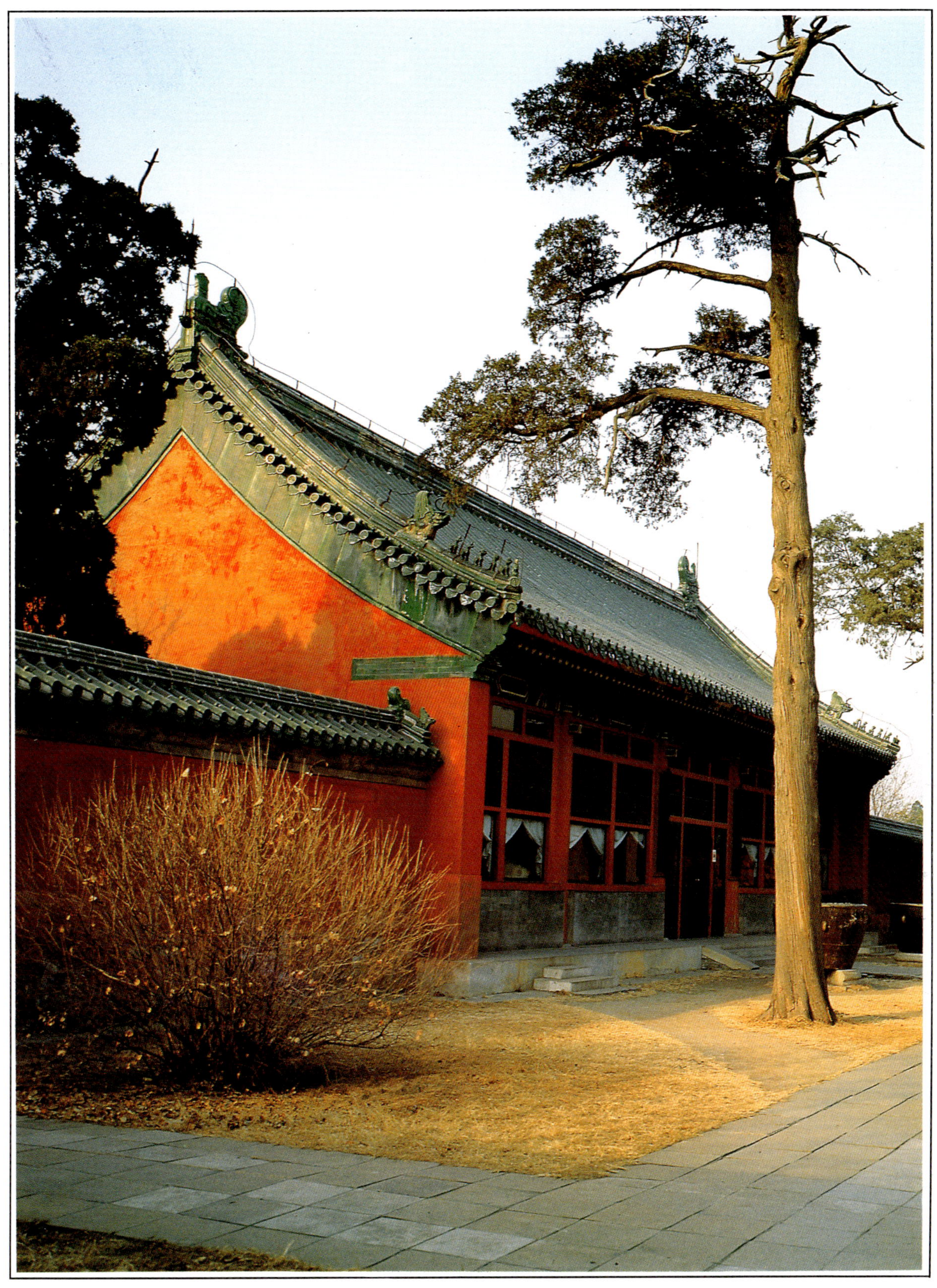

寢宮，又稱柏堂，爲皇帝齋戒時住宿之所。三間開，硬山式建築、環境幽雅。明間門額懸“敬止”匾，寓意謹愼對待自己的言行舉止。

Sleeping Palace was where the emperor resided when he was fasting. It is a 3-bayed construction that is quiet and elegant, In Ming Dynasty, a plaque with inscription was hanged in the room, which implied that one should be careful about his own words and deeds.

寝宮は、柏堂ともよばれていた。皇帝が斎戒するときに宿泊するところである。三軒幅硬山式の建物で、環境も幽雅である。あけている部屋に、“敬止”の額が門の上にかけられて、自己の言行を特別に注意する意味だ。

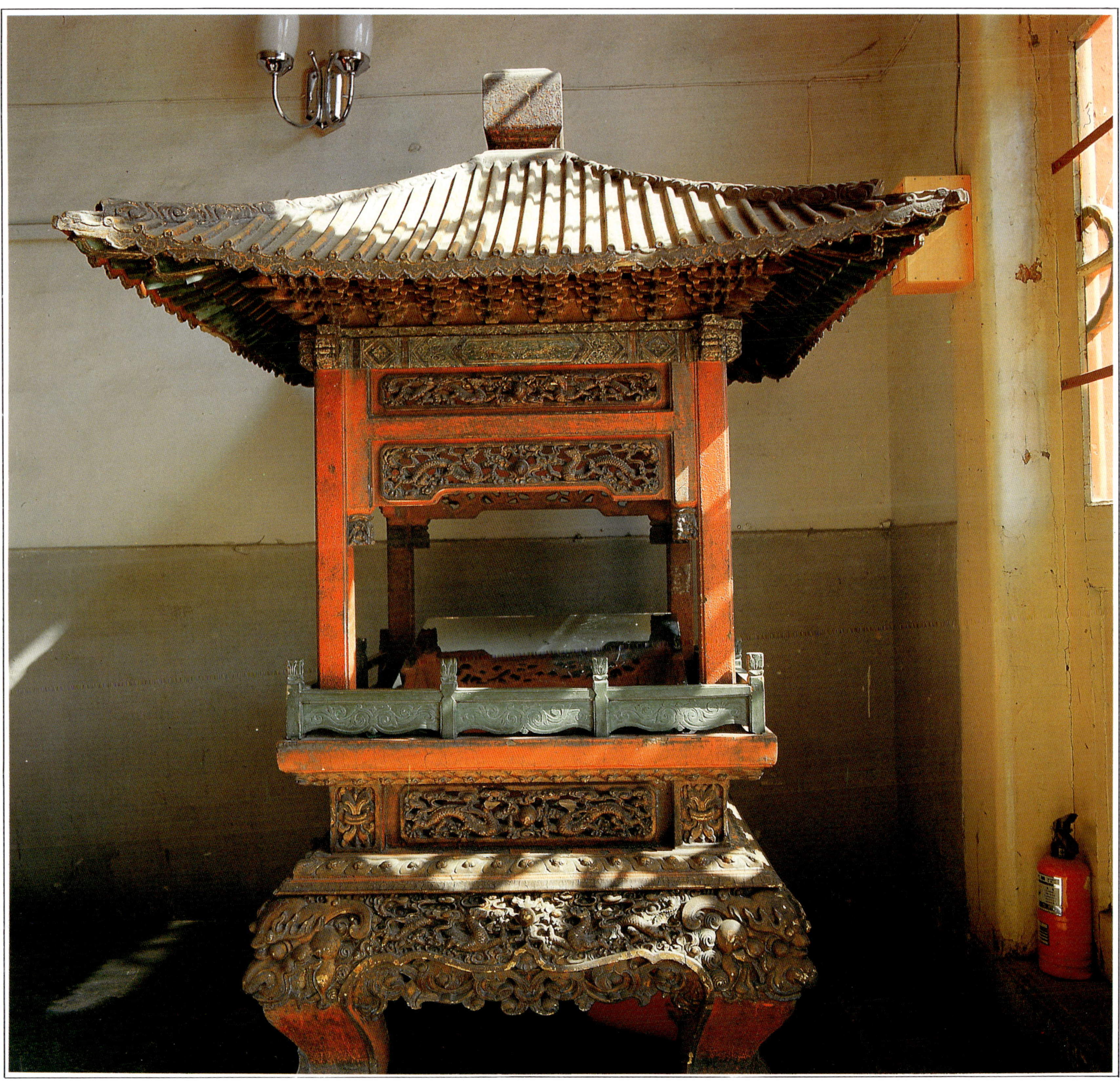

寢宮南殿　夏季陳設的情景

Furnishings in the Southern Hall of the Sleeping Palace

寝宮の南殿　夏の装飾。

◀祝版亭　皇帝祭天時的祝文，在祭天時用祝版亭由太和殿抬至天壇。祝版亭構造異常精巧，全身遍布龍浮雕，帶斗拱、彩畫，各浮雕、彩畫均貼金泊、華貴精致。

The Pavilion for the Memorandum Board　Prayers of emperors were written on the Board. When sacrificial ceremonies were going to be held, the Board was always put into the Pavilion which was carried from Taihe Hall to the Temple of Heaven. The Pavilion was meticulously constructed with reliefs of dragons all over the body, and decorated by brackets and coloured paintings. The reliefs and coloured paintings were all covered by gold foils, thus looking splendid and delicate.

祝版亭　皇帝が祭天をするときにつかう祝文は、その儀式が始まり前に、祝版亭で太和殿から天壇へはこんでゆく。祝版亭が非常に精細で巧妙にできて，竜形浮彫いっぱいで、斗棋と彩色絵画がある。浮彫と彩色絵画が金箔をきせて、立派で精巧なものだ。

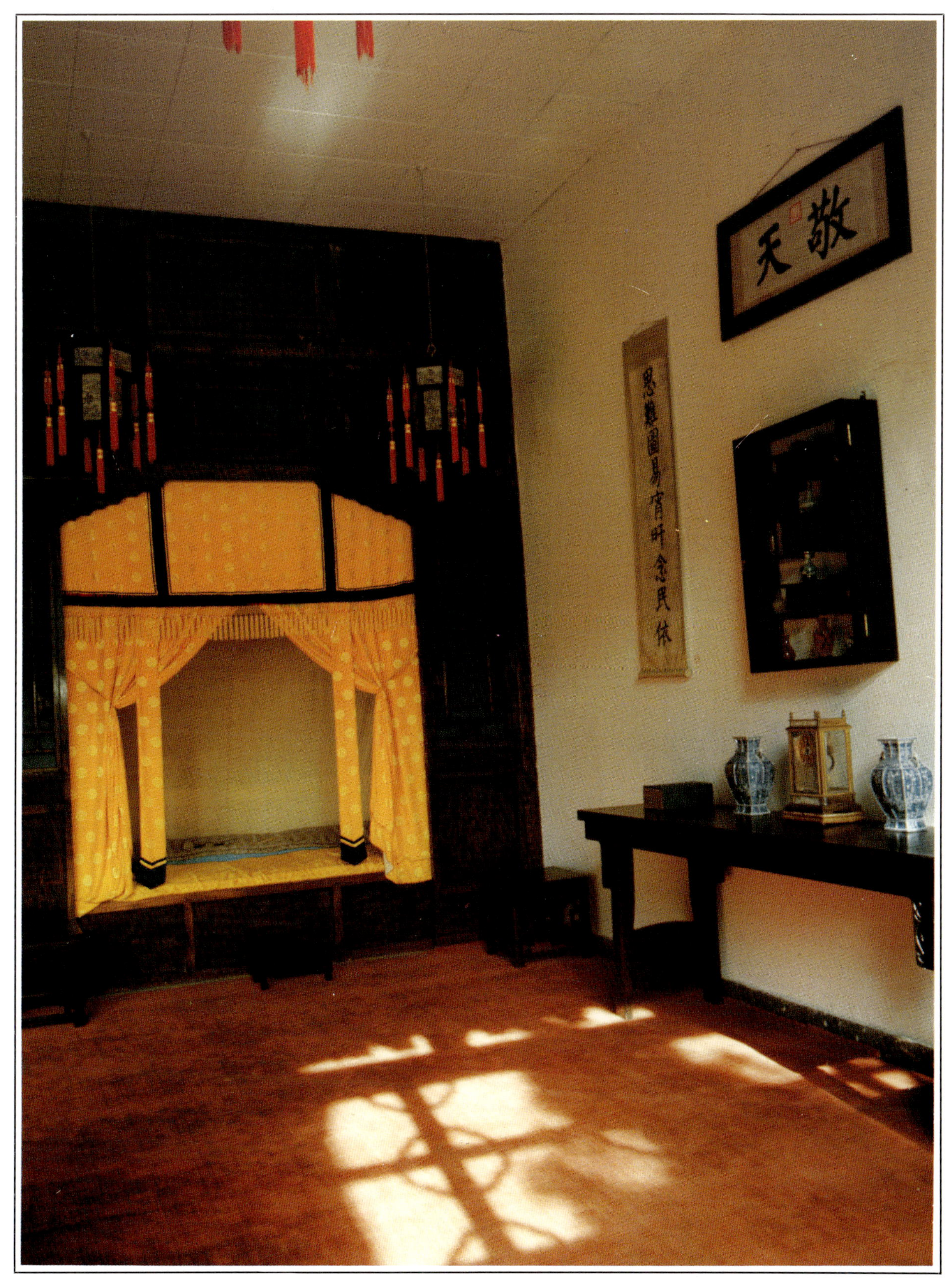

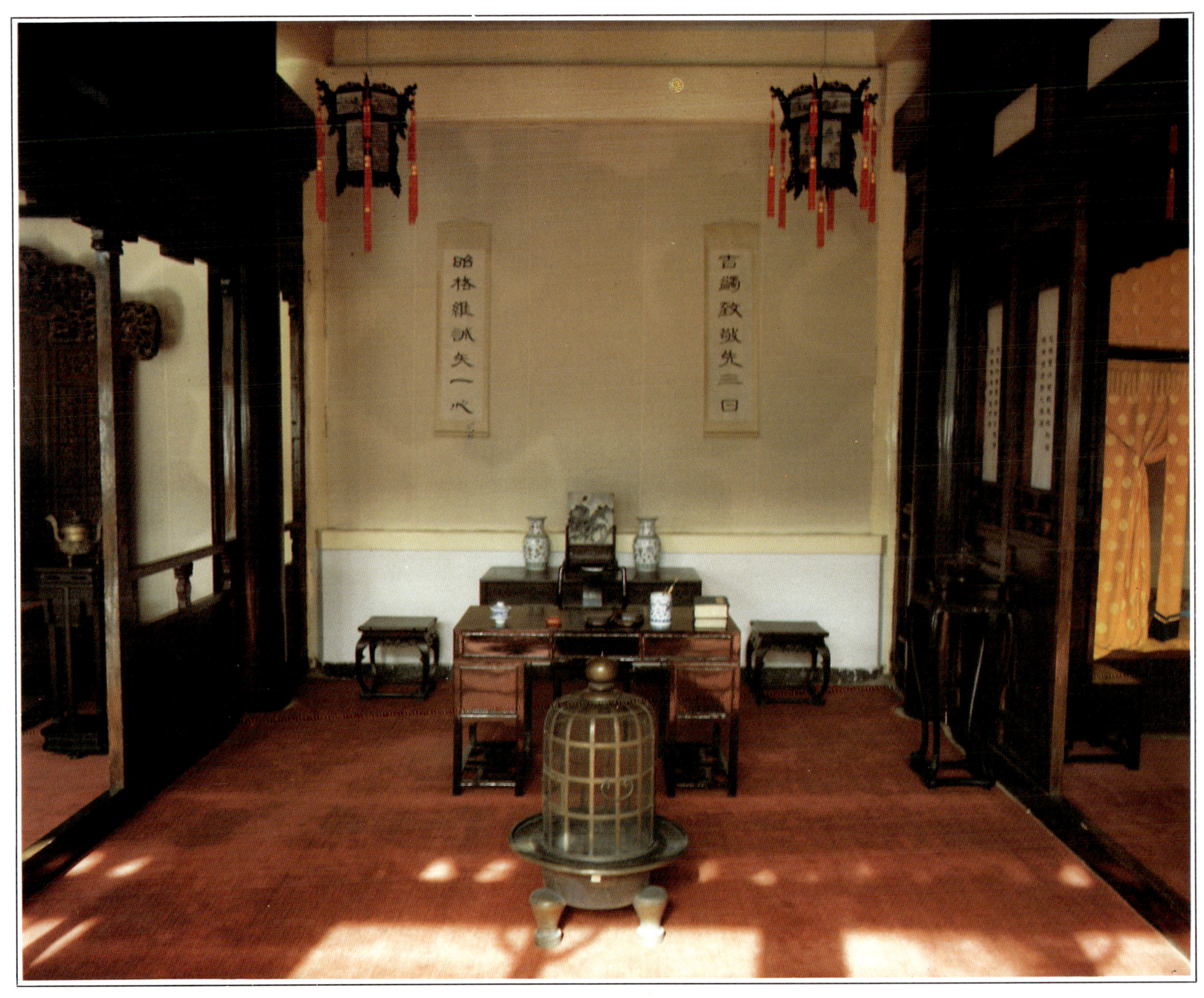

寢宮北殿之一　陳設冬季時所用的火爐等物。

A Room in the Northern Hall of the sleeping Palace　A stove, etc, needed in winter, is furnished there.

寝宮の北殿(一)　冬につかう暖炉など陳列品。

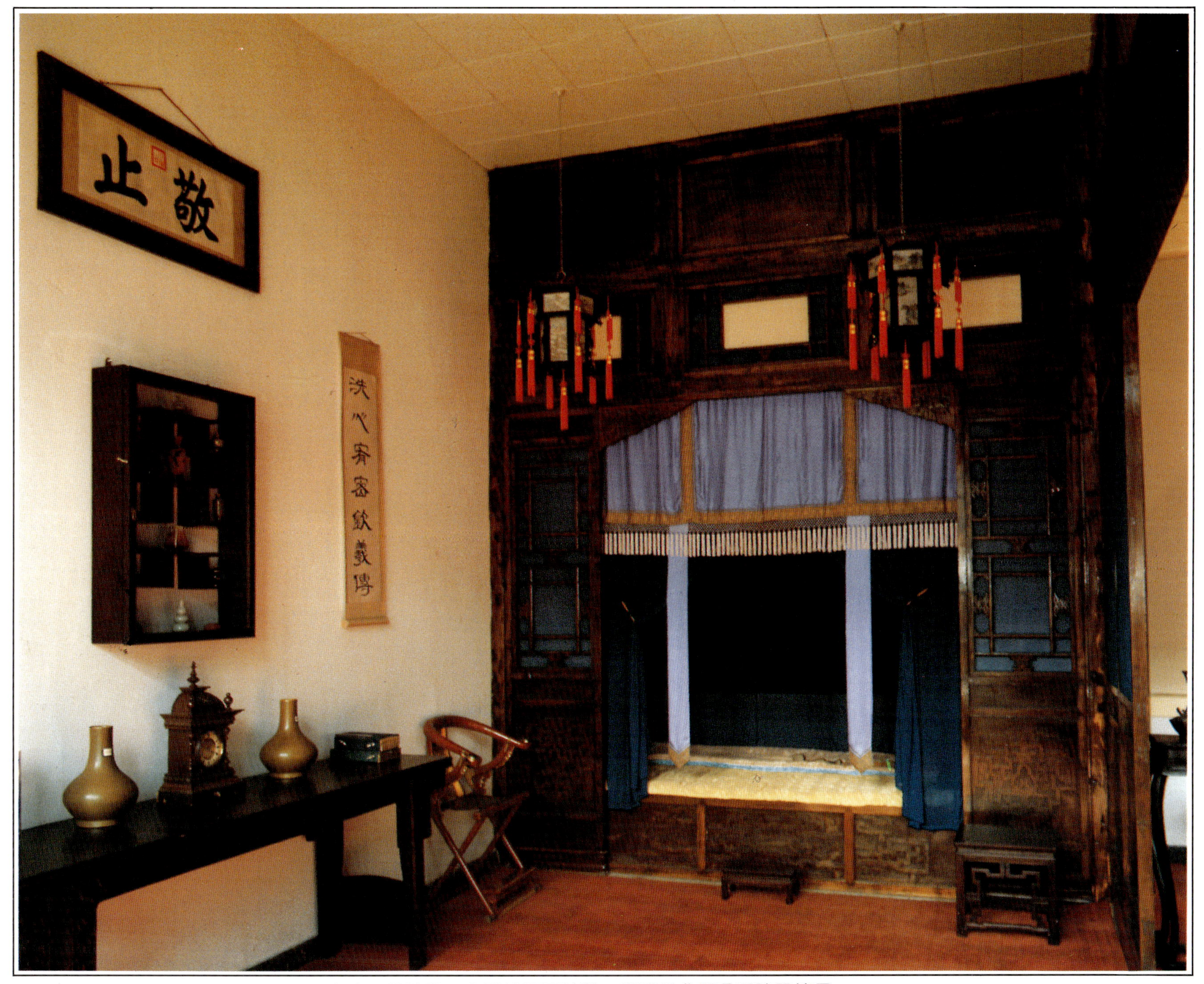

寢宮內部陳設南北相異、北間按冬季齋戒所需陳設，南間按夏季陳設、圖示爲北間冬季陳設情景。

The southern and northern rooms of the Sleeping Palacc were differently furnished. The northern room was set up in a winter style according to the demands of fasting, while the southern one was in summer style. Picture shows the winter styled furnishings of the northern room.

寝宮の中、南北両方の陳設がちがいである。北の部屋は冬の需要によって、南の部屋は夏の需要によって陳設されている。写真は北の部屋にある冬の陳設。

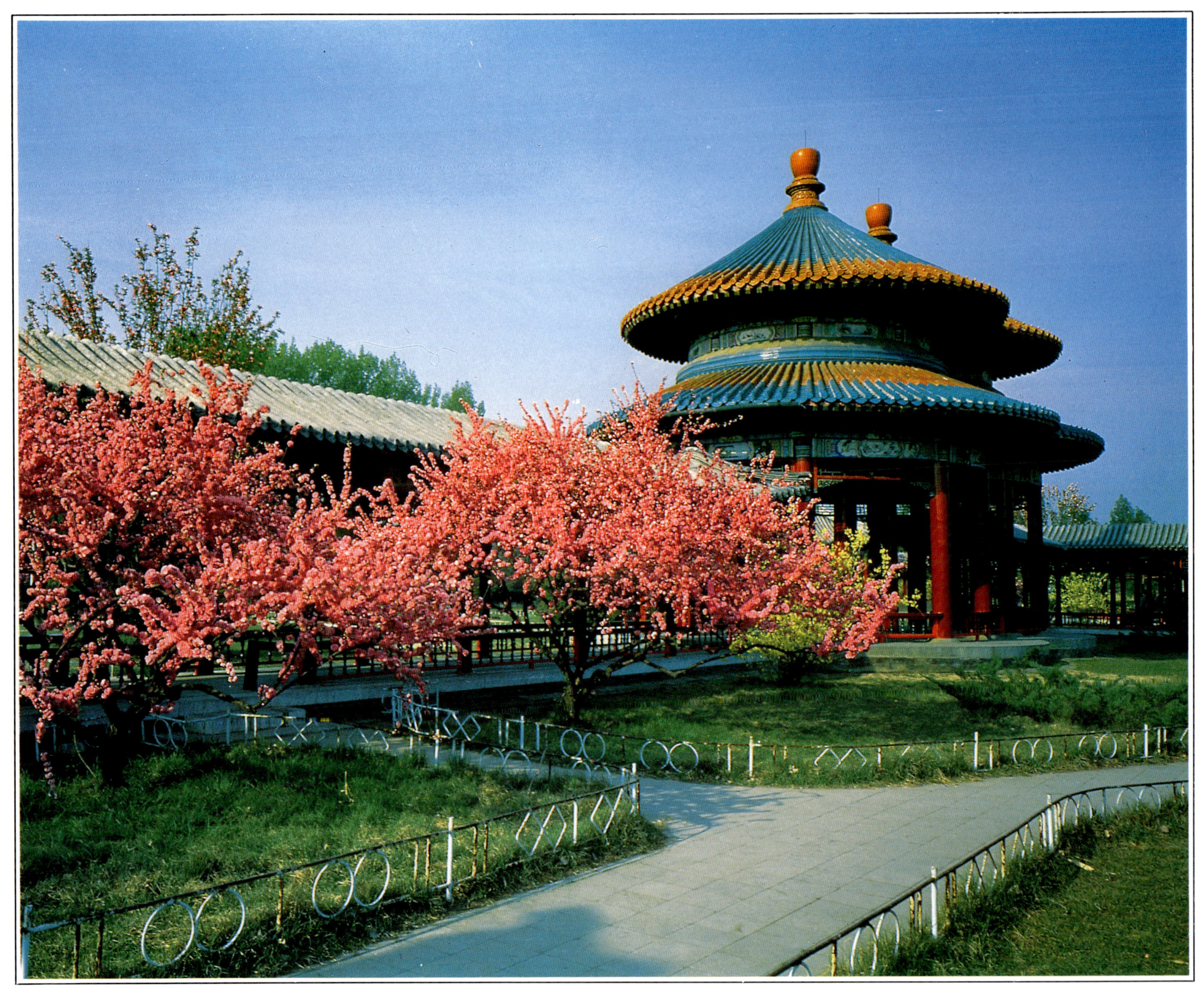

雙環萬壽亭，爲乾隆皇帝爲其母五十大壽而建，原存中南海，1975年遷建天壇。

Being built under the order of Emperor Qianlong for his 50th birthday anniversary, the Double Ring Longevity Pavilion was originally in Zhongnanhai. It was moved to the temple of Heaven in 1975.

双環万寿亭が、乾隆皇帝は自分の五十歳誕辰日を記念するために建てさせた。もとは中南海に立てて、1975年に天壇へはこんだ。

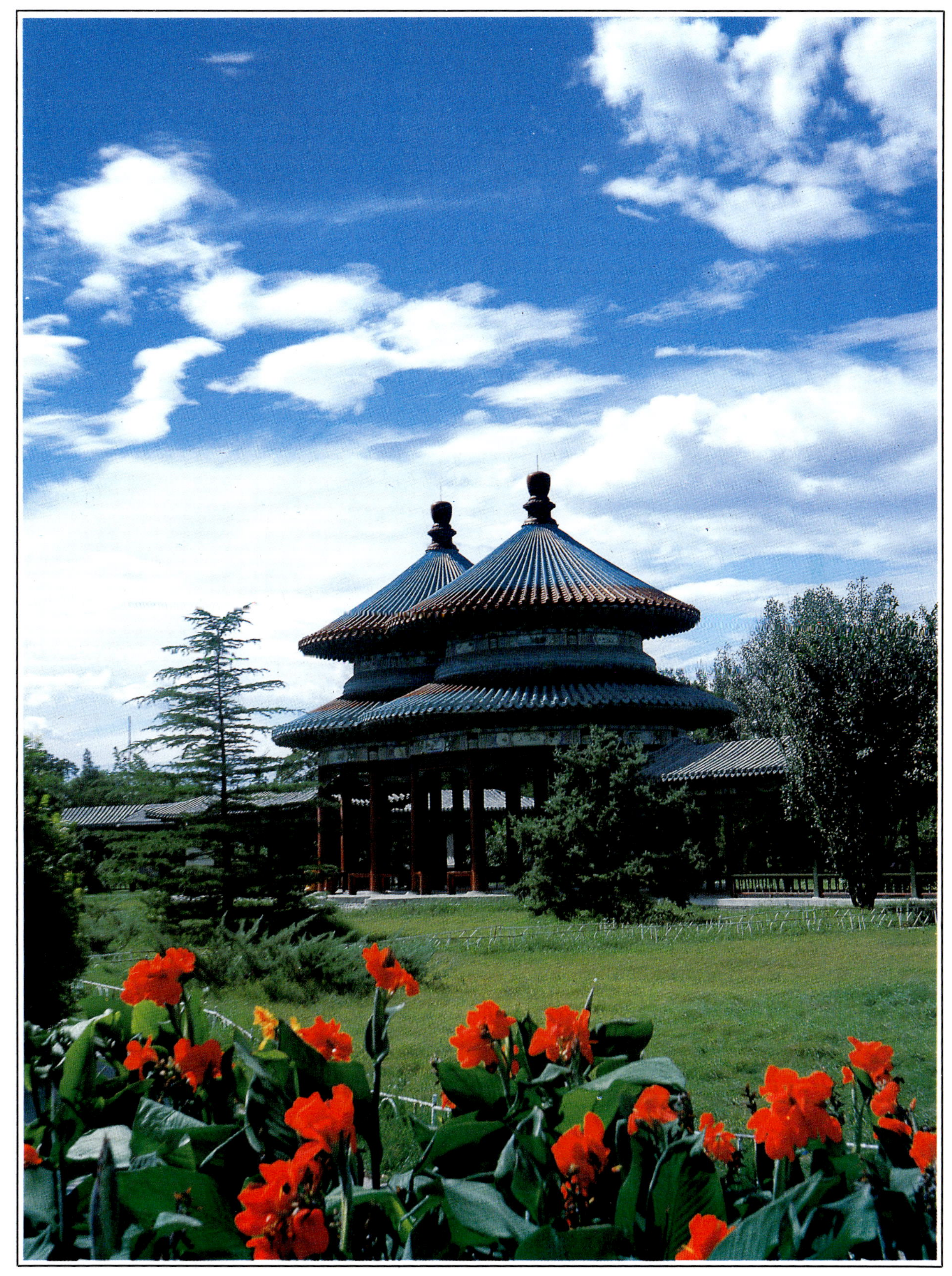

雙環萬壽亭之春

Spring in the double Ring Longevity Pavilion.

双環万寿亭の春

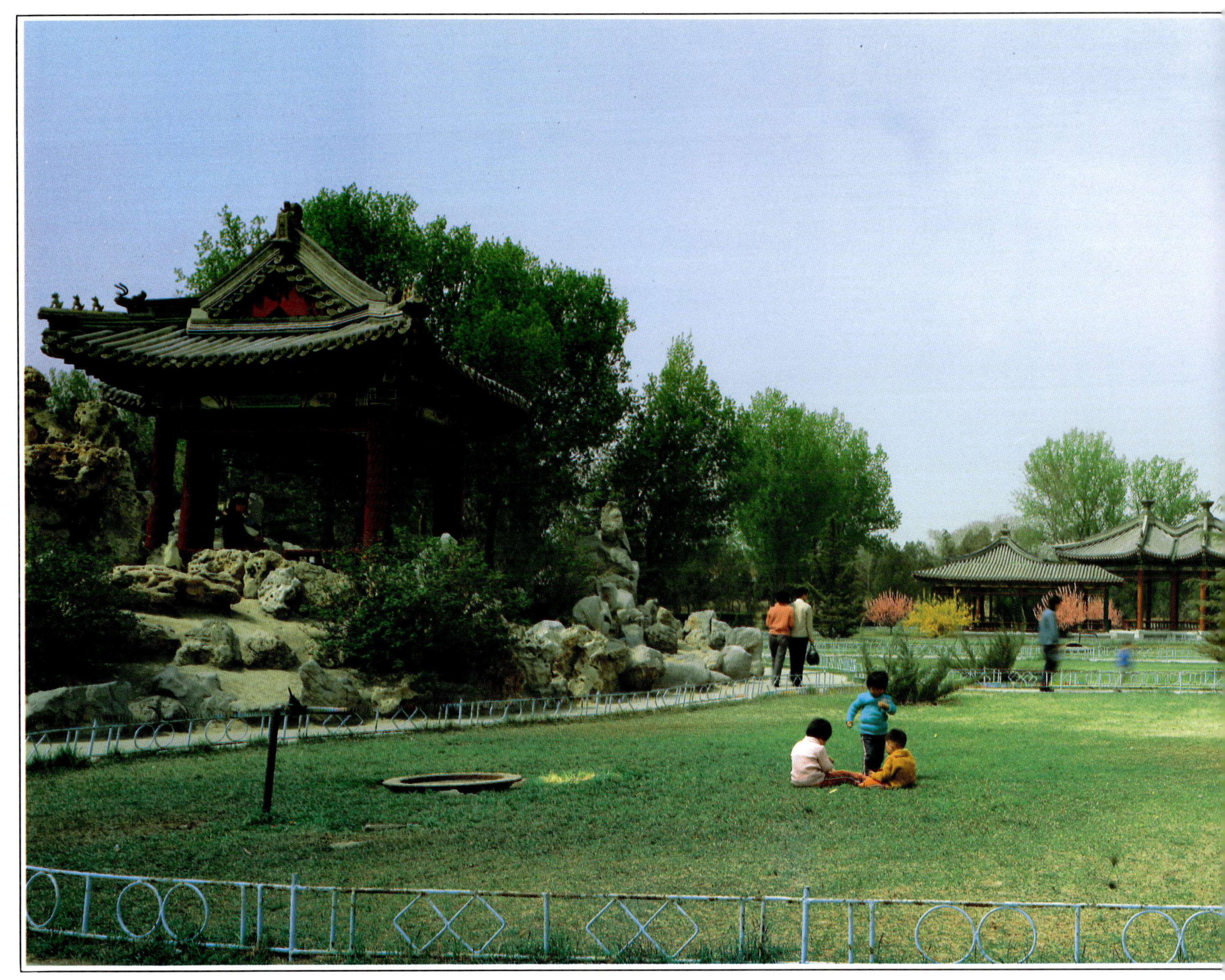

雙環萬壽亭之夏

Cool summer in the Double Ring Longevity Pavilion

双環万寿亭の夏

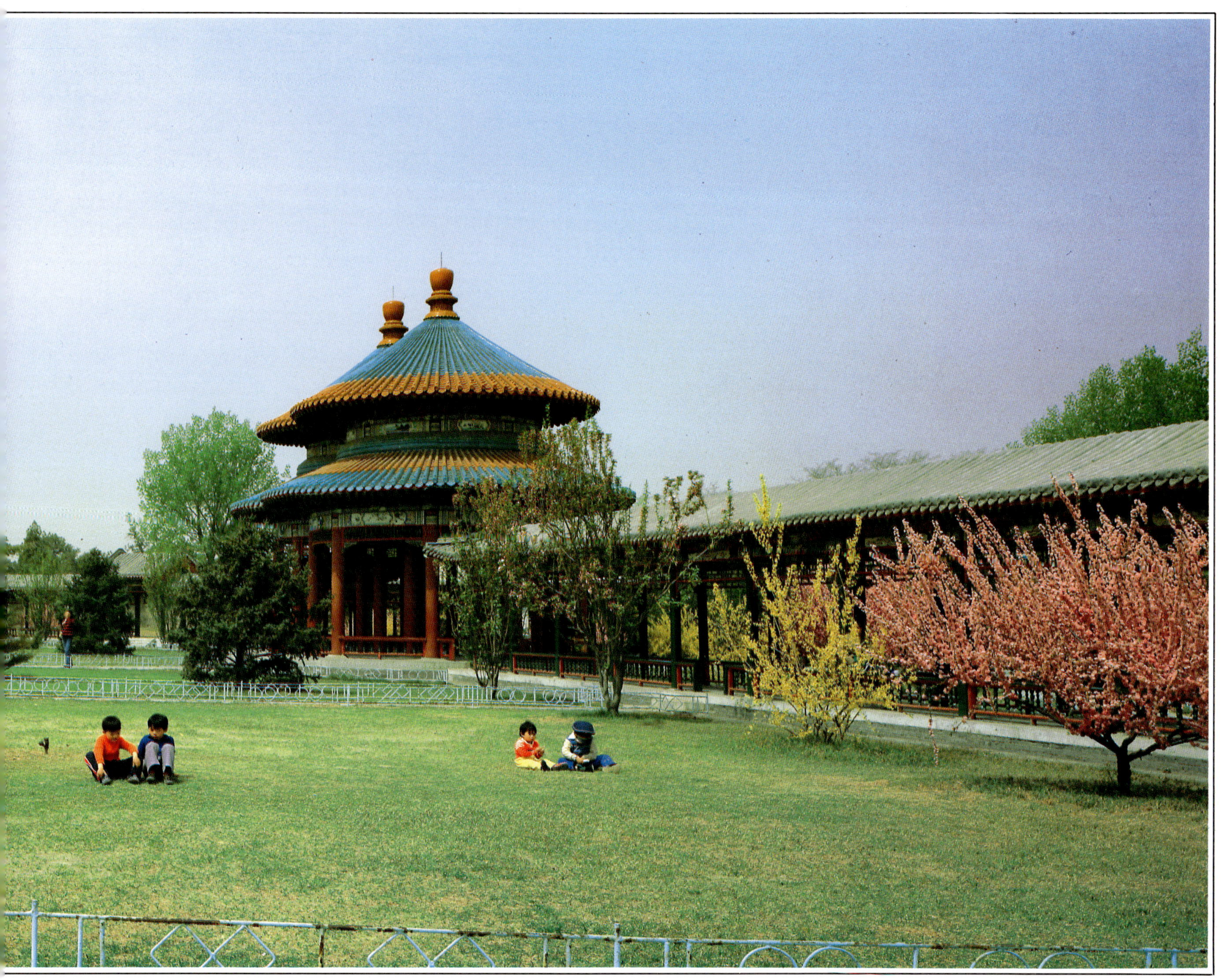

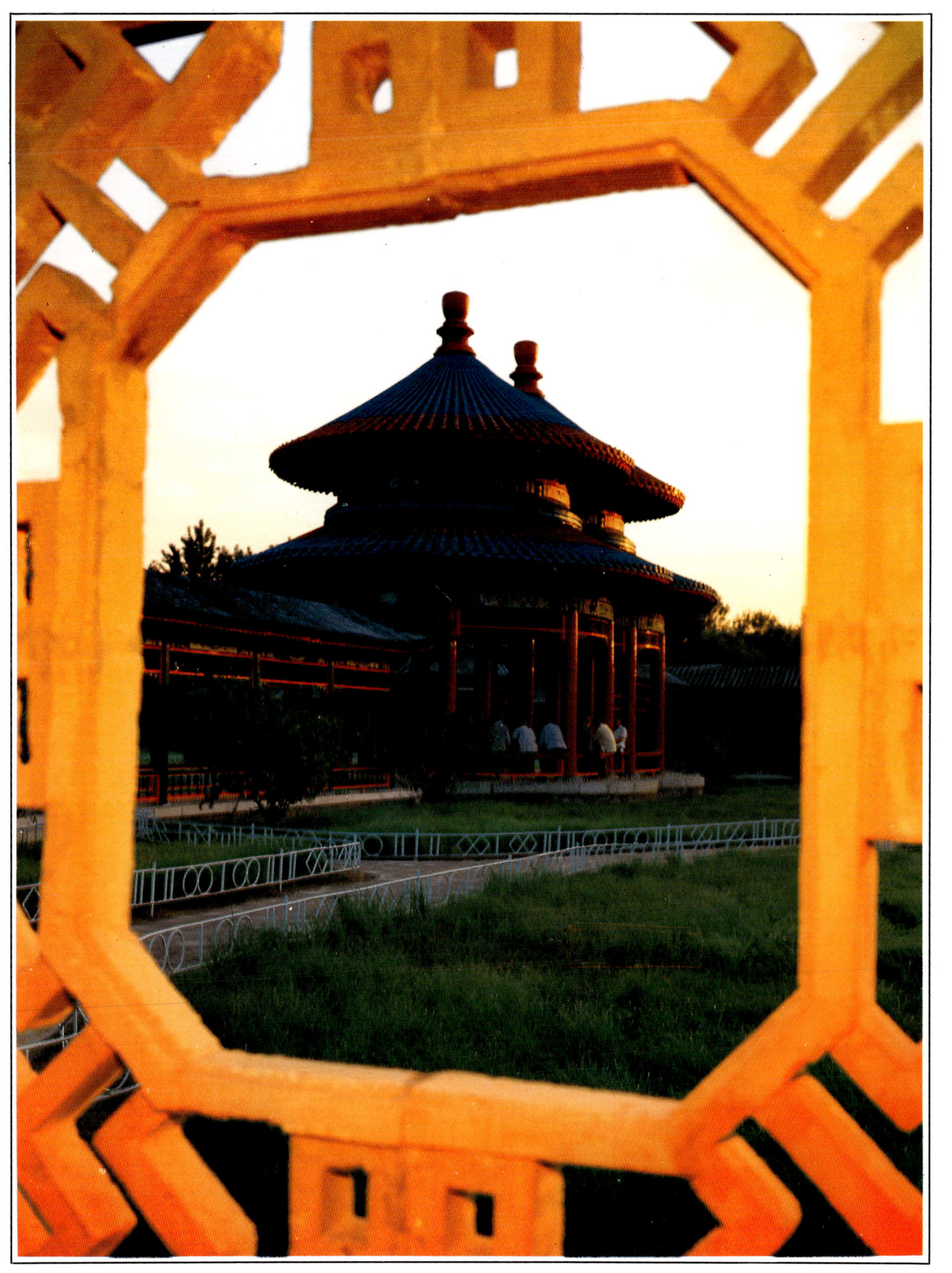

雙環萬壽亭

The Double Ring Longevity Pavilion

双環万寿亭

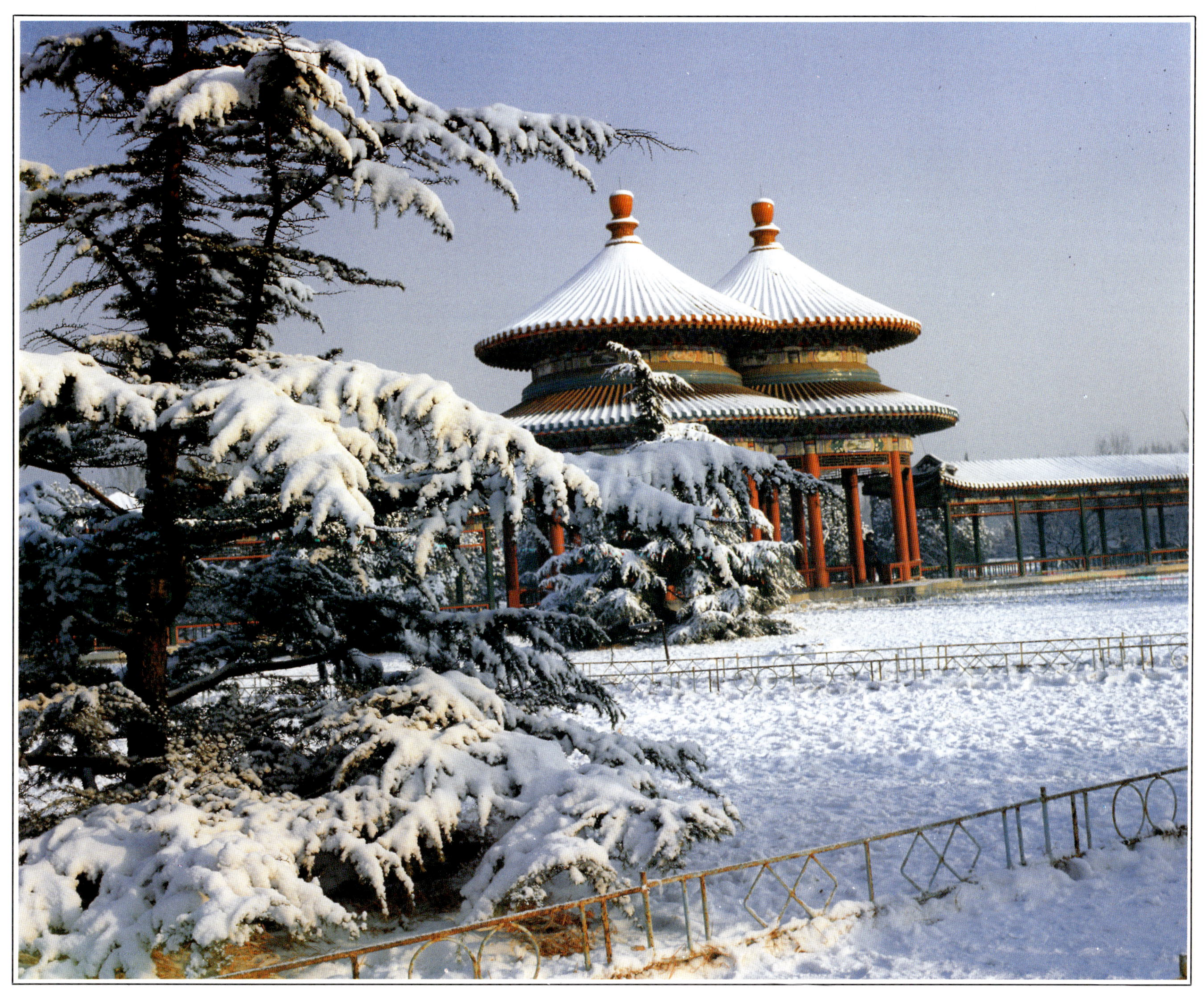

雙環萬壽亭之冬

The Double Ring Longevity Pavilion in Winter

雙環万寿亭の冬

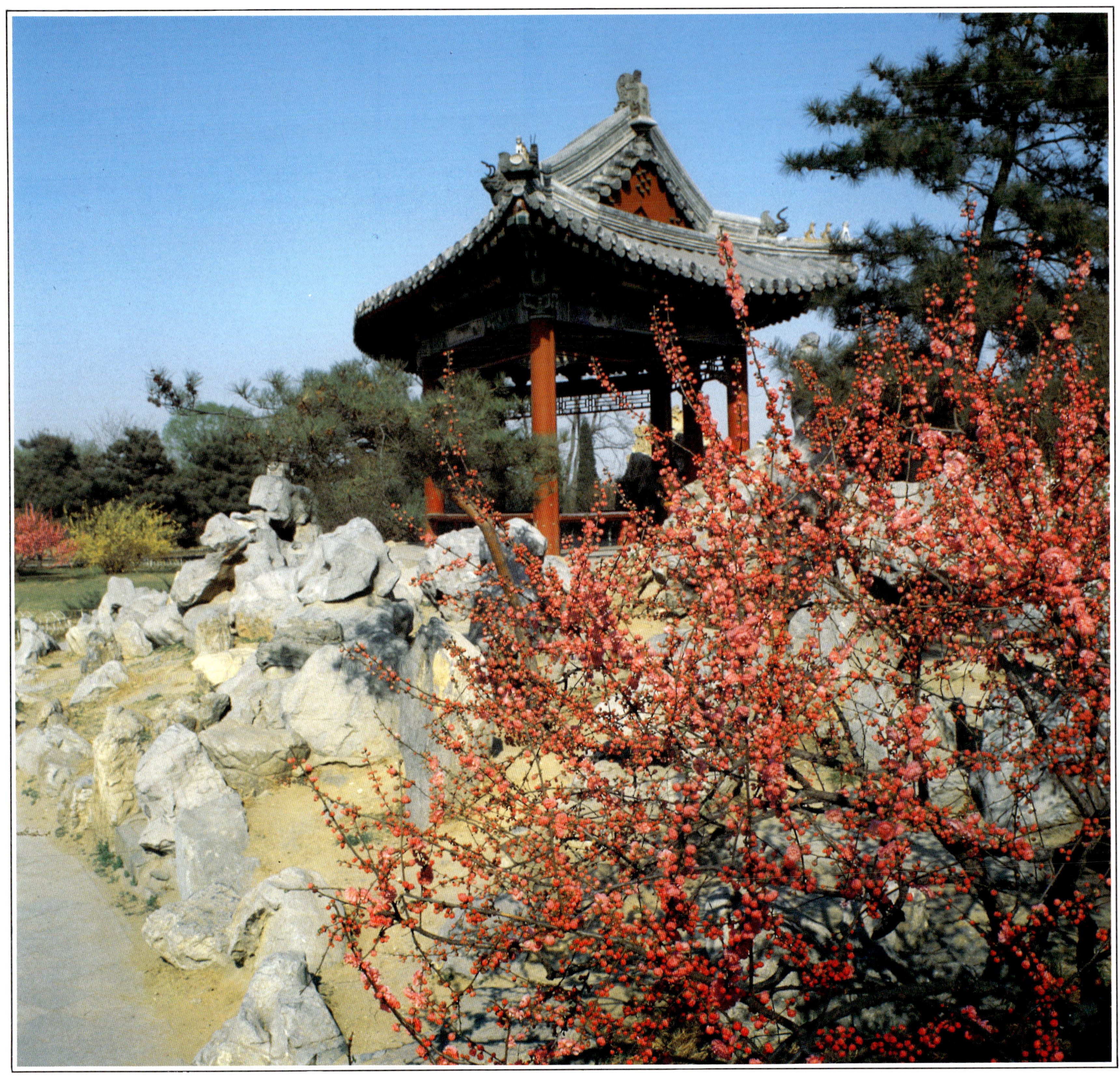

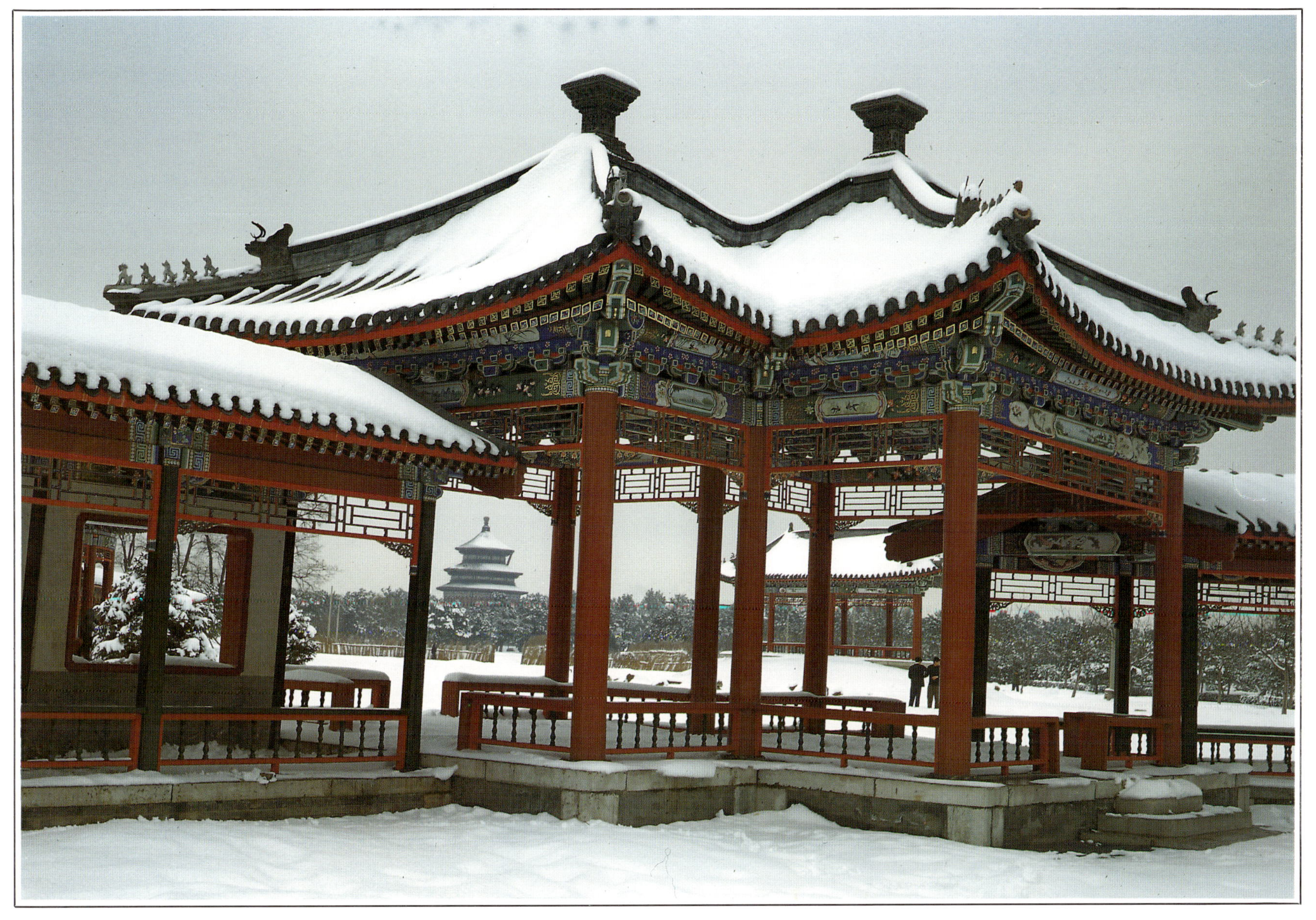

方勝亭與雙環亭相連，遙對扇面亭，內外滿施蘇式彩畫，漫步其間，物隨景移，情趣不凡。

Fangsheng Pavilion　Being linked to the Double Ring Longevity Pavilion, it stands against the Fan-shaped Pavilion. Surfaces in the inner and outer sides are decorated by Jiangsu-styled coloured paintings. Wondering in the Pavilicn, one will be highly interested for the ever-changing view.

方勝亭　亭は双環亭とつながって、遠いから扇面亭に対している。内部と外部にとも、蘇州式の彩色絵画がいっぱい。そこであるけば、景色の変化で、かなり風情がある。

◀扇面亭與雙環亭相對，亭頂爲歇山式的扇面變形。造型輕巧，躍躍欲飛。

Fan-shaped Pavilion　Standing at the opposite side of the. Duble Ring Longevity Pavilion, the Pavilion has a top of deformed shape in Xieshan style. With a light shape, it looks as if going to spring up.

扇面亭　亭は双環亭に対して、屋根は歇山式の、形が変化された扇子の形で、軽巧に見えるで、とびるようとしている。

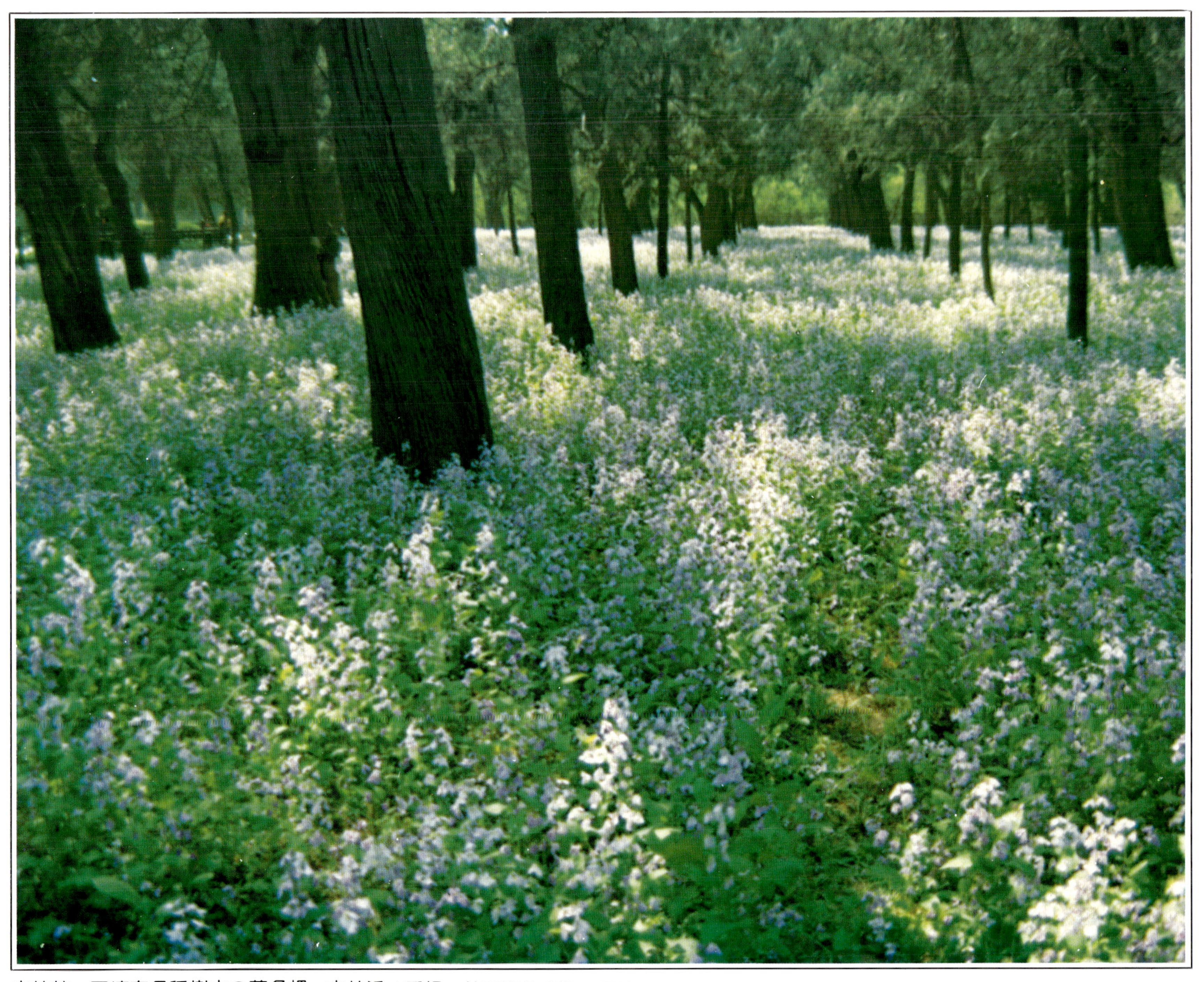

古柏林　天壇有各種樹木８萬多棵，古柏近４千棵。林下野花成海，環境靜雅宜人。

Ancient Cypress Forest　There are over 80000 of trees in the Temple of Heaven, among which nearly 4000 are ancient cypresses. On the ground where the forest grows, wild flowers look gorgeously flourishing. The environment is quiet, elegant and pleasing.

古い柏の木の森林　天壇に、各種類の木が80万本以上もある，その中、古い柏の木が4000本ある。林の下に花いっぱい、環境が典雅として、人によい感じを与える。

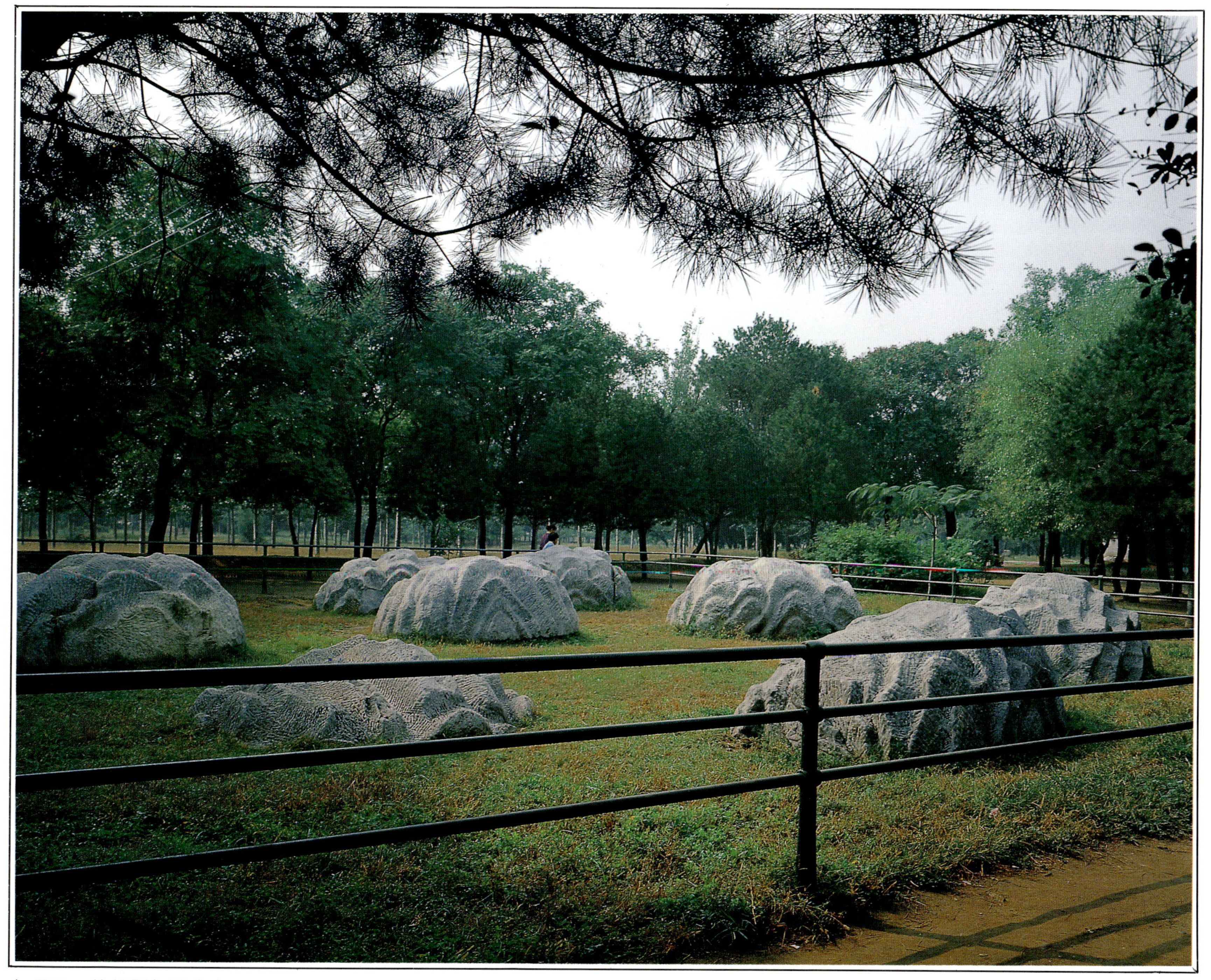

七星石　位於祈年殿東南，一共八塊，上刻山形，相傳爲嘉靖皇帝所立鎮石，一說爲明朝道士祭祀北斗七星所用。

Situated to the southeast of the Hall of Prayers for Bumper Harvests, the stones are 7 in number, and patterns of mountain are carved on them. A legend says that they are guarding stones set up by Emperor Jiajing. Another saying goes that they were used by a Taoist Monk of the Ming Dynasty when worshipping the Big Dipper.

七星石　山の形を彫刻してある八枚の石が，祈年殿の東南にある。伝説によれば、これらは嘉靖皇帝が立てた鎮石だという。ほかの説が違い——明代の道人が北斗星を祭するにつかったものである。

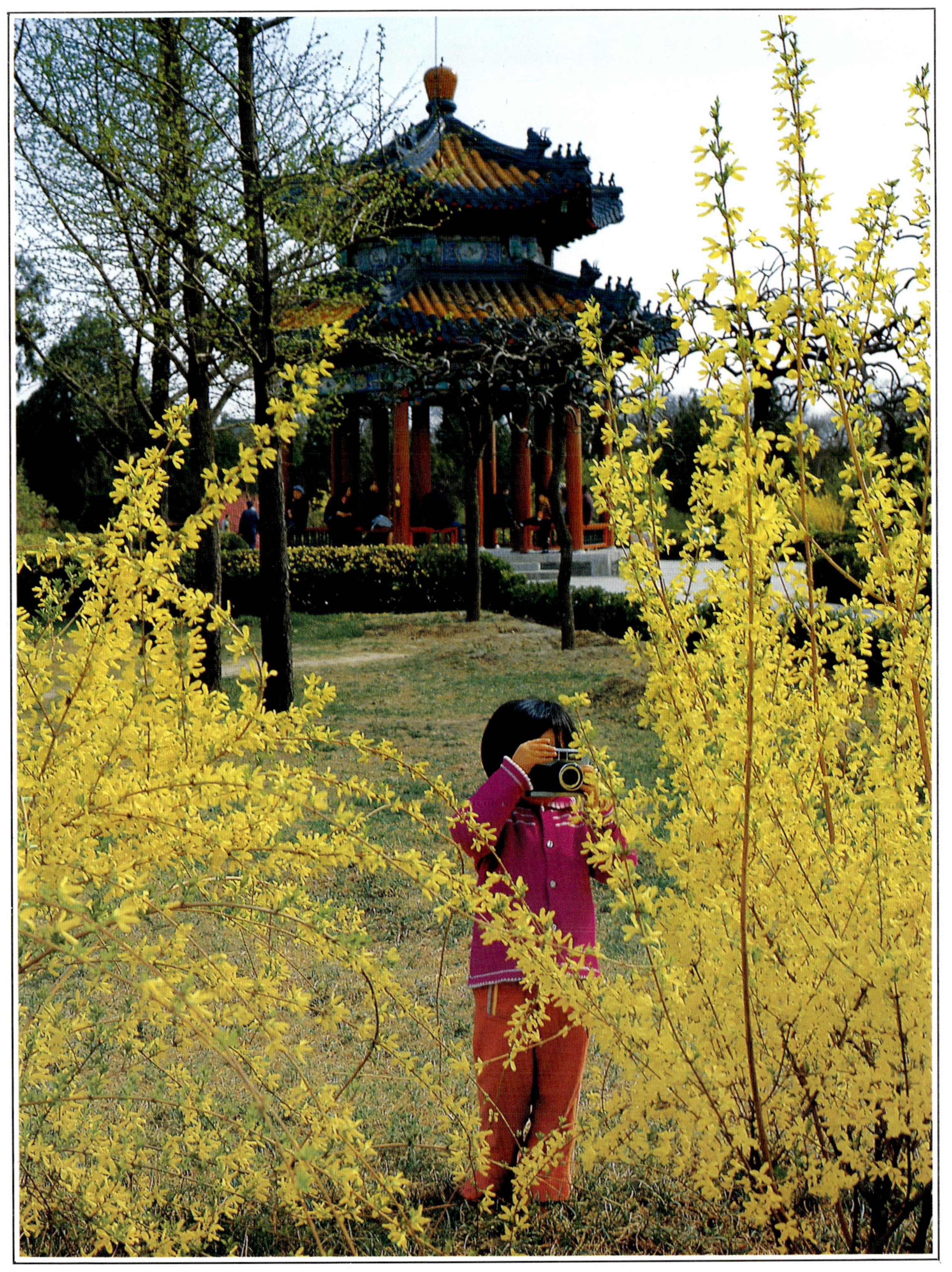

百花亭　位於天壇百花園內。重檐攢尖頂，六角亭，內外施蘇式彩畫，畫題以花草爲主，固得名。

Multi-flower Pavilion

Situated in the Multi-flower Garden in the Temple of Heaven, the Pavilion is hexagonal with doubled eaves and gradually rising pointed top. The inside is decorated all over with Suzhou-styled coloured paintings. Most of the subjects of the paintings involves flowers, hence the name.

百花亭　これは、天壇の百花園の中にある二重檐、とがた屋根が持っ六角の亭である。亭体内外に蘇州式彩色絵画がいっぱい。絵画の題目が主として花草で、このなまいをつけた。

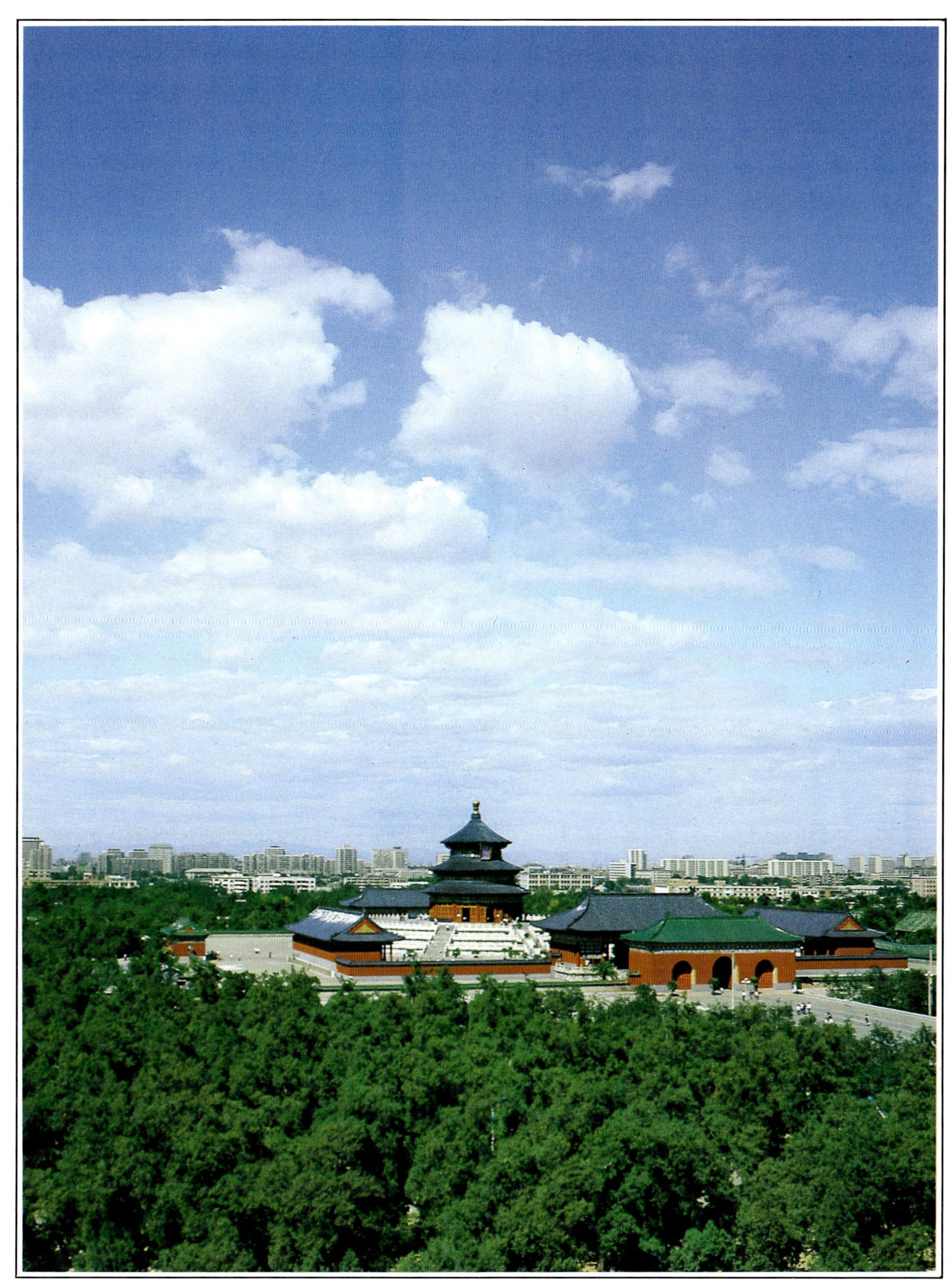

祈年殿

Hall of Prayers for Bumper Harvests

祈年殿

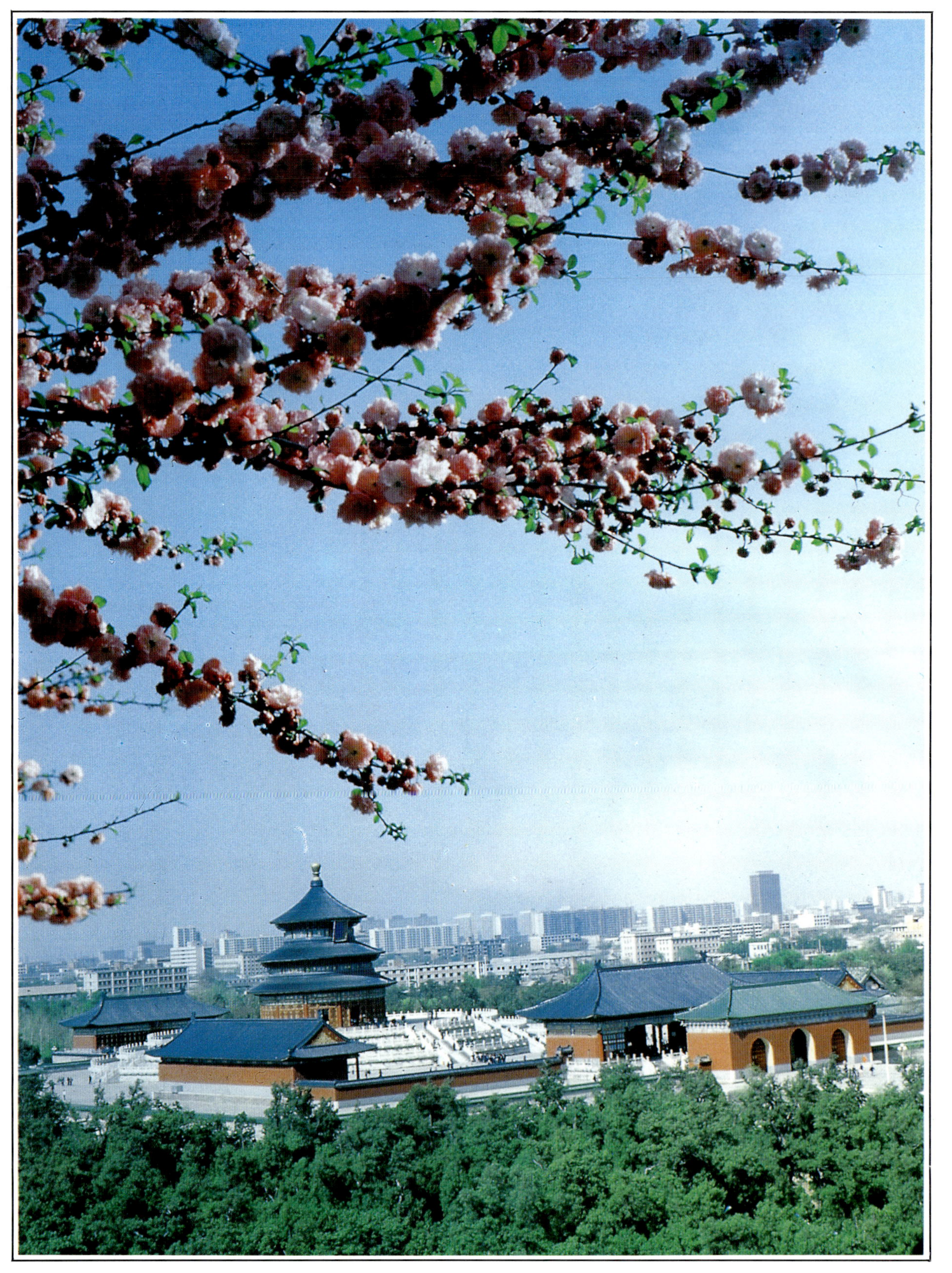

祈年殿春色

A spring view of the Hall of Prayers for Bumper Harvests

祈年殿の春光

祈谷壇主體建築坐落在一個方形基座上，高出地面３米多，東、西、南三面之內壝牆上出磚門，外又增一道外壝牆，布局渾然一體。建築氣勢磅礴，松柏相間，宛若人間天宮。

The Altar for the God of Grains is set on a square base over 3m high. On the east, west and south sides of the inner surrounding walls, doors are open, and an outer surrounding wall is added. The integrated layout looks magnificent, and just like a heavenly palace in the world.

祈穀壇の主体建物はひとつの方形の基座の上にある，地の平面より、三メートル以上も高くになって、東、西、南三方の内塀の上に門があけて，その外に、外塀場が加えられて、布局がまったく一体になった。建物は意気偉い、松と柏がかわるがわるで、人間の仙境のようた。

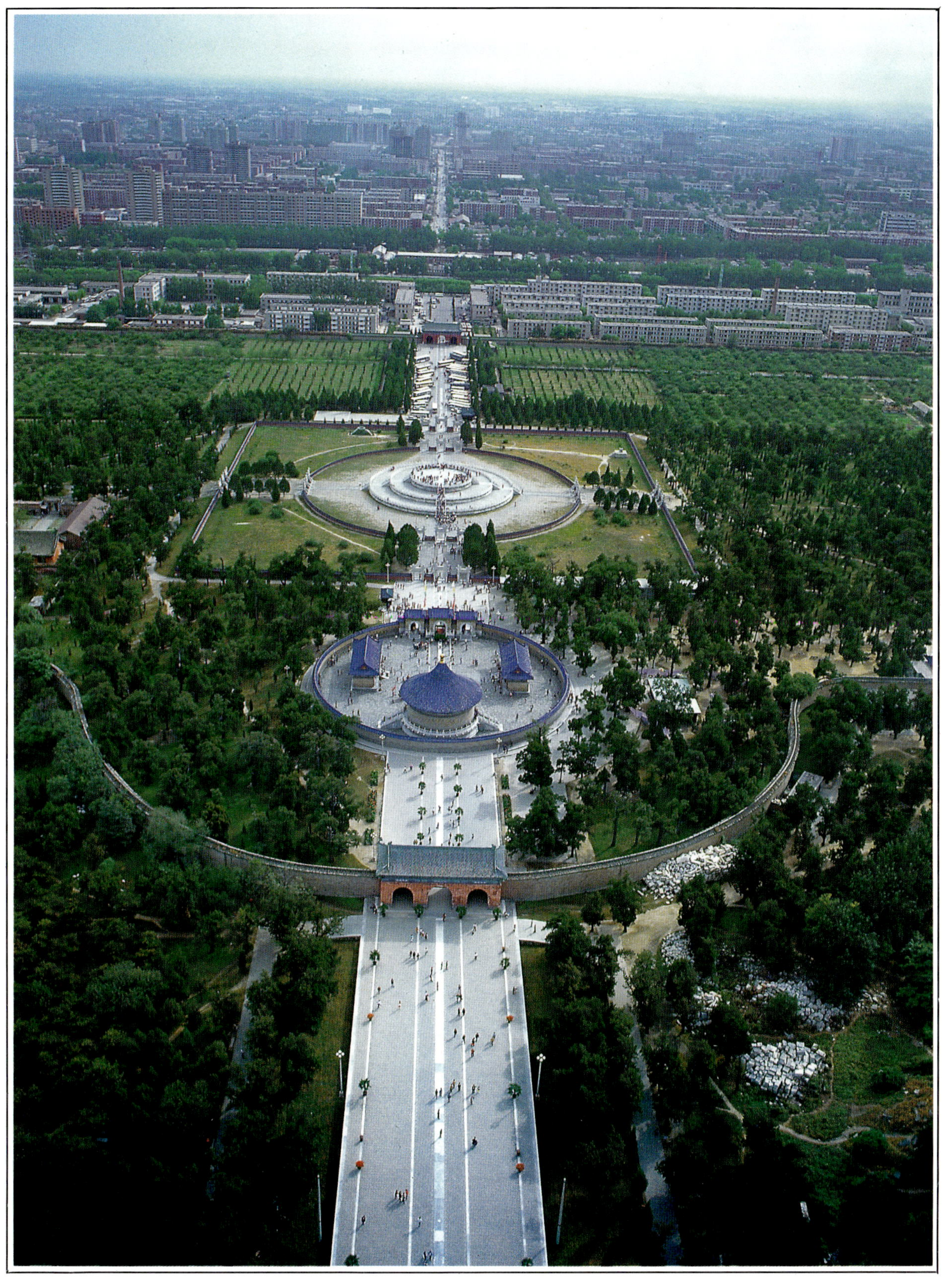

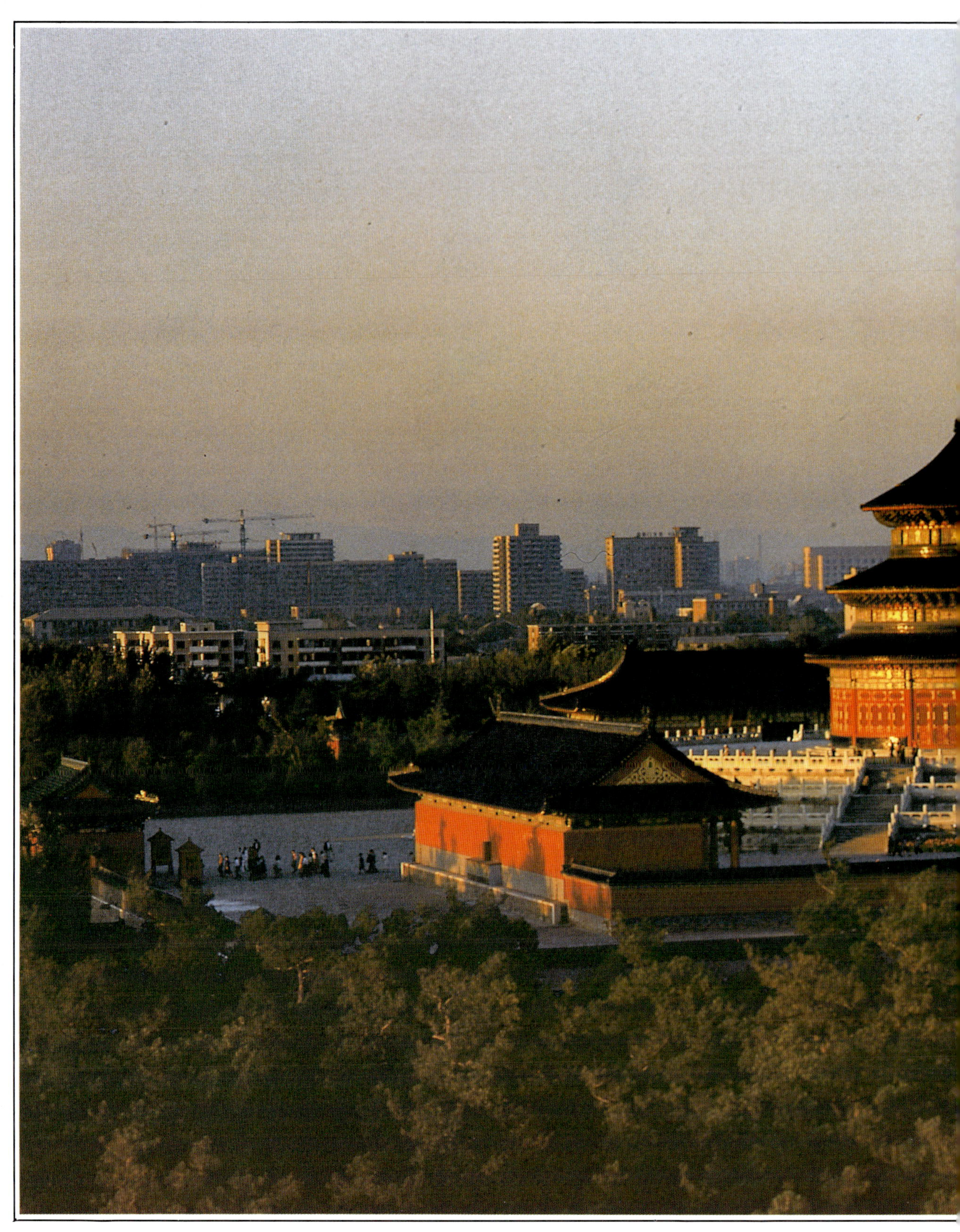

祈年殿
Hall of Prayers for Bumper Harvests
祈年殿

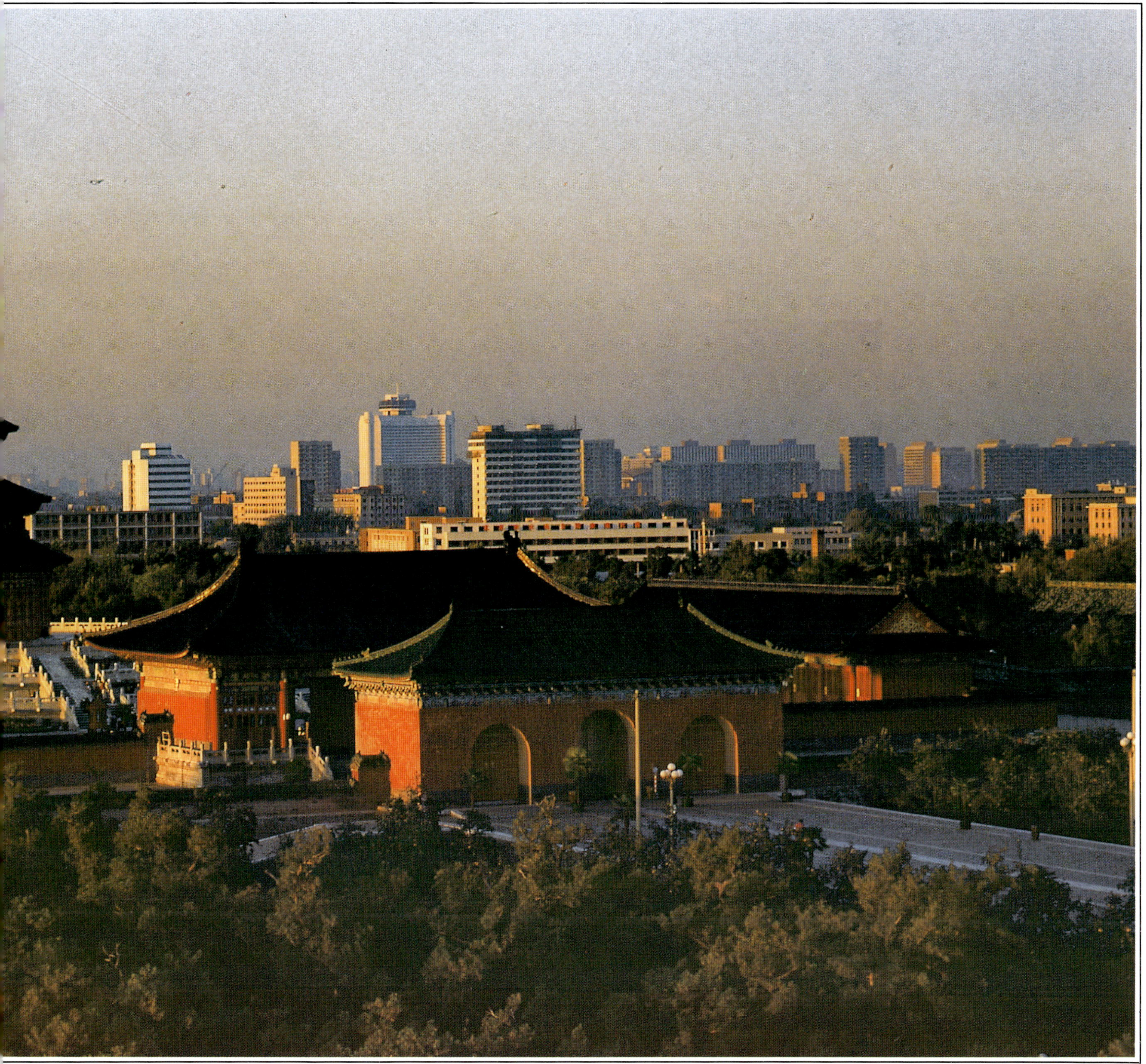

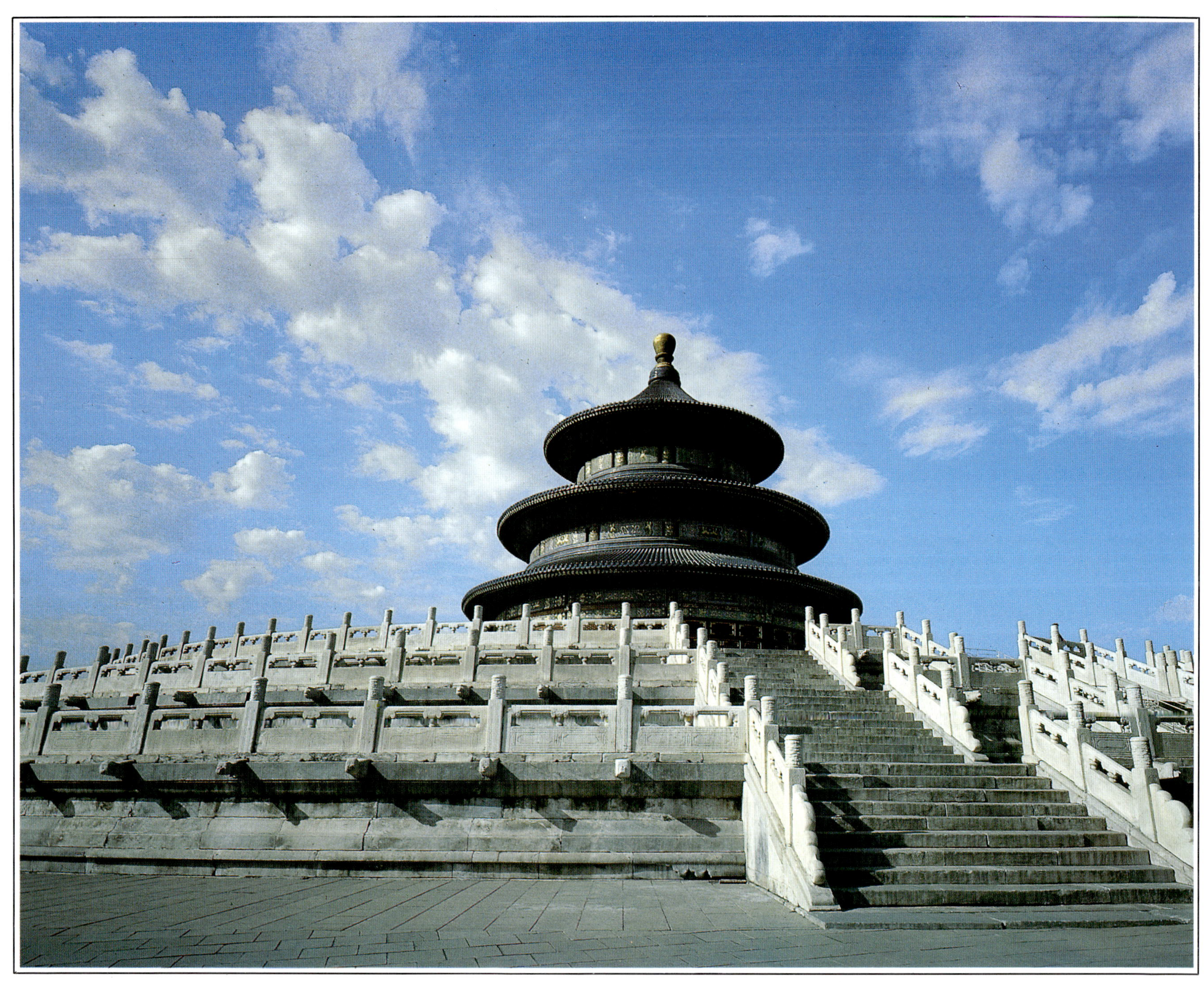

祈年殿

Hall of Prayers for Bumper Harvests

祈年殿

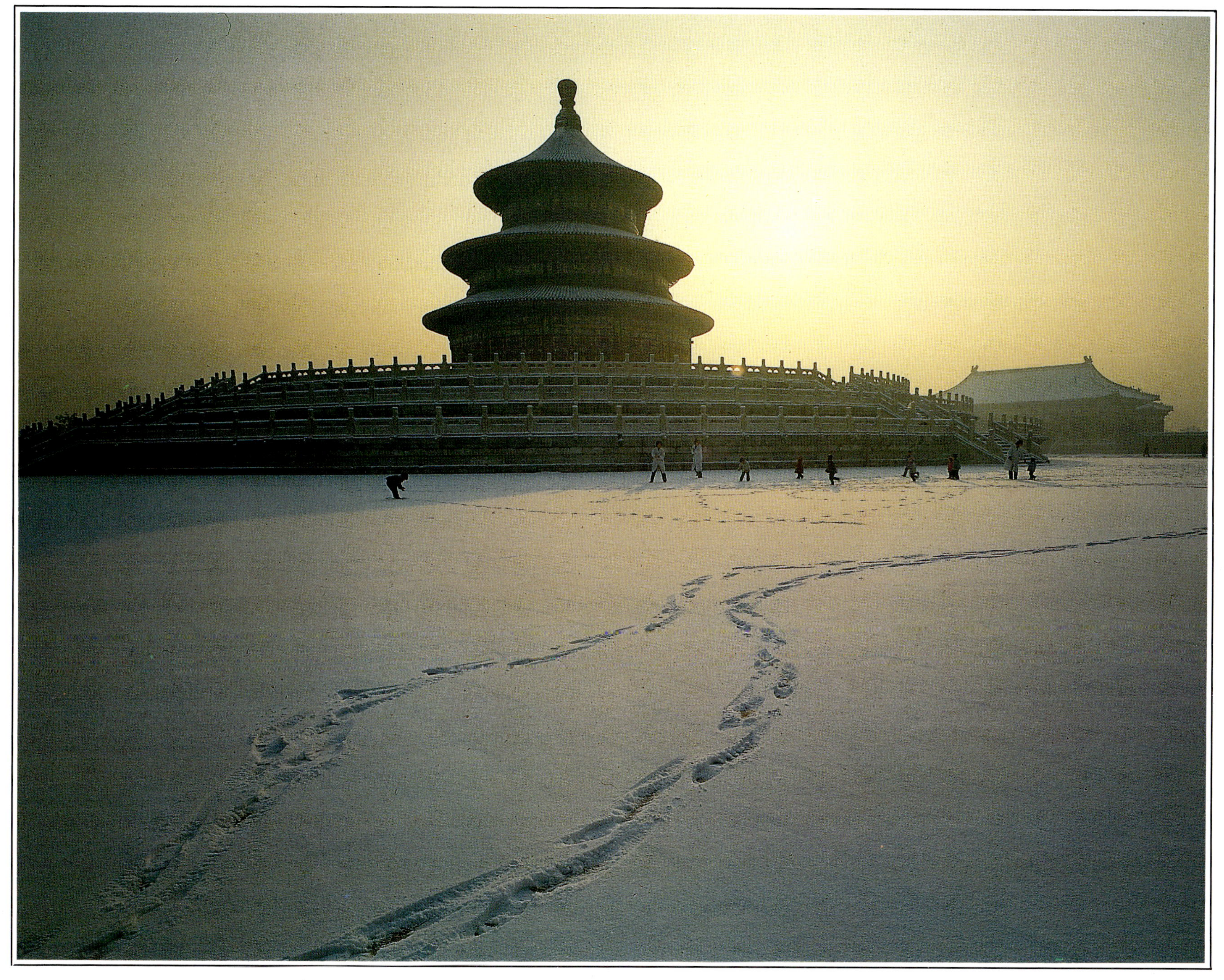

祈年殿建築高低輝映、方圓相接，充分體現了中國古代“天人合一”、“陰陽合諧”的自然哲學觀。雪中的祈年殿更顯其神韻。

Buildings in the Hall of Prayers for Bumper Harvests vie with each other: The high ones with the low ones, and square ones with round ones. They fully embody the natural philosophy of ancient Chinese that “Heaven integrates with human being” and “the Negative is harmonins with the Positive”. The Hall in snowfall presents more charms.

祈年殿の建物は、高さちがのと形がちがいのが互いに映えて、よく、中国古代にある“天人合一”と“陰陽和諧”の自然哲学観を具体に表現している。雪降ったあどに、祈年殿は一層壮観である。

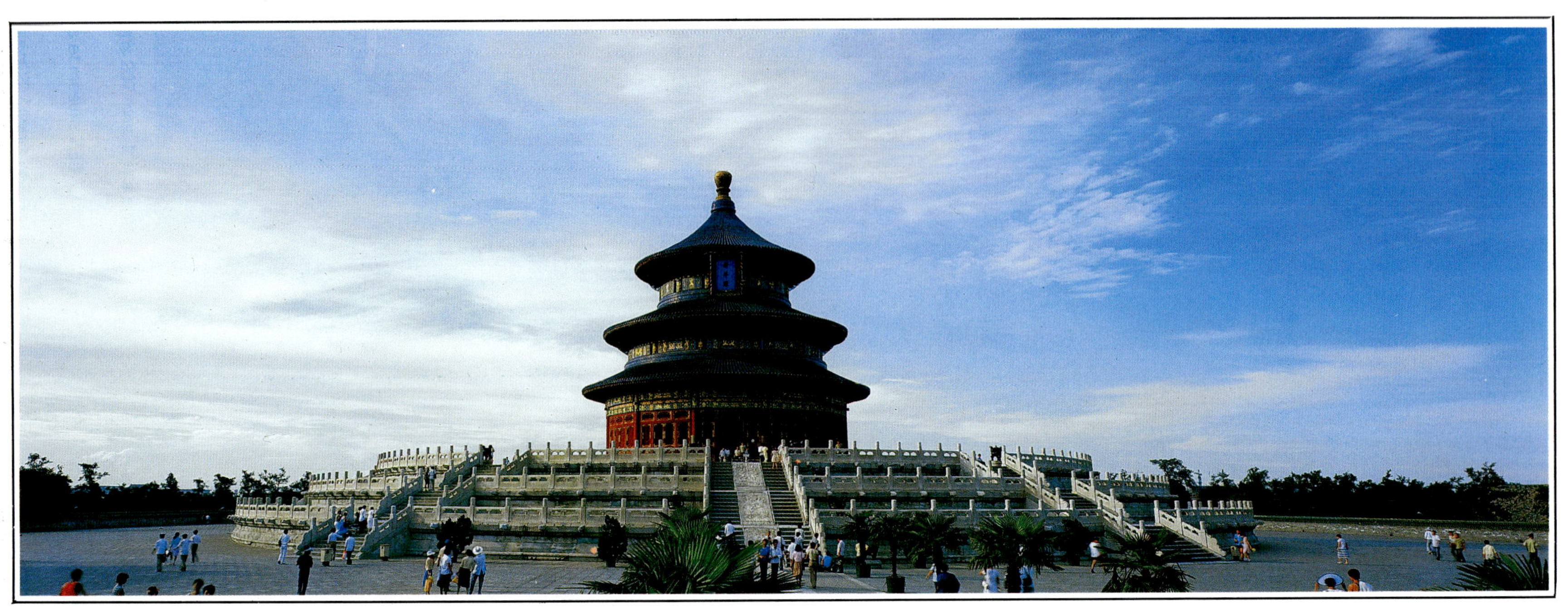

祈年殿

Hall of Prayers for Bumper Harvests

祈年殿

▶天壇始建於明朝永樂十八年(1421年)，是明清兩朝舉行祭天、祈谷、常雩大典的祭壇。天壇分南北兩壇，南圜丘、北祈谷、另有齋宮、神樂署等建築。天壇許多景點中外聞名：有三音石之音、回音壁之趣，天心石之樂、七星石之謎；壇內古樹千株，森然成蔭、環境幽雅，祥和寧靜，爲中國旅游之勝景。

Built in 1421 (the 18th year of the reign of Yongle, Ming Dynasty), the Temple of Heaven was the sacrificial altar where ceremonies of worshipping Heaven, those for the God of Grains and other important ones were held. It contains the southern and northern altars——The Circular Mound in the south and the Hall of Prayers for Bumper Harvests in the north, In addition, there are constructions like the Fasting Palace, the Office of Sacred Music, etc. Many scenic spots there are well-known at home and abroad: The sound of the Triple Sound Stone, the interest of the Echo Wall, the merth of Tianxin Stone and the riddle of Seven-star Stone. The forest there forms a quiet, harmonious and peaceful environment. The Temple is really a famous scenic spot for tours in China.

天壇は1421(明代永楽十八年)に建て始まり，明清両代に天を祭る、穀を祈禱する、またはほかの儀式をおこなわれる祭壇である。南と北の両部にわけており，南には圜丘壇、北には祈穀壇で、ほかに、斎宮と神楽署などの建物がある。おうぜな天壇の景色が国内でも、世界でも有名である。たとえば、三音石の音、回音壁の趣味、天心石のたのしむ、七星石の謎、皆、人をひきつけることだ。公園の中に木千枚あり、環境がたいへん奥ゆかしく上品で、吉祥と和諧の感じがおこさせる。このところは、中国旅遊のすぐれて良い景色である。

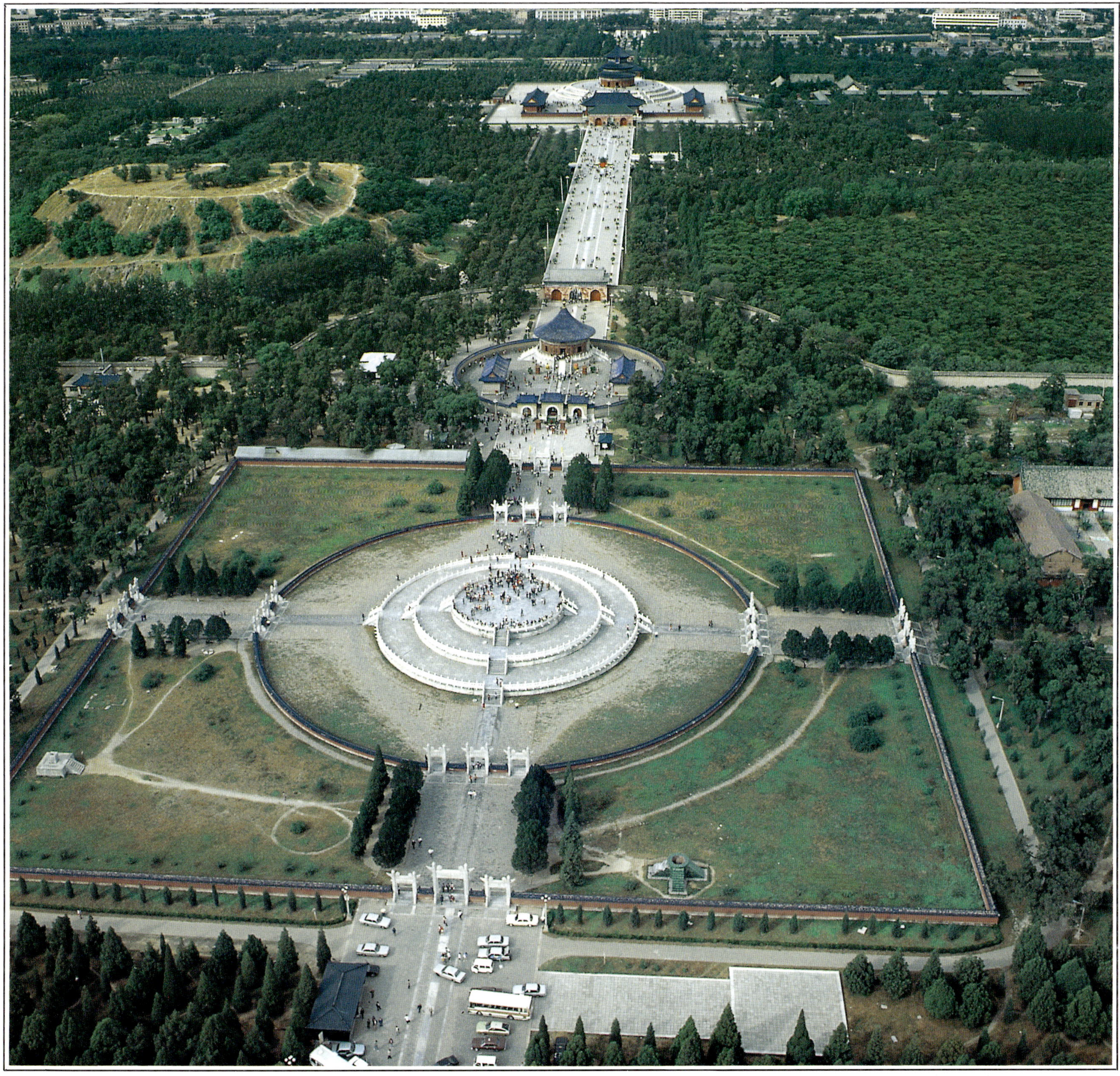

顧　　問：穆　青　石少華　楊牧之

編委主任：許　邦　閻振國　張萬舒

編委委員：（按姓氏筆畫爲序）

牛嵩林　卞志武　甘純庚　何世堯

邵柏林　周　毅　吳庚新　茹遂初

柳成行　胡維標　華仲明　陳　勃

陳長芬　鄂　毅　馮法光　許安寧

景長順　程克雄　張家驊　楊春華

熊迪強　劉　軍　劉　毅　劉世昭

主　　編：楊春華　馮法光

執行編輯：陳衛東　徐文金

撰　　文：周慶生

翻　　譯：麥仰曾（英）　計　傲（日）

裝幀設計：徐文金　董英傑

書名題字：徐楚德

攝　　影：胡維標　劉啓俊　董宗貴　牛嵩林

周　毅　鄂　毅　鮑　昆　華仲明

張肇基　徐志長　柳　琴

Advisors: Mu Qing　Shi Shaohua　YangMuzhi

Directors of Editorial Committee:

Xu Bang　Yan Zhenguo　Zhang Wanshu

Editorial Committee:

Niu Songlin	Bian Zhiwu	Gan Chungeng
He Shirao	Shao Bolin	Zhou Yi
Wu Gengxin	Ru Suichu	Liu Chenghang
Hu Weibiao	Hua Zhongming	Chen Bo
Chen Changfen	E Yi	Feng Faguang
Xu Anning	Jing Changshun	Cheng Kexiong
Zhang Jiahua	Yang Chunhua	Xiong Diqiang
Liu Jun	Liu Yi	Liu Shizhao

Editors-in-chief: Yang Chunhua　Feng Faguang

Managing editors: Xu Wenjin　Chen Weidong

Text by: Zhou Qingsheng

English translation: Mai Yangceng

Art designer: Xu Wenjin　Dong Yingjie

Title Inscription: Xu Chude

Photographers:

Hu Weibiao	Lin Qijun	Dong Zonggui
Niu Songlin	Zhou Yi	E Yi
Bao Kun	Hua Zhongming	Zhang Zhaoji
Xu Zhichang	Liu Qin	

顧　　問：穆　青　石少華　楊牧之

編輯委員会主任：許　邦　閻振國　張萬舒

編輯委員：（苗字の筆画数の順にもとづいて）

牛嵩林　卞志武　甘純庚　何世堯

邵柏林　周　毅　吳庚新　茹遂初

柳成行　胡維標　華仲明　陳　勃

陳長芬　鄂　毅　馮法光　許安寧

景長順　程克雄　張家驊　楊春華

熊迪強　劉　軍　劉　毅　劉世昭

編 集 長：楊春華　馮法光

執行編輯者：陳衛東　徐文金

文章担当者：周慶生

翻　　訳：計　傲

装丁デザイン：徐文金　董英傑

書名かき：徐楚德

写　　真：胡維標　劉啓俊　董宗貴　牛嵩林

周　毅　鄂　毅　鮑　昆　華仲明

張肇基　徐志長　柳　琴

《天壇》

（中、英、日）三種文版

新華出版社出版發行

北京利豐雅高長城印刷有限公司

787×1092　12開　印張：8

1994年10月第一版　1994年10月第一次印刷

ISBN 7—5011—2651—8/J・118

05000